S0-EDK-731

Make Your Life Magical

Make Your
Life
Magical

Creating Wealth from Within

Tony Kent

DENVER, COLORADO

The opinions expressed in this manuscript are solely the opinions of the author and do not represent the opinions or thoughts of the publisher. The author has represented and warranted full ownership and/or legal right to publish all the materials in this book.

The author of this book does not dispense medical advice or prescribe the use of any technique as a form of treatment for physical, emotional, or medical problems without the advice of a physician, either directly or indirectly. The intent of the author is only to offer information of a general nature to help you in your quest for emotional and spiritual well-being. In the event you use any of the information in this book for yourself, which is your constitutional right, the author and the publisher assume no responsibility for your actions.

Important: This book was conceived and written as part of a complete program and, to learn more, I would invite you to visit:

www.MakeYourLifeMagical.com

Although I feel that the book will also stand alone, the exercises, ideas and teachings, especially those from my spiritual teacher, will have greater value and deeper significance if you go through the interactive multimedia modules. The complete program will help you to integrate and implement everything to achieve change and transformation, as it takes you step by step through applying the concepts.

Make Your Life Magical
Creating Wealth From Within
All Rights Reserved.
Copyright © 2013 Tony Kent
v3.0

Cover Design by Purple Fish Media- all rights reserved.

This book may not be reproduced, transmitted, or stored in whole or in part by any means, including graphic, electronic, or mechanical without the express written consent of the publisher except in the case of brief quotations embodied in critical articles and reviews.

Outskirts Press, Inc.
http://www.outskirtspress.com

ISBN: 978-1-4787-1957-1

Outskirts Press and the "OP" logo are trademarks belonging to Outskirts Press, Inc.

PRINTED IN THE UNITED STATES OF AMERICA

This book and the program is dedicated to my partner in life and my beloved wife, Dr. Elizabeth Rose.

We share a common dream of serving God through helping others, and through this sharing, I feel we are growing more and more into one heart, one body, one mind and one soul.

The love and support she has shown me in our time together has been one of the deepest blessings in my life, and I really hope that everyone gets to experience with their partner what I have been blessed to share with her.

She has truly helped to
MAKE MY LIFE MAGICAL.

CONTENTS

PREFACE

Are you happy with your life?

Are you satisfied with how things are for you?

Are there things you want more of?

Do you know your life purpose?

Do you love enough?

Are you earning enough income?

Do you feel that you're making a difference?

Have you mattered enough?

My purpose in this book is to help you turn your answers to these questions into a resounding "Yes." I know what it's like to be in the space where a lot of the answers would be "No." I spent far too much time in this space myself, so I know it intimately. What I will be sharing with you are the things that I learned that have allowed me to turn my pain into passion, and to transform my life so that it has become truly magical.

What do I mean by magical? I mean that my life feels as good as I could imagine it to be; in fact, I couldn't even *imagine* it would be this good when I was struggling. My vision is that the material I'm presenting will empower you to lead a more magical life. I've been using this information for more than two decades now, and I know that it works.

So why would you listen to me? Well, what I have to share is how I went from being quite successful doing what I loved, to losing basically everything, and then bouncing back to do even better.

I moved to France in my early 20s and built a life as a very successful fashion photographer. I worked for all the best magazines, such as *Vogue, Elle, Marie Claire,* and so on, and photographed some of the most beautiful models while traveling all over the world to exotic places. I was the official photographer for Princess Grace and the royal family of Monaco for a while, photographed Presidents Mitterrand and Nixon; as well as personalities such as Raquel Welch, Catherine Deneuve, the Rolling Stones, and numerous others. You can see a lot of these photos on my website: www.tonykent.com

Starting My Family

I met and fell in love with a French lady, Nathalie, and we started a family together, moving to the French countryside about 30 minutes from Paris while we restored an old country estate. We then decided to move back to the States, had children, and eventually moved to Santa Fe, New Mexico, where everything started to fall apart. I can still remember the day when Nathalie told me she had met someone else and wanted to leave me. My entire life turned upside down. I had never experienced such emotional turmoil. There were days I honestly had trouble breathing properly. I had such severe pain in my stomach that I went to the doctor thinking that I had ulcers or something. I couldn't think, much less work, and my expensive lifestyle started to eat away at my financial reserves as my depression totally overwhelmed me.

I started seeing different therapists, reading a ton of self-help books, and talked to anyone and everyone who would listen, desperate to try to figure out what had happened.

I tried shaming Nathalie into coming back, but all I did was push her farther away. And from what had felt like living the best life possible, I found myself in a walking nightmare, drowning in my own self-pity.

When I had just about gotten to the end of my emotional rope, a series of circumstances led me to end up in Jerusalem in the home of a very holy man who was really a hidden teacher. Slowly, bit by bit, he shared teachings that helped me not only turn things around, but eventually led me to a place of genuine happiness and contentment.

What I've done in this book is to share those teachings, as well as others that I've learned to apply to my daily life. I've also created a sort of how-to series, which I believe can help anyone looking to transform their life into a more positive experience.

I am someone who likes great processes, but what I love are systems that make those processes work—those systems that help us grow spiritually, emotionally, and financially. This is what I want to share with you. I want to give you hope—hope that change is possible. The hope that no matter who you are, you can still grow more. I want you to know that there are limitless possibilities for you, and that living joyfully is a choice. And I want you to know that there are ways to further enhance that joy by sharing what you've learned with others.

"Your time is limited, so don't waste it living someone else's life. Don't be trapped by dogma, which is living with the results of other people's thinking. Don't let the noise of others' opinions drown out your own inner voice. And most important, have the courage to follow your heart and intuition: they somehow know what you truly want to become. Everything else is secondary."

— Commencement speech to Stanford students in 2005
  by Steve Jobs

INTRODUCTION

Many great people have mentored me along the way. I've spent years reading, studying, going to seminars, and working in companies with some really powerful business builders and creators. But without a doubt, the greatest teacher I have ever encountered has been my spiritual guide—who is known around the world as Sidi, which is a common term of endearment.

Not only have I been blessed to meet him and study his teachings, but as you will learn also, I have spent years by his side, traveling with him and sitting next to him during all the teachings he has given in this country and abroad. The love I feel for Sidi really has no limits, and the gratitude that wells in my heart as I mention him is immense. There's no doubt in my heart or mind that it is through him that I have learned the most, and have grown the most, and owe the most. I love him deeply and unconditionally; and it has been a truly great honor to serve him and help him share his message of peace, love, mercy, justice, and freedom.

Up until now, I have not really introduced him fully in any of the books I've written, other than my personal story of meeting him. Here I will focus on him to a greater extent—more than just mentioning some ideas he has taught me. I've actually transcribed excerpts from his talks and plan to insert them in various chapters. I believe, without any doubt, that if we want to really grow and experience a fulfilling life, we must develop ourselves spiritually and have a connection with God or the Divine, or however you choose to call the Creator. Sidi has guided me to understand this more than any person I have ever met. I hope that you will enjoy his teachings, and that they will have the impact on you that they've had on me. I have not edited his talks, other than adding a comma or two, so there are grammatical and syntactical errors. But I wanted you to experience their original flavor.

Sidi's natural language is Arabic, and he is what is called a "Sufi." Rumi is probably the best known Sufi in the Western world. Sufism is knowledge of God through the heart; it is what I call the mystical side of Islam, just as the Kabbalah is the mystical side of Judaism, or the Philokalia is from the mystical side of Christianity. The message of Sufism contains the religion of Unity and the religion of all the Prophets, peace and blessings be upon them all. Sufism is a complete religion embracing the spiritual laws as well as the inner truth. Sidi teaches that we are all one heart, one body, one mind, and one spirit; and he says that he is the guide of love, peace, mercy, justice, and freedom. He believes we all come from Adam and Eve; and that Abraham, Moses, Jesus, and all the other prophets teach the same thing and carry the same message.

I think that as you read his words, you will come to have a deeper understanding of the universal truths we all share, regardless of where we live or which spiritual tradition we follow.

When I first met Sidi, one of the things I strongly felt was the immense possibility of the human being to live in a manner much greater than the way most of humanity seems to function. Now when I look into and feel Sidi's heart, I feel the heart of those he lives to serve and the devastation of their experiences, the pain of their suffering, and how easy it is to disconnect from the heart wrenching sadness of their pain. I feel the power of the faith that allows him to work so tirelessly to bridge the gap that opens the roadway between people who can give to those who need. And I hope that by sharing many of his words in the following chapters, you will be moved to stop thinking for just a minute about all the things you *don't* yet have, and instead look at that which you *do* have, and that which you can share with those in need.

As I said, I've drawn a lot from Sidi's teachings, but I've also learned a lot from other spiritual traditions, and they have helped me learn about the power of acting in harmony with spiritual truths. I spent a year of my life living in India immersed in Hindu teachings, a lot of time focused on Buddhism and Vipassana meditation, years studying the great Christian mystics and a wonderful book called the Philokalia—which was about the "prayer of the heart"—and a long time with the Tarot and the mystical studies of Judaism, especially the Kabbalah. I have endeavored to share a lot of my favorite quotes from all these traditions to substantiate the fact that they all share the same truths and have a common meeting ground, and that there are many paths that lead to the Truth. (Please note that I have capitalized certain words intended to express the Divine.)

I chose my path because of the man who introduced me to it, and had he been from another tradition, I would have immersed myself in *that* tradition. I wanted a guide who I could have a relationship with, to hold my hand and walk me through all the different paths of the journey. I wanted to learn from someone from whom I could feel a connection with God that was complete, and whose life was one of service.

For now, I want to share a bit more about me, because I'm sure that within my story you will find pieces of your own.

Chapter 1

Secrets of Wealth Creation

I went to some of the best private schools and absorbed a lot of great information, but I never learned in those institutions how to take that information and make *money* with what I knew. I actually dropped out of Yale University to pursue my passion for theater, and have never really looked back since.

I am a great believer in self-education and personal growth, and have spent a considerable amount of my time and income learning from leaders in marketing, sales, and personal growth. Within these pages, I've distilled a lifetime of learning, the thousands of dollars that I've invested in those lessons, into an effective way for you to benefit from what I've learned.

But make no mistake. If you don't actually go out and *do* the things I share here, then I cannot imagine anything changing in your life. What has made a difference for me is putting into practice what I have to share. I have actually implemented the systems and processes that are described here into my own life. And, for example, if I mention the name of a book and you don't read it, then the knowledge within that work is pretty worthless in terms of creating a better life for yourself.

I found a quote on Facebook that said:

"Nobody can go back and start a new beginning, but anyone can start today and make a new ending." — **MARIA ROBINSON**

Recently I was driving somewhere with my wife and we saw a poster for Prudential Insurance that said: "Live your life without outliving your income," and one of the things I would like to accomplish here is to help you figure out how to do that in the most enlightened way possible. I had a good friend who made millions on Wall Street, and he was even featured on the cover of *Time* magazine, but he had such a strong drug habit that everything sort of crashed down around him, and one day I asked him what had happened, and he said, "I don't know. I think I always thought I would die before I ran out of money."

A few miles past that billboard on the highway, there was another one from Prudential that read: "We're all living longer. Our money should, too." I think we all want our wealth to outlast our lives, and one way to accomplish this is to create residual income, which is income that continues working even when we do not. It works even while we sleep; it also continues on after we die. So when you're building a business with residual income, you're developing an asset that will live longer than you do. So I strongly recommend finding a business that has meaning for you and that can also create this type of income.

An example of residual income is a song, a book, or some other creation that earns income on a continual basis. A fully paid-off piece of real estate that receives rental income is a form of residual income. In my case, I've built a network marketing business that has paid me month in and month out for over a decade now.

The Importance of Giving

I have been abundantly blessed, and I feel it's because I believe so strongly in giving in order to receive, which is a concept I'm going to be stressing over and over again within these pages. Giving opens the gateway to the heart so that you can receive. I believe that how much money you earn in life is frequently in direct correlation to how much value you deliver to others on a consistent basis. I say frequently because this isn't always the case. There are many teachers who offer tremendous value year after year to our youth and are not paid what they're worth, yet their internal rewards might be immense. Generally, I've found that when we give a lot of value to people, we generally receive a lot in return.

Like many secrets, once you actually understand them, then they don't really seem like such big secrets. For example, a lot of magic tricks involve a secret you need to understand if you want to know how they're done, and once you know the secret, then it might not feel like such a mystery. For me, I know that a magic trick is a really good one when I still like it after I understand the secret. And the same is true for many things in life. Once you learn the secrets of how to open your heart and really start to connect with others, the more you will penetrate into the mystery of love, and the more your appreciation for everything in your life will grow.

Our destinies are often decided by moments that take our breaths away, stop our hearts, and touch us in places where we have not yet been touched. Sometimes those moments are joyous, sometimes painful, and sometimes we don't even realize at the time how important they may be. How many people met their future life partner and never knew at that moment they would have such a deep connection? I never realized when I saw my first magic trick how much passion I would develop, how many hours of my life would be dedicated to learning and mastering certain sleights-of-hand, and lead me into a fascination with understanding the psychology of the human mind. I definitely fell in love with magic from the first moment I was exposed to it, but for years it was really just a hobby.

All the lessons, ideas, teachings, practices, and systems that I share here have really worked for me, and have also worked for countless others. What I love most about all of them is that I feel that I've been able to develop so many different areas of my life, and I can't really take credit for what is shared here other than being a funnel for others' generosity. That is, they shared the thoughts, feelings, and extraordinary abilities that allowed countless others to learn how to become empowered expressions of the Divine creation.

Why I Wrote This Book

I have created this book and program not because I want to earn more money, but because I want to give back all I have already received. One hundred percent of the profits from the last book I wrote were donated to those in need. I don't know what I will do *here* yet, but I am hoping to do something similar. At any rate, if what you find in this book or in the membership site, which will be a place to meet with me and other seekers, is not worthwhile to you, I will refund your money, no questions asked.

I am not scared of work, but find that I'm often busy with things that are not as productive as I would like them to be. And being busy is not the same as working, as you well know. Creating wealth is a process that requires intention, as well as attention to detail and focus.

This is a story with no beginning and no end. I want to share with you a process, one that totally transformed my life and helped me create the wealth I desired. Many of the things that occurred during this process are archetypal, and I'm sure that you'll see some of your own story within mine.

I've written a number of books and ebooks, and some of the material that I've shared in those works is presented here as well, so if some of it seems familiar, it is, because you might have seen it before. I have selected what I feel are the core ideas that have worked best for me and have continued to build on these concepts as I've applied them personally.

Where I Am Today

I am currently living a life that is so filled with abundance in so many areas, and in my heart I truly want that for you. There's a saying in my spiritual tradition that goes: "No man is a believer unless he desires for others what he desires for himself." I hope that by sharing my journey with you, you will find ideas that will add immense value to your life. I am committed to doing everything I can to help you, and I am always available to answer questions. You can e-mail me at: tony@tonykent.com, and I will usually respond within a few days. If you don't hear back within 24 to 48 hours (e-mails get lost), please go to my websites: www. MakeYourLifeMagical.com or www.TonyKent.com and fill out one of the forms requesting a consultation. There is no charge for this service at this time.

I believe my examples will empower you to follow your dreams, create wealth, and experience abundance. In the current marketplace, we are seeing more and more successful people who have not been to college, but who followed their passions and attained so-called street smarts. I am a big believer in having the courage to be one's own boss, and feel that the rewards are so immense that they far outweigh the risks.

There are a number of young, exciting entrepreneurs creating really wonderful web-based programs, which are heavily focused on personal growth and spiritual principles. One of my personal favorites is a young man of 27, Jonathan Budd. Just the other day, I was listening to one of his webinars, this one about Facebook, and after buying his program, I went online to search for some videos of his I'd seen in the past that I loved, both for their extraordinarily beautiful images and for the content. I don't remember whether it was from the webinar or the video that I took the quote below, and I'm not sure I even got it exactly right, but in general he was talking about systems, and how important it is to test your systems and to test your ads to learn what works and what doesn't. It's necessary to test these things if you want to reach your goals and manifest your visions.

And then he said: "If you want to master life, you have to also test yourself." I found this to be a really awesome way of presenting a truth that is so important. And I loved the connection between one's business and personal life, which is really what this book is about. So as you read these chapters, please take the time to do the exercises suggested and test the teachings that I'm sharing here. I have tested these concepts over and over, and I'm sharing them with you because I believe in them and they have worked for me, which has allowed me to manifest so many of my visions. But I cannot stress enough that if you just read these pages and don't actually *do* something with the information presented, it won't have much value for you.

Chapter 2

My Background

Let me start by giving you more in-depth information about my background than I offered in the preface. I was born in New York City on August 29, 1941. I spent the major portion of my adult years living in France working as a fashion photographer. I had a very successful career and was fortunate to work for many of the best magazines. During one of my assignments for French *Vogue*, I met and fell deeply in love with a French woman by the name of Nathalie, who was at that time an editor for the magazine. We subsequently married and had four children together. Sharing my life with Nathalie felt like a constant showering of magical dust sent down by the Divine, and my life prospered in many ways.

In the safety of the love we shared, my heart opened up in ways I had not previously known, and the more my heart opened, the more I felt that I grew as a person. For more than 20 years I lived in the blessing of this love until the early 1990s, when, as I mentioned earlier, Nathalie felt the need to experience life on her own.

My heart shattered when she left, and the pain rendered me totally dysfunctional. For the next four to five years I was obsessed with my misfortune while raising our four children who stayed with me, and I was feeling very angry and desperately sorry for myself. One of the therapists I was seeing, a wonderful and loving woman named Ava Brenner, said that one day I would build an altar to commemorate this event in my life, and my thinking at the time was: *I can't believe I'm paying $100 an hour to hear this.* (Yet she turned out to be right, and you will see why this is so as you read on.)

The whole thrust of what I want to share with you here is that the future you're going to have tomorrow, you can actually start creating today. If you want to create enough wealth to feel financially free, start now by developing the habits that will produce this wealth. Sometimes very small actions that we take have great and powerful consequences. When we feel that the time has come to change our life, one of the first things we need to do is accept personal responsibility. This means that we stop blaming other people or outer circumstances for what has happened, and realize that what we have created in our lives is our own doing.

As my life fell apart, it took me years to turn my attention to myself and stop blaming things or people outside of me. It felt like an impossible task at the time. There was no way I was ready to accept that a part of me had been responsible for the falling apart of my marriage and my life. I really felt at the time that it *wasn't* my fault, and while I was stuck in that attitude, it became really hard to instigate change.

The Tapestry Unravels

I had saved some money over the 25 or 30 years that I had worked as a photographer, because I knew I had to. Being self-employed, I wasn't privy to benefits or pension programs, so I was responsible for providing for my latter years myself. But I ended up going through my life savings very quickly. In fact, it was gone in less than two years.

It was amazing how I had miscalculated. Sometimes you think $50,000 to $100,000 is a lot of money. I'd never actually accumulated much more than that because I was always doing things, buying things, spending money, and living well. I made a lot of money, and my cash flow was always pretty consistent, so I never imagined it would stop. So even though, in my mind, I thought I had a lot of money in reserve, when the time came that I stopped working for six months to a year, or wasn't working at the same rate that I'd been working at previously, it was amazing how fast the money disappeared.

Imagine a big tapestry of the picture of my life—that is, what I *thought* it would be like. I imagined myself to be a successful father, husband, and photographer, with a certain lifestyle, kind of like one of those Norman Rockwell paintings that used to be on the cover of *The Saturday Evening Post*. It was a pretty secure picture, one that I had formed, obviously, pretty early in my life. That picture fell apart; all the threads of the tapestry unraveled on the floor, and I was in a lot of fear. I would lie awake at night and worry to myself, *What am I going to do?* I was very depressed, and wondered what would happen to my children. My wife had really been the social person, and she had a very large family with lots of brothers and sisters. That was my connection to the world at large. We had been living well with a big house and a pretty high mortgage, spending a lot every month to keep up our lifestyle.

Fear is really just imagined pain.

One thing I've learned since all this fell apart and I was lying there in fear, is that fear is really just imagined pain, because most of the things that I feared during that time of my life never came to pass. I would sit there and imagine a lot of negative things. I think I could have stopped all of that worry a lot sooner, but I didn't realize how important it is that our attitude (or change of attitude) can really change our lives. I was convinced that if I could just change one person's viewpoint—that is, convince my wife to come back to me—that everything in my life would be on-track again. It was a very controlling and manipulative way to think, but it was where I was at the time. I wanted the love from one source, and in the exact form I'd always had that love. But because I wasn't getting it in the way I wanted, I felt that I wasn't getting it at all. I realize now that we don't ever fall *out* of love. The love just gets blocked, and blocked love creates pain, which renders us dysfunctional.

Love is eternal and it is always present, even if we can't feel it. We are all children of God. We might not know this consciously, we might forget it, but we will always be Divine creations.

So as I was lying in bed (on those evenings I probably never slept more than two hours at a stretch), and I was in a very bad state. I would go into my office during the day and start looking through my papers and try to figure out who I was going to call for jobs. I had no motivation to go out and take photographs because I'd only been doing it the previous few years to support my family. My passion was gone. And unfortunately, I had no idea how to turn that *into* passion. There was nothing that I was passionate about except my children. I used to sit there and think to myself, *How am I going to get out of this hole?*

How Small Actions Can Lead to Big Results

I had a basket on wheels in which I kept my in- and out-boxes for my mail. When I was sitting at my desk, I could touch it with my arm. I had papers in one of the baskets, and I had books in another. In another basket I had a dozen or so cassette tapes I'd received in the mail, most of them promoting home-based businesses. When I first moved back to America, I'd read in various newspapers and magazines about starting a secondary business, and I thought this was something that would create cash flow in addition to photography. I'd sent away for a few things, so I guess I was on a lot of mailing lists, and I was constantly receiving offers in the form of letters and tapes in the mail. I threw out most of the letters and magazines but happened to keep the tapes.

I lived in Europe for almost 25 years and had never received tapes in the mail, so the novelty of the idea made me hold on to them. I started seeing a lot of promotion for businesses that helped create residual income, and I knew something about this topic because I had friends who were artists, rock 'n roll stars, or movie people, and the royalties they earned were a form of residual income.

My sister, Jill Krementz, is a very well-known photographer and author who was married to Kurt Vonnegut, an enormously successful writer. (He is no longer with us in body, but his spirit and writings are still very much present.) Jill has created a number of wonderful books on her own, including *A Very Young Gymnast* and *A Very Young Rider,* from her *Very Young* series. And also, *How It*

Feels to Fight for Your Life and *How It Feels When a Parent Dies,* from her *How It Feels* series. These books contain beautiful photographs of young kids, with sensitively written testimonials and first-person narratives. I knew she was doing very well selling these books over the years. The same was true of my friends who were artists. They would create works of art that would then allow them to earn residual income. So I knew about this concept and appreciated it.

I did many things to try to create residual income that didn't work. But I didn't quit. I kept going until I found something that worked for me. I had tried real estate development, the stock market, commodities, taking photos that would be resold more than once, and many other endeavors. The problem was that I hadn't found an opportunity that I really wanted to do because I *loved* it. More often than not, I was doing something because I thought I could make money from it, and that, in itself, never worked for me. Whenever I encountered obstacles, unless I had some passion and deep belief in what I was doing, I would end up focusing more on the resistance or rejection of other people than on my own desires.

Without that passion, I kept saying to myself, "God, why am I in such pain? I've been a good father. I'm a good husband. Why do difficult, challenging, bad things happen to good people?!" Little did I know that each day all I had to do was reach into my basket and listen to a particular tape to find the solution to my current situation. I had the tapes for months (I think I had 10 to 15 tapes; I'd never really counted them). In other words, the solution to all my challenges was right in front of me, just a few feet away, but I didn't recognize it.

We have windows of opportunity surrounding us at all moments that we actually don't recognize.

It's like the person who loses a piece of gold and walks right by ten piles of silver because he's just looking for that gold. I thought about this for months afterward. One day I was walking out of my office to my car and I just reached into the basket and took out a tape that ended up putting me on a path that would lead to a tremendous life change. What made me pick up the tape that day?

I thought to myself that if I could figure *that* out, I might have a key to help *other* people create change in their lives. But I *did* pick up the tape, and as I told you, at the time it didn't seem like a very important gesture.

A small gesture can make such a big effect as it leverages out.

I suggest you try a little experiment to illustrate this idea for yourself. Stand with your feet together and point yourself toward a spot in front of you—say, the middle of a wall, and start walking. You will be moving in one straight line and end up in the middle of the wall; but if you make a slight alteration now and just turn a few degrees with your feet and point yourself toward the door, then you will walk in that direction instead. If you don't make a small adjustment now, when you get to the middle of the wall, it takes a lot more energy to change direction, walk along the wall, and then out the door. So a small adjustment now will save you a lot of effort down the road.

So, back to that tape I listened to.

We tend to take things for granted when they're going well, but if we're sick, for example, we start to really appreciate what it feels like to be well and decide to pay attention to our health. Taking care of ourselves physically is of vital importance, and I believe it is one of our most vital responsibilities. Earth's topsoil is so eroded now that most of the food we eat is lacking in mineral content, and if our food is lacking in mineral content, it stands to reason that our bodies are also lacking minerals. The food that they talked about on the tape that fateful day—blue-green algae—is mineral-rich and full of trace minerals, amino acids, vitamins, chlorophyll, and protein. Almost immediately upon eating it, I started to feel better; and eventually I created a business where I shared this food with other people. The reason that I started doing so was that I was so passionate about the improvements in my health and well-being.

me: not once or twice, but numerous times. And I'm sure that we're not that much different.

Whether it was business, personal growth, relationships, spirituality or any other aspect of my life, I would read, study, attend seminars, or do whatever else I could to grow in every way possible.

So take things step by step, and stay committed and persistent.

An Important Tip

Here is one of the most important tips I can share with you: What you focus your thoughts on is going to be a huge factor with respect to where you end up. I will tell you over and over about my belief that vision can and does become a reality, so where you look and what you think about is going to determine where you end up. I choose to only think about things that I want to see happen in my life, and will always avoid spending time in a negative space.

One of the great commonalities I've noticed with every teacher, almost without exception, is that they build upon what they have learned from other experts in their field and their life experience. They then shape that into what they feel is a cohesive learning experience, and then go out and share it with others in the hopes of being able to help them on their life journeys. That's what I'm trying to do here.

For example, my spiritual teacher, Sidi, has learned from some of the greatest teachers in the Middle East; has studied the Bible, the Torah, and the Qur'an; and knows the teachings of all the prophets. He is a master of what he teaches.

In September 2011, I went to a seminar given by Brendon Burchard, the founder of Experts Academy (a training academy for authors, speakers, and more), and he shared that not only does he read books by those he admires, but has also worked with Tony Robbins, Frank Kern, David Bach, and a long list of experts in all the fields he's been interested in mastering. He is now changing lives by teaching what he has learned to others.

Anyone who wants to master something must spend thousands of hours working at whatever it is they want to master, but first they have to take that first step.

**No matter where you are in your life today,
you are free to change your circumstances
by changing yourself.**

I think we all want to keep changing, evolving, and moving forward to manifest our greatest potential. If you're like me, deep in your heart you want to make a difference in the world. You want to be someone who helps improve the lives of others. We sometimes think that we just want more for *ourselves,* but really the source of this desire turns out, for many, to be the desire to do more for others.

The purpose of this book is to share the philosophies, techniques, thought processes, and methods I have used to create a life that I believe is truly magical; and in so doing, help you to **MAKE *YOUR* LIFE MAGICAL.**

Chapter 3

My Love of Magic

I've had a lifelong romance with magic. Before I stated to write this book, I looked up the word *magic* on Google, and this is what appeared:

Magic: The power of apparently influencing the course of events by using mysterious or supernatural forces.

It really brought a big smile to my face, because it seemed to sum up what I want to share with you here. I've had such a blessed life, and I have a passion to share some of the things I've learned along the way, because in my heart, I truly want to see more people living out their dreams.

I love magic, and I think the most beautiful thing we can *experience* in life is magic: the magic of God, the magic of love, the magic of a beautiful day, the magic of being able to turn pain into passion . . . which is not as hard as many people think.

When you look at painters' canvases, you can see their art in how they go from white to black, in the stroke of their brushes, in the choice of their colors. When you watch dancers, you can see their art in their technique and form, and in their grace and fluidity, but when you watch a magician, what you *don't* see is the art involved.

So when we look at that definition of magic and read "the power of apparently influencing," we can see how in alignment this idea really is. For example, if you're selling something, when you see the selling, it is not really magical, but when you *don't* see the selling, it comes across as teaching, educating, or adding value to someone's life.

There are so many things in life that remain mysteries to the unenlightened. When I turn on a light switch, it is magical to *me*, but not to an electrician. The way my car works is magic to *me*, but not to a mechanic. And some of the magic performed by magicians would be a mystery to most people, but not to me. I find that when things are explained and I can understand how they work, it makes me just as happy as I would feel witnessing the beauty of the mystery behind it.

I don't think that the beauty and majesty of a sunset is diminished when I understand the science behind it. Magic is the same thing. When *how* something works is explained to me, it's as if a lightbulb has gone on inside me and a ray of illuminating light shines on everything. I enjoy it immensely. As certain spiritual truths have been explained and I've come to understand them, I get the same feeling. Many times I'm just as happy to be humbled by the mystery as I am to understand it. In fact, knowing how something works actually improves things for me because getting to the core of the truth of things is so deeply meaningful.

When we allow ourselves to trust enough to give ourselves completely into love, it's like sinking into the heart of God. Everything disappears but love itself, and then we are in a truly magical moment. When you meet people who are bubbling over with joy, you don't see the struggles in their lives, and this makes them very charismatic. It doesn't mean they haven't struggled, or that they're not struggling in the moment. It's just that it's more hidden, and the individuals have usually gotten to a point in their lives where they are more in the flow, and where they trust their higher selves more. That is, they've started to overcome the fear and negative self-talk that holds so many people back.

My life doesn't seem to take a lot of effort because I spend so much time doing things I love. To someone else it might appear to be a nightmare, but I am blessed to absolutely *love* my life. But this has not always been the case.

How I Got Started

My introduction to magic occurred when I was around ten years old. I had a neighbor, who was one of my best childhood friends, named Jeff Gillespie. We shared a passion for baseball. He was a Yankee fan, while I was a Dodgers fan, and we had a lot of good arguments. I had to eat a lot of humble pie, as the Yankees constantly beat the Dodgers during that time.

One day Jeff showed me a couple of card tricks, and I was immediately mesmerized and just had to know how he did them. He was pretty clever, and got me to trade every Yankee baseball card he coveted before he would explain the tricks to me. But as soon as he did so, I got quite upset, as I had given him some pretty valuable cards in exchange for the information, and I didn't feel that I had received that much value in return. However, once I started showing those tricks to friends at school, I used them as leverage to get a lot of things *I* wanted, so it turned out to be a great deal. Also, whenever I showed those tricks to people who also knew a card trick, they would teach me one of *their* tricks to learn how I did mine. Within months, I knew a dozen tricks and was on my way to a pursuing a hobby that became a lifetime passion.

Not long after, I fell down at school and suffered a concussion and a fractured skull, which laid me up in bed for a while. My mom went to the local library and got me some books on magic. One of them was on a *different* kind of magic, almost like voodoo, talking about how to make offensive friends disappear through spells, and so on, and this was actually my introduction to mysticism. My mom used to pay me 25 bucks to learn the tricks she couldn't figure out, so I got a lot of mileage from the two tricks Jeff taught me. I haven't seen him since those days, and I can't imagine he has any idea of how sharing a couple of tricks with me so changed my life. As an aside, when I went to Paris for the first time, I supported myself by doing magic in clubs there.

A Hidden Secret in the Declaration of Independence

Here's a good trick that can make you look deeper into the mysteries of things, because my guess is you've seen the following words a number of times without ever imagining that there are secrets hidden inside. The following is a fun example of some hidden magic, and the words are divided into three segments: **bold**, *italicized* and underlined for a reason. They make up the first paragraph of the Declaration of Independence, and they go as follows:

When in the course of human events, it becomes necessary for one people to dissolve the political bands which have connected

them with one another, and to assume among the powers of the earth, the separate and equal station to which the Laws of Nature and of

Nature's God entitle them, a decent respect to the opinions of mankind requires that they should declare the causes which impel them to the separation.

You are instructed to pick any word in the first (**bold**) section of the text. Then, skip as many words as there are letters in your chosen word. For example, if you picked the fourth word (**course**) you have to skip six words (**of human events, it becomes necessary**) to end up on the word **for.** Repeat the same process by skipping as many words as there are letters in the successive words you land on.

What's the first word you encounter in the last (underlined) section?

Answer: God. And if you did everything precisely as explained, this is always the word you will end on.

I don't know if you're aware of it, but some authors go to some pretty unusual lengths to hide keys in their books. Sometimes the last word of every chapter will spell out the text of a hidden secret. I think *The Da Vinci Code* revealed some of these coded texts. I have heard that if you take the shortest and longest psalms in the Bible and go to the middle word, this is the exact center of the Bible, and the Book of Psalms was written years after most of the Bible was. Our dollar bill has hidden symbols, so we are surrounded with mysteries and magic that abound in so many unexpected places, but once they're explained, we're still amazed.

In many of the teachings that will be shared here, you might at first wonder what is so special about them—that is, where the magic is, but I want to encourage you to read them over and over. There's a lot of wisdom from some very magical people, and if you spend the time, you will unlock many keys. Later, if you want more help, there will be a membership site with special lessons to allow you to go more deeply into each chapter, and give you the opportunity to ask questions and engage in a dialogue, which should help you immensely.

Another thing I love about magic is how it pushes boundaries and belief systems. I was watching someone called Marco Tempest on TV the other night, and he mentioned that he feels that magic blurs the lines between truth and lies; and that with magic, we can create our own reality.

By using our imagination, we can see differently, and this is so important in life. We can make the impossible seem possible, which is such a powerful tool. When we were young, so many things appeared magical, but we lost this sense of wonder as we grew older, so it's important to rediscover that magic.

That's why I love using magic as a way to reexperience this sense of wonder. As I found my spiritual path and devoted myself to a life of service, I began to regain this sense of magic. Some days when I look out upon the magnificent universe that God created, I am completely in awe—a much deeper sense of awe than I ever experienced as a child.

Just like most people, I've had some extended periods where getting through each day was agonizingly painful. Who I am today is a result of having worked my way through those struggles using the information I'm about to share with you.

I've had an amazing journey, started a new business, remarried, moved to a different state, started a nonprofit that now has thousands of people involved with it, and a number of other things that I will share with you as we move forward.

My new wife, who has a Ph.D. in psychology, shared a joke with me: "How many psychologists does it take to change a lightbulb? One, but the lightbulb has to want to change."

If you're reading this book, I imagine it's because *you* want to change, or want to learn more about how to help others do so. And I thank you for taking the time to look at what I have to offer. I hope you'll find information within these pages that will be helpful in getting you from where you are to where you want to go.

I've spent most of my adult life pursuing spiritual teachings and studying personal growth, and have been truly blessed to encounter some phenomenal teachers, so I almost can't find the words to tell you how honored I am to share my journey with you. It seems that more and more, I run into individuals and groups who have a sincere passion for helping others, and I keep meeting so many people who have tremendous talents and abilities. The majority of lessons I've learned, though, have come through my spiritual guide Sidi, and are based on teachings from the Bible, the Torah, and the Qur'an; and have been taught by the prophets for centuries.

Awaken Your Inner Magician

I have had a number of great teachers in the field of magic, but as I've mentioned, the most magical teacher I've ever met is Sidi. I shared that story in a book called *My Journey to Know the Truth: Healing the Broken Heart*.

As we individuals accept and take on the task of being the best we can be, we can lead by example and inspire so many more people to simply stop accepting a life of mediocrity and live as fuller expressions of God's creation. Stepping out of our comfort zones has risks, but that's far less risky than living a life that doesn't really make us feel fully alive. As we reach out to work collectively in a spirit of co-creation (I am not referring to co-creation with God, but co-creation with other people) instead of competition, focused more on what we *want* to create rather than on *who* creates it, we will move toward the realization that we are one heart, one mind, one body, and one soul. And that if each one of us does everything we can to realize our potential, we will make our lives magical.

Hidden inside of all of us is our own personal magician, someone who can turn pain into passion, struggle into ease, sorrow into joy, tears into laughter, and poverty into richness. I want to show you how to connect with this magician and change the things in your life you *want* to change.

If I were to show you a magic trick now, you might say something like, "No way, that's impossible!" but if I revealed the process I used, you might say, "Wow, that's really easy." Some of the effects have taken me literally years to learn, but others, I learned very fast, once I knew the secret. There are some things that you can learn that you can start applying today so you can make immediate changes, and there are some that will take longer. The ascension of the highest mountain starts first with a desire to climb it, and then taking a first step. You don't need to be a genius, you just need to learn to be more effective, and you can do this by *deciding* to make changes, and then just taking one step at a time.

Even though you may think you're stuck and see no light at the end of the tunnel, once you start walking, the light can appear very quickly. In a recent seminar, Brendon Burchard conducted a group process where the entire room focused their attention on one person and then extended their arms and wiggled their fingers and said "Shazam." I hope that what follows is a "Shazam" for you. As a young magician, I would say "Abracadabra" when I wanted something to either disappear or appear, so I say "Abracadabra," and may all *your* challenges disappear, and may all your dreams be realized.

The universe is full of magical things, patiently waiting for our wits to grow sharper. —EDEN PHILLPOTTS (1862–1960)

That must be wonderful! I don't understand it at all. —ANONYMOUS

"Any sufficiently advanced technology is indistinguishable from magic."
— THIRD LAW OF ARTHUR C. CLARKE (1917–)

EXERCISE

Make a list of five to ten different action steps that you feel you could take that might help you get from where you are to where you want to go. They don't have to be big steps, but be sure they're steps you're willing to take, and set a definite date for accomplishing them.

_____

_____

_____

_____

_____

_____

_____

_____

_____

_____

_____

_____

_____

_____

_____

_____

_____

_____

_____

Are you ready to take the step to Awaken Your Inner Magician?
Join me in our 8-week program for in-depth support.
www.MakeYourLifeMagical.com/explore

Chapter 4

.ఇ☆ఇ.

More on Wealth Creation

(Much of this chapter is taken from an ebook I wrote called *The Art of Abundance.*)

"Material success may result in the accumulation of possessions, but only spiritual success will enable you to enjoy them."
— NIDO QUBEIN

One of the keys I've used to create real wealth is developing a *feeling* of living in abundance. I've learned that wealth for one person does not necessarily translate to wealth in someone else's eyes. It has different meanings for different people. To one individual, maybe a million dollars represents great wealth, while to a billionaire, that amount may not seem very significant. Some people measure wealth with money, while others might say their real wealth lies in their health or overall well-being. Still others might value time and freedom above everything else, or say that true wealth lies is in love for their family.

Financial wealth starts by feeling deep within your being that when it comes to earning money, there is *no* lack of money in the world. Also, you need not think that because you earn a good income you're depriving someone else of his or her rightful share. There is nothing unfair about having a good income if you fill a legitimate need and help others get what they want.

There's a direct relationship between how much money you earn and how much value you offer to others.

There are too many people who compensate for their inability to manifest money by criticizing those who *do,* saying that money corrupts or whatever other phrase they find appropriate. If you're not earning what you'd like, take time to explore your own core beliefs about financial issues. Be honest with yourself—brutally honest—and if you have trouble getting to the root of your issues, ask those close to you what creative avoidance they feel you're adopting that has put you in your current situation.

Certainly enough stories abound about people who have started with nothing and who've achieved financial freedom, so really explore what's blocking your path or standing in your way. You have to eliminate all your own dysfunction around money and open yourself to stepping into the stream of abundance that others enjoy. If you look at *anything* with anger and resentment, it will create a life of limitation for you in that area.

Definition of Wealth

"Wealth is having the abundance of resources necessary to fulfill your life purposes."— From *10 Keys to Create Wealth,* by Michael Ellison

From the Internet: *Wealth: welfare; prosperity; good; well-being; happiness; joy; Riches; valuable material possessions; A great amount; an abundance or plenty; Power, of the kind associated with a great deal of money*

I agree with this definition. I also feel that wealth is having an abundant connection with God and being full of Divine Energy. This connection is the power behind everything that I have attained in life. It is the power that allows me to express myself in ways that help me to pursue my purpose. Abundance is a natural expression of life, as exemplified by how much abundance we see in nature. I believe that our Creator has already given us huge wealth through the abilities He has given us, which when used correctly, allow us to really live a magical life.

For out of His fullness (abundance) we have all received [all had a share and we were all supplied with] one grace after another and spiritual blessing upon spiritual blessing and even favor upon favor and gift [heaped] upon gift. — JOHN 1: 16

For me, success is all about helping others improve their lives, and if just one person is helped by something I say or do, then I can feel really positive about all the effort it takes just to complete one book such as this one. Success is also about being committed to, and moving toward, the realization of something that is bigger than we are, about moving forward as we contribute to a cause we believe in, and about doing something where we feel we're making a difference.

In fact, I feel that knowing what your purpose is and being able to clearly share it is so important that I plan to share a system with you to help you do just that.

If you look into your heart and seek your Creator, and continue seeking the Creator, you will eventually meet Him, because He is always seeking those who want to meet with Him.

Every book I have ever read about success that has had a major impact on me has had a focus on personal growth and a connection with God. I love what Carl Jung said when asked if he thought there was a God. He replied, "Do I think there is a God? I don't *think* there is a God. I *know* there is a God."

And I have that kind of certainty as well. Whether you refer to the Creator as God, Allah, Spirit, Love, or any other name, it's not as important as believing in something greater than yourself. The reason this is so important is that it goes hand-in-hand with having a purpose that is bigger than your self. And it is in connecting with that purpose that true wealth is attained.

When the voyage becomes more important and joyful than the destination, when the outcome is not as important as the experience, when the intention is what creates the fulfillment, then we are living in harmony with Divine principles. This is because it is in giving that we can experience some of our greatest feelings of joy and fulfillment.

We might think our happiness is dependent on what we receive, but I believe true happiness comes in giving, and can far outweigh the joy we experience when receiving. I have heard it said that our wealth is not truly ours until we give it away.

Your success in life, your ability to create wealth (abundance) in all areas—not just financially, but emotionally, personally, spiritually, and physically—will have more to do with your passion, your desire to make a difference, your ability to be persistent and consistent, and your faith, than depending on others to come up with the answers. Every great idea still needs great follow-up, dedication, and belief—not only in what you are doing, but in who you are *being.*

Following these paragraphs is a picture of a sign I saw many years ago while on a photo assignment in Thailand. It shares an important message, and is an example of how we can find truth in many different places. The sign was on a tree in a remote village, and none of the other signs I saw were in English, but I think this one was meant for me. I was spending a lot of my prayer time asking God to send me what I needed, and I figured if he gave me more, I would have more to give, and then have time to do good things. Since then I've learned that by first giving, by first doing good… this is what opens our hearts so that we're in a place where we can receive blessings. I've also learned that when we trust enough, we no longer have to ask for anything for ourselves because God knows what we need better than we do.

In case you have trouble reading the sign below, it says:

"Do good is better than asking for blessings."

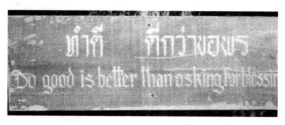

In the beginning, as my heart opened up to experience the spiritual side of my life, I was pretty amazed and in awe of creation, and had a hard time grasping how anyone or anything could possibly create all that exists. Yet years later, I am even more amazed by how magical it seems that all that exists is sustained. How many birds will be fed today? How many fish will have their needs met? How many people will experience moments of deep joy and fulfillment?

Dealing with Pain

Often when people get involved in personal-growth programs or are looking for change, it is pain that motivates them to look for something different.

"Pain is a common denominator drawing people together. The greatest pain is separation from God, and drawing nearer to God lessens the pain; because with proximity comes immense relief from pain, and immense gratitude fills our being, filling and replacing the void previously experienced." — **QUOTE FROM MY GUIDE, SIDI**

A lot of this program is not only about creating that connection, but also about maintaining it by following the spiritual laws passed down to us through all the holy books. It is about applying ancient wisdom to our modern lives to give them meaning.

"Thousands of candles can be lit from a single candle, and the life of the candle will not be shortened. Happiness never decreases by being shared." — **BUDDHA**

There's a saying in my spiritual tradition, which God said through the angel Gabriel: "If I were to give to every living creature everything he asked for, it would not diminish the splendor of My abundance any more than dipping a pin in the ocean would decrease its depth."

I've thought a lot about this saying, and I realize that within it is a real key to opening one's heart to accept the limitless ability of God to offer each and every living creature whatever is needed. So there's no reason for anyone to worry that his or her abundance might detract from anyone else's. I've come to believe that millions of dollars does not represent even one grain of sand in the hand of God, and that there's more than enough to go around.

I've also come to believe that there's no limit to God's generosity, just as I believe that there's no limit to our own potential. And with this limitless potential, we can not only *be* more, but *have* more, and thus have more to give. In accepting this in my deepest heart, it eradicates all feelings of guilt that if *I* have something, it means someone else is deprived.

Does my use of air take air from someone else? God loves us because of His nature, not because of us. He loves us and forgives us because this is His quality. He gives us all we need for survival because of His generosity and not because of what we do or don't do. If things aren't going in a way that pleases me, I look at what I need to change to tap into this abundance that is constantly flowing to His creation.

"To understand everything is to forgive everything." — BUDDHA

When we love someone, does that detract from the amount of love available to others? No, it doesn't. In fact, it *adds* to the amount of love in the world. It is magnetic, and it inspires others to love. It makes us feel good and others around us feel good. When we love, we are living in harmony with Divine principles and as an extension of our Creator, who loves unconditionally. When we are living from a place of love, we feel happy; which is a sign that we're connected to God. When we feel bad, it is a sign that we're less connected.

Clear your heart as a home for the Beloved. There He will unveil His beauty. — SHABISTARI

A Key to Creating Wealth

Now I want to share one of the true keys to creating wealth or abundance:

**We must discover our purpose,
and then live for this purpose from a place
of so much love that it becomes a passion.**

Without love, passion is empty. It's like a relationship based on physical attraction rather than deep emotion. Those of you who have had both experiences would, I hope, choose the emotional connection. Yes, there might be some pain involved, because there can be disagreements, rejections, hurt feelings, and so on, but there can also be moments of bliss that change us forever. Author Robert Fritz said, "The nature of creating is that we connect with the deeper spirit of ourselves throughout the process." And also, "The beauty of the human spirit: we can see beyond the current situations, and evoke the creative process." And then he shares what I want you really to get: "Exercise your imagination and you build the capacity to see beyond the circumstances, but imagination without work won't lead to anything."

When we are thoroughly committed to a purpose, we are lovers who are vulnerable. We can experience rejection, the pain of people not understanding our vision, and the disappointment of not being able to accomplish all we might want to. And yes, this can be painful, but it is nothing compared to the vast wasteland that people find themselves in when they live without passion and purpose. Remember the line from that well-known song: "It is better to have loved and lost than to have never loved at all"?

But love is what fuels the vision. Love is like the power of Divine connection. Love is a fire that you can fuel the flames of through constant, persistent, and consistent effort. And as the love grows and passion becomes ignited, the effort grows, but seems more and more effortless. Love is not the only powerful emotion. Desire, anger, fear, sadness, hope, and envy are also powerful; and they can fuel truly majestic experiences for us that create rich and transcending moments. Or, they can cause us to be real jerks and badly hurt others.

Our world progresses when mankind masters these emotions, and we slide backward when the opposite is true. Fear is normally thought to be such a negative thing, but fear of good things disappearing if we don't take action, fear of losing our home if we don't get out and do something, fear of losing our marriage if we don't change our ways, are just a few examples of how we can use a strong emotion to improve our situation. Fear can also paralyze us, so it can push us to a negative outcome. This is where spiritual strength can help us master our emotions and channel them into performing positive acts that can change our lives in a beneficial way.

"All the holy words you read and all the holy words you speak are as nothing if you do not act upon them, Even if you read little and say little but live the right way, forsaking craving, hatred and delusion, you will know the truth and find calmness and will show others the path." — BUDDHA

A Lesson from Sidi

Here are some excerpts from a talk given by Sidi in the summer of 2011 on the subject of love.

> *When you find the love, you find yourself. The secret is in the love. You are the love, not another. Everything is in the love, and everyone needs the love. If you find this, what more could you want? When you know, what could you want? When you have the knowledge of the love, you feel peace in your hearts. The jewels are inside you. This is the holy meaning.*
>
> *We ask God to surround us with peace and love, the everlasting love, the love that the human being could never do without, the true love that God wanted for us, for all the worlds, not just only for the human being.*
>
> *He made this love, also, between the animals and the birds and even the fishes. There is no creature that will do without this love, and this love cannot be expressed by the tongue. This love also*

has to be embodied in the hearts, in the bodies, in the souls. The human being should love his fellow human being. From wherever the person comes it doesn't matter, because the one who created him is God. He is the only One Lord.

We are all from one earth and from one drop of water. And the first item that God put in the human being is the love, and he did not come to this life without the result of the love. If it weren't for your father, your mother, and the love, you wouldn't be here. This is true. We should not deny it; we should keep it holy and make it pure.

This all resulted from a Divine command. God said, "I created you from one self."

He created the male and the female. Although your ways of living are separate and different, this is the wisdom of God. God said, "I created you from a male and a female. I made you into tribes and communities so you may know one another. The whole of creation are the dependents of God. Those who are most beloved to God are those who love His creation."

The truth of love is the essence of God. All this creation of God began with love. For this reason, this creation cannot continue unless we return back to the true essence of the creation, which is love. We must return and go back to the fragrance of love, the everlasting fragrance of love. If you accept this, accept it. You did not come to this earth as you wished. You came from the womb of your mother because you came through love, and the love is stronger than you are. The love forced you out of the womb of your mother. Then you have to prove yourself in this Divine test. The human being would be dignified or disgraced when he was put into a test.

Whether you are a man or a woman, we are all the same. You cannot say you are a man, you say that you are a human being. God did not say, "Oh, you man." He said, "Oh, you human being." What deluded you about your Lord? He perfected you and created you in the best image. God did not address the man or the woman singly. He addressed, "Oh, human being."

Take your mother who gave birth to you. She was in pain when she gave birth to you, tremendous pain. But after she gave birth to you, she held you in her arms and put you toward her breasts to feed you, and you started drinking milk from her breasts. She gave you the love from the first drop. At the time when you were coming out, you gave her a very painful labor and birth, but she gave you an exchange for that pain. She gave you the love, the love of this life. This is the beginning of the journey. Don't you remember that?

His Love is constant, for it is a continuous expression of affection. There is no other possibility except that God loves the world. Could the Maker dislike His own creation? We are made by Him; He is our Creator and the Creator of our provision and the Creator of everything.

He brings clear evidence, casting into our hearts the light of faith, making faith lovable to us and beautifying it within our hearts, while making wickedness and disobedience intuitively distasteful to us. And thus, we believe and have faith, and He then grants us success and uses us in what is pleasing to Him. Thus, we know that except for His love for us, none of this would ever have been.

What This Means

What this all means is that whether you are a man or a woman, from one culture or another, we are all from Adam and Eve, the first couple, so we are all related and all connected. Existence continues through love, and this is how we came into the world; so choose your actions in a loving way, follow what all the holy books tell you, love one another, and do everything you do in a loving way.

This is the way to open the doors of happiness, and when you are happy, your life will flow and you will have everything you need. Even when something happens that hurts you, continue to open your heart, and continue to let yourself love.

Our pain increases when we stop loving, because we are really going against our natural state of being. Not only is God the Creator of everything that is, but He is also the sustainer and provider that keeps everything going.

One of the reasons I am always so grateful is because God's ability to sustain everything is so awesome to me. I have worked for a few companies where the owners were unable to sustain the growth, so the companies crashed. As for me, I was unable to sustain my marriage and keep my family together. The human being is the one who is weak and makes mistakes. So why not turn to and trust the One who has proven what real sustainment is?

When choosing a business, it's important that it is in harmony with our purpose, because then we know that all the actions we are taking are helping us fulfill that purpose. The same is true about goals. So often I see people set goals that are not in alignment with their purpose. More often than not, this is because they don't have a clearly *defined* purpose.

But even if we don't consciously know our purpose, I believe our inner selves know what it is. And if we choose a goal that is in conflict with this desire, even if it is subconscious, then we will struggle to attain that goal.

Most people have jobs that are furthering someone else's purpose, and they perform that job just to put food on the table. They aren't happy with the position because it isn't furthering their own purpose. Someone who owns the business has bought them wholesale and is selling their efforts retail and pocketing the difference.

I have always worked for myself; so I make a conscious effort to choose activities that further my purpose and also help my businesses grow.

I have learned that sometimes I will spend six months to a year working to build an organization within the structure of a company and see very few real results. It feels like I'm struggling. Then I might change and go to another company, and everything seems to go so smoothly. What I've learned is that this is because, on a deep inner plane, I am more aligned with the real purpose of the individuals who run that company. This creates an atmosphere where things seem to flow more.

**When my goals are in alignment with my purpose,
all seems to go really smoothly.**

So what if you don't know your purpose? How can you make choices that are in alignment with it? If the quality of your life is determined by the quality of your choices, then it's important that you know your purpose. The next two chapters are going to show you a system to determine what your purpose is and help you express it so simply that a ten-year-old could understand what you're saying.

When reading the chapters on purpose, I invite you to take a pen and paper and do the exercises. Just reading the chapters won't change you. The change comes in the *doing*.

"No one does it until they do it." — **LAYLA KENT VIEL**
(my five-year-old granddaughter in 2011)

EXERCISE

Write a simple sentence expressing what you think your purpose in life currently is before reading the next chapter, and then see what changes occur, if any.

_____

_____

_____

_____

_____

_____

_____

_____

_____

_____

_____

Not sure what your purpose is? Join me in our 8-week program for in-depth support. www.MakeYourLifeMagical.com/explore

Chapter 5

.ঙ৵ঽ.

Defining Your Purpose

"Let yourself be silently drawn by what you truly love."

"Let the beauty of what you love be what you do."
— JALAL AD-DIN RUMI

"Many people have a wrong idea of what constitutes true happiness. It is not attained through self-gratification, but through fidelity to a worthy purpose." — HELEN KELLER

"The purpose of life is a life of purpose." — VICTOR FRANKL

People often ask me what I think the key to my success is, and I always answer that everything in my life comes as a result of my faith in God.

In terms of what the most *important* action step is, I would have to say it is in defining my purpose in life and constructing a written, memorized statement that a child could understand. I have been blessed in that I have had some wonderful teachers along the way, and the system that I'm going to share with you now is a blending of all of the information I've acquired.

When I first started leading seminars, I always tried to communicate the importance of a purpose statement. I think that one of our biggest fears is to lead a life without meaning, a life where we don't feel that we've made a difference.

Unless we know why we're here and what our unique gifts are, it's difficult to find a path of action where we feel we're making a significant contribution.

All too often we get caught up in existence mode, and then this develops into a pattern. Years go by and we never want to face the fact that we're on a course that leads nowhere. When someone or something in the form of a wake-up call confronts us, it is frequently depressing because we feel we've been wasting our lives. When I would bring up this subject in seminars, after a while I realized that when people were confronted with the question of what their life purpose is, they would get stuck in a place that didn't always feel good. The reason is that, for many people, it is a seemingly overwhelming task to state their purpose in clear and concise words.

I worked for a long time on how I could help people overcome this challenge, and I feel I've made some progress. I started by going to the bookstore and was astonished to find so few books about defining a purpose statement.

Our lives are simply too short to spend our time living someone else's purpose unless it is in total alignment with our own purpose.

I read once that Steven Covey, one of the foremost teachers and motivators in the country, took eight months to define a purpose statement for his family. The reason is that there is a process involved, and a purpose is more an ongoing situation rather than something finite, like a goal or a mission.

The Difference Between a Goal and a Mission

A goal or a mission is something that can be accomplished within the framework of a time limit. An example would be the goal of buying a new home by the end of the year, or within two years. A mission is something that is greater than a goal, and usually involves a cause. Gandhi had a mission of home rule for India; JFK had a mission of putting a man on the moon. In a sense, a mission is bigger and more important than a goal, and is usually in alignment with someone's purpose.

A purpose is something that is bigger than we are, something that no matter how much or how often we do, always allows room for more. There's no limit to how much we can love or be loved, there's no limit to how much faith we can have, and there's no limit to how much we can serve.

Purpose is something that comes from the heart, is full of passion, and fuels you so powerfully that no challenge is insurmountable. When you know your purpose, every choice you have to make in your life is simplified, because all you have to ask yourself is which of the things you're choosing between will help to further your purpose the most.

Living without knowing your purpose is like driving without knowing where you're heading. I know many times just taking a walk without any apparent destination can be a wonderful experience, but if you have an appointment with someone and don't know how to get there, it can be frustrating. When you know your purpose, that's a tool that will help you meet your destiny, and this is one appointment we should all want to keep.

We are, each one of us, unique individuals; each of us carries special gifts, and our life's journey is a path, which points the way and guides us to knowing why we're here. The clearer we become about our purpose, the more defined our path; and as our inner path gains clarity, the outside path becomes more focused. We see more clearly where we're going because we understand why we're going there. Each action we take resonates with our inner life, and we connect with other people who are clear about *their* life's purpose. And because focused energy is so powerful, a few people with a sense of purpose can break through the inertia of a large collective consciousness that is drifting along without any particular direction, or just resisting an idea whose time has come. That is why we have so many visionaries who have, by themselves, changed the direction of a nation.

Michael Ellison, the co-founder of a company I work with, is just such a man. With the power of his vision, he attracted people into his life who were necessary to help him get where he wanted to go. Starting with his wife, the two of them have touched hundreds of thousands of lives. There now exists a core group of people, each with similar visions, who can attain more as a group than each can individually. These people are seekers with a vision of world peace—a group of passionate and energetic individuals mutually interested in creating a team of socially conscious, environmentally aware, spiritually and physically healthy souls united together with the intention of drawing others to support this vision. All of this came about because one person started with a strong sense of purpose and was motivated day after day to find a way to attain a goal.

Michael has a passion for helping people experience wellness and create residual income to live their life purpose. He plans to expand his $100 million company into 100 countries over the next ten years. My wife and I just returned from Australia, where Michael traveled to bring a group of entrepreneurs to our current team.

With all the challenges he has encountered, it was the fuel of this sense of purpose that drove him to keep persevering, and today the company stands poised at the threshold of its greatness. It took him and his wife over a dozen years to get to this point, and I believe the company is now poised for hyper-growth. He works with his sons as well, so this is an added benefit.

Because each year there are more and more committed and connected people joining in this vision, there will soon be a force big enough so that the word of its existence will be heard and felt over larger and larger areas.

Choosing to Make a Difference

There are many people who lie awake at night and wonder what happened to their dreams as I did. They yearn for a sense of feeling connected; they are thirsty for a life where they can be part of a team and can make a difference. They know that deep in their hearts they are here for a purpose, and they are desperate to know what it is and how to express it.

They are tired of the struggle of their daily lives, and lack energy because they're eating food that doesn't nourish them because it comes from depleted soil. When they're exposed to a large group of people who are connected through a sense of purpose, they are drawn to this experience because these people are so charismatic. People with a clearly defined purpose are like magnets, because they mirror something of our own potential greatness back to us. In them we see a spark that is bright, because it accentuates our own darkness. This sense of contrast serves to awaken us. Their knowing awakens our own; their love and passion serve to remind us of how glorious it feels to be passionate and love ourselves, and gradually it becomes impossible to return to the station of our previous existence, because now we sense its emptiness.

We are not taught in school how to define our sense of purpose, we are not guided to express the beauty of our individuality, nor are we usually rewarded for being different. Fortunately, there are increasingly more educators offering forms of alternative education. I see a day coming when parents will not only trust the process of a more creative system of education, but will demand it, because scores of young people are graduating from these systems and serving as examples that are like shining beacons of light to their contemporaries.

My son Jason told me that when he was attending college, he was told that the universities were seeking people who have been to alternative-type schools, where personal responsibility is taught and the kids are free to study what they're truly drawn to. These individuals revere values and a sense of purpose more than an A-plus. Personally, if I were looking to hire someone to work with me, I would rather have one individual who knew his or her purpose than a bunch of college graduates who weren't sure why he or she were here on Earth.

How can we discover our purpose and put it in writing? This is surely one of the most challenging and thought-provoking issues we have to deal with. Often we find it frightening to confront such large issues without the benefit of guidance, and what I want to share with you now is a system devised through studying with many different teachers, and I apologize before starting for not remembering all my sources and all the names of the people who have contributed to this process. I kept many notes over the years, but sometimes it seems so obvious when I'm taking notes that I will never forget the source, but later this is not always the case.

What I hope is that in learning this system yourself, you will be able to pass it on to others and help them consciously embark on a path with clear purpose. For this to happen, I will explain along the way why I do things in the order I do, but feel free to change and adapt the process to suit you. I know that those who have contributed to this approach did so because they wanted to serve, and I cannot imagine that they'd be upset if you use the information as you see fit. I will mention the sources where appropriate—at least those that I can remember.

Chapter 6

Constructing Your Purpose Statement

The two most important books that I used in developing this technique were *The Path,* by Laurie Beth Jones, and *The On-Purpose Person,* by Kevin McCarthy. And, of course, numerous conversations with Sidi. So let's get started.

Start by making a list of what you believe are your ten best qualities and your ten best talents. Talents are things that you do well, such as cooking, driving, gardening, writing, speaking, and so on; while qualities are more about being. Some examples of qualities might be *kind, generous, compassionate, patient,* and *loving.*

During this entire process, it's important to avoid filtering any information. Anything that comes to mind should be noted, and can be eliminated or discarded later. For now, try to remember every flattering thing that your mom ever told you. Be kind and love yourself a lot, and don't judge yourself too harshly.

If you have a hard time coming up with positive qualities, think about what annoys your friends about you, and then go to the other extreme. For example, if they call you nosy, write down that you are curious; because *every good quality taken to an extreme can lead to a dark side, and every dark quality has an opposite side of goodness.* When you pick up one end of the stick, you also pick up the other end.

Our path is to integrate and embrace all parts of our nature, just as we need to learn to embrace each other.

Peace in the World

If we are to find peace in the world, we must learn to love as God loves—that is, unconditionally. Then we become a true extension of our Creator, and we can live in, and from, the love that created us. Global change starts with personal transformation; and personal transformation starts with personal truth, which culminates in global transformation.

Here is a passage that I hear often from Sidi that comes from his spiritual tradition, and are God's words revealed by the angel Gabriel to the prophet Muhammad:

My servant continues to draw near to Me with voluntary works,

More prayer, more remembrance, more good actions,

Until I love him.

And when I love him,

I am his hearing, with which he hears,

His seeing with which he sees,

His hand with which he strikes,

His foot with which he walks.

And were he to ask something of Me,

I would surely give it to him.

And were he to ask Me for refuge,

I would surely grant him it.

And if he says, "Be" then it is."

For God says,

"O, My worshippers, be to Me as I want you to be,

And I will become as you want Me to be."

So beloveds, would you not like to be in that loving state?

This love is so glorious.

This is the way. Amen.

When we align ourselves with teachings such as this, then we can more easily access our Divine nature, and our real purpose for being here becomes clearer. All religion is based on remembrance, so the more we remember our Creator, the more that Divine essence becomes actualized within us.

The Next Step

Once you have listed all your qualities and talents, take a moment and circle the two or three that you feel you use the most. In all of these exercises, the numbers are just indicators, and do not need to be exact. You can circle two or four or whatever number works for you. The purpose here is to start making conscious choices.

The reason I start with this exercise is that I want you to have a feeling of self-worth, and when you actually write down a list of your qualities and talents, you are committing not only to this process, but are also able to see in a material form that there are good things about yourself that contribute to your uniqueness.

I believe this process helps us feel more positive about ourselves and helps with self-esteem. I want all of us to feel the courage to stretch ourselves when we write down our purpose, and I want us all to sense that we are all Divine and thus potentially great.

> **Too many people allow themselves
> to be diminished by an internal dialogue
> that destroys their self-confidence.**

I like to use this part of the process to reverse the direction of this type of thinking. Also, you will see later how referring back to this step can help you construct an action plan that will be in alignment with your talents and passions.

Once you've circled the qualities and talents that you feel you use the most, underline the three of each that you would like to use more often. Some of these might be the same. For instance, maybe you circled "good listener" as one of your talents, and you would like to use this talent more often, so you might underline it as well. The reason for doing this is that later it will help you make choices about what actions you should take by knowing what you would like to draw out of yourself.

When you're writing down your purpose, one of the ways to know if you're on the right track is to see if the attainment of that purpose would necessitate the use of these talents and qualities. If this is true, you know that you're in alignment with who you'd like to become.

Once this stage has been completed, I use a method taught to me by Laurie Beth Jones in her book *The Path.* I really give thanks to her for this; because it was really the missing piece of the puzzle for me in helping people get so much closer to writing down a statement that would work for them.

She shared the idea of providing a list of words from which people could actually choose, so that they could accurately write down their purpose. What had happened in some of my earlier seminars was that many people could not find the words to express such a profound idea such as "What is my purpose in life?" and when they couldn't find the words, it left them feeling negative about themselves, the process, the seminar, and me.

When you share this process with friends or loved ones, or individuals in the world you want to help, please realize that for many people there's a lot of fear related to looking so deeply at their lives. As I've said before, not many people rejoice at the idea that they might not be doing as much with their lives as they'd like. When people start to beat themselves up about having wasted so much time, tell them that instead of feeling bad about themselves, they could choose to feel good that their inner selves have brought them to this opportunity for change.

How I Share This Process in My Seminars

There are three different lists of words that I project onto a screen, and I ask the seminar participants to write down a few of the words that truly resonate in their hearts. I ask them not to worry or think about how they will *use* the words, but to just see if they're attracted to them, and then to note them down. I'm not going to print the entire list here, but I will suggest that you read *The Path,* which is available in most bookstores.

Here are a few of the words that I see people choosing a lot. They will allow you to can get an idea of how the process works:

affect, affirm, build, connect, create, delight, dream, educate, embrace, encourage, enhance, enliven, excite, facilitate, heal, help, inspire, light, love, manifest, motivate, nurture, open, promote, realize, serve, share, support, team, travel, work, worship . . .

What you would do is circle the two or three words that you feel the most connected with, and that touch your heart the most. Then go through a list of groups or causes, and select the one that most appeals to you. Here are a few examples:

environment, family, homeless, youth, spirituality, people, human development, children, animals, the poor, sports, community service, gardening, women's issues ...

The last list Laurie calls "key phrases," or values, and includes words such as the following:

God, joy, service, justice, being present, creativity, integrity, excellence...

Please remember that there are a lot more words in *The Path.* I have also added a lot of words to the list over the months, as people who took the seminar would offer suggestions.

So what you can do now is try to write a short purpose statement using the words you've chosen. A few examples of statements that people have come up with during the seminars make up the next list. Laurie Beth also suggests keeping the statement so simple that a ten-year-old can understand it.

My purpose is to: live each moment joyfully...be a light that inspires others...be present always...help people help themselves ...serve God by loving others...help children heal...educate others about health...

Have fun with this. My experience has shown me that very often, the more the phrases are shortened, the more powerful they become.

(A special word of thanks to Laurie Beth Jones for her book, and for her team who helped come up with all the words.)

EXERCISE

Write down your purpose statement. Make a list of your qualities. Make a list of the words you feel attracted to. See how you feel when you've finished doing so.

_____

_____

_____

_____

_____

_____

_____

_____

_____

_____

_____

_____

_____

_____

_____

_____

_____

_____

Need support to uncover your purpose in life?
Join me in our 8-week program for in-depth support.
www.MakeYourLifeMagical.com/explore

Chapter 7

❦

The Wheel of Life

"For the past 33 years, I have looked in the mirror every morning and asked myself: 'If today were the last day of my life, would I want to do what I am about to do today?' And whenever the answer has been 'No' for too many days in a row, I know I need to change something."— **STEVE JOBS**

This introduces another tool that has been absolutely phenomenal for me in helping to make my life magical. It has helped me so much, and I'm always amazed by how few people actually use it on a regular basis even after they've been introduced to it.

I know so many people who attended the same seminars I went to, or studied with the same teachers, or read the same books, or took the same online training courses, and are given so many keys to help them move forward; yet they absorb it all but then never make the effort to implement it. It's like setting a goal and then ignoring it.

I have a training modality on my website that is the key method I've used to build large organizations in multiple companies, and it's free for people to look at. Hundreds of thousands of dollars of research went into the information by those who taught it to me. I emphasize its power and usefulness over and over to everyone who wants to build a home-based business, and not one in a hundred will really do it. I know this because part of the process necessitates them calling me up in the earlier stages. And I see that they hardly ever actually build a big business.

Very few people will ever go through the building of a purpose statement either. They read it, think about it, kind of get a loose idea, and then forget about it.

Change takes some effort. It doesn't have to be a *huge* effort to start, but it has to be *something*, otherwise you're just going to stay where you are. One of the most popular phrases in personal-growth books is: "A definition of insanity is to keep doing the things you're doing and expecting things to change."

One tool that has helped me along the way is the wheel of life The wheel of life is about creating balance. I first learned this years and years ago when I was following the teachings of Paul Meyer, who made the first record (not CD, but record) about personal growth. He created a company called Success Motivation Institute, which created and sold programs focused on personal growth. I marketed those for a while, and they helped to change my life.

This is what the wheel of Life looks like:

I have worked a lot with this diagram and have incorporated some of my own ideas, which I hope you will find useful and you will give a try. Try it as it is first and see what your life looks at.

Look at the lines in the center as if they are two intersecting Y's. The first Y is an image of the human being from behind, standing with his arms outstretched reaching up to embrace Divine energy. The other Y is upside down, and it is Divine energy reaching down to embrace the human being.

Where they intersect in the circle is called the Kiss of Life.

The diagram is very similar to the Tarot card called the Wheel of Life. And the lessons one can take from it are found in many explanations of the Tarot.

Take a piece of paper and draw the wheel in *pencil*, not ink. You will see why later.

We'll look at each section now, and I'll explain the basic idea. Let's start with **Financial & Career.** On a basis of 1 to 100 percent, 100 percent being the most satisfied, draw an arc in the triangle of Financial at the level of satisfaction where you currently feel you are now. Let's say you're about **90 percent** at this time. This would mean your line is an arc closer to the outer edge.

Now let's move on to Physical & Health. Say in this area you are at **50 percent** satisfaction, so your arc would be midway between the edge and the rim.

Now let's do Mental & Educational. Say that you're pretty happy with your continuing education programs. That is, you are involved with some personal development programs that you find satisfying. Your line could be at about **80 percent**, so much closer to the outside edge. However, if you are doing nothing along these lines to really further yourself, your line would be closer to the center.

Let's look at Family now. Let's say you're so involved with your work that you hardly have time to spend with your family or significant other, then the line might be close to the center; while if you're very satisfied and fulfilled with this part of your life, then your line would be closer to the outside of the Wheel.

So go on and draw the line in all the other areas. Once done, your Wheel might look like this:

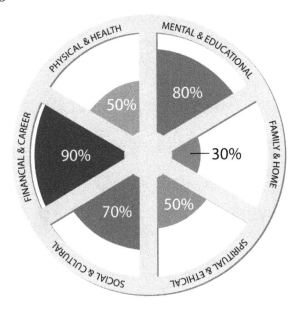

Now I want you to erase the outside rim and all the lines that go past the line that you drew, and now your Wheel might look like this. I think it should be powerfully clear that this is going to give you a pretty rough and bumpy road:

Your scenario might be different . . . you might be very satisfied with your family life and social contacts, but your career and financial situation may not be as rewarding. Your Wheel might look like this:

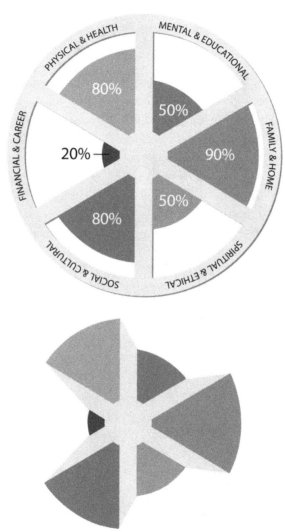

After erasing the lines as before, your wheel might look like the above wheel.

Often we think we're having a rough time because the road is not smooth, or the path we have chosen appears to be full of obstacles, when in reality, it is our wheel that is causing the bumpy ride.

Now let's look at how to fix this so that you have a smoother ride. In the previous diagram, you can see that the financial section is the one with the lowest level of satisfaction, and I deliberately did that because after doing this exercise with a lot of different people, I have seen that this is the area that troubles them the most. So it becomes painfully clear that this line must move to a greater level of satisfaction if we are to improve our ride.

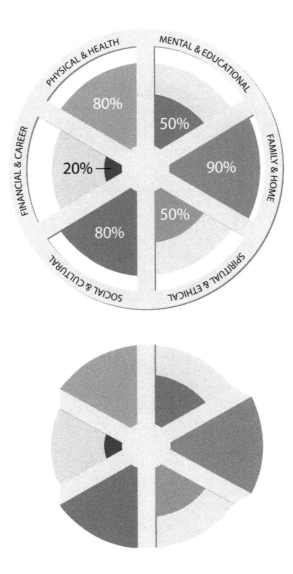

What I love about this system is that it visually connects you to an image of your life that, once seen, is almost impossible to forget. If you were to improve the areas in your life with low amounts of satisfaction (as in the diagram on the previous page, where the shaded areas are extended toward the edge of the Wheel), you would discover that your Wheel is much more balanced, and will roll with greater ease.

Here are some other images of Wheels that you might be familiar with. I just typed in "Wheel of Life" into Google, and these are just a few of the things that came up:

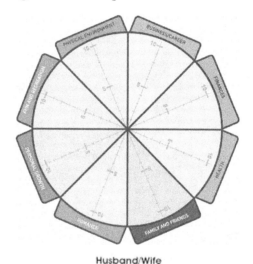

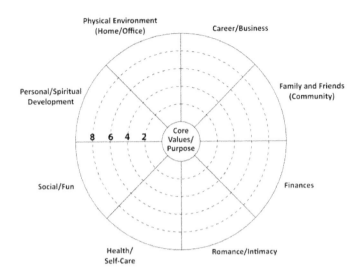

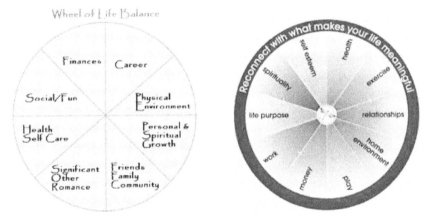

Explanation of the Tarot card

This particular Tarot card (the Wheel of Fortune) was actually my first introduction to the Wheel of Life, even before I got involved with the Success Motivation Institute, because when I lived in France, I did a tremendous amount of research, study, and work with Tarot cards; and my favorite deck was the Tarot of Marseilles. I loved the Tarot for a number of reasons, and I discovered the cards because of my passion for magic, especially card magic, which has always been the area I've been most interested in. One of the reasons I loved this particular Tarot was because all the other decks had a known author, but this Tarot was anonymous, and I felt at the time that sacred art should be anonymous.

When I fell in love with card magic, I started researching their origins, and what I learned was really fascinating, because it was so connected to developing our spiritual side. I spent many years of my life studying cards, especially the Tarot, and even today I spend many hours working with mathematics to help with some of the magic tricks I do.

Cards have always been important to me and have brought a lot of value to my life. First, having a hobby that became a passion early in my life taught me a lot about the rewards one gets from really loving something and committing to learning as much as possible about it. The hours and hours of practice and self-discipline that have gone into becoming good at card magic has opened so many doors for me.

When I traveled with my sitar teacher, and we would show up in ashrams looking for food and a place to sleep, Pramod would play his music and I would do card tricks, and sometimes the yogis would ask me, "What Spirit do you call upon?"

My guide Sidi would just laugh and say, "These are games."

It takes a lot of persistence and consistence to get really good at difficult sleights, and it takes hours of practice for which you're not paid. There was a movie with Anthony Hopkins called *Magic,* where he had a ventriloquist's doll and was performing in a nightclub in front of a lot of people who were talking and drinking, and I remember him getting upset and very loudly saying something like, "Excuse me, but you are looking at thousands of hours of my life here."

As for me, I have some tricks I've been working on for years and have never done publicly because I just haven't gotten good enough, and wonder if I ever *will* get good enough. But I love practicing them, and I enjoy the process so much that it doesn't really matter to me if I ever get to do them for others. When I read some books on magic, it's like taking a trip inside and around someone's mind as they explain how they came up with the idea, and how they like to present it, and they run through all the psychology of the way they want it to work.

Also, when I'm doing magic, I learn a lot about people's personalities, because of the cards they choose, due to their resistance or lack of resistance, and whether they enjoy being fooled or not. I have a lot of great stories about working in Paris nightclubs while trying to break into photography and supporting myself as a magician, but will share more of those in the modules that will be online.

I know that when I was taking photos, many of my clients used to love it when I did magic tricks for them, as did the models and other people on the shoots. Magic has really opened so many doors for me, and even today as I'm creating this program, the people I speak to seem very excited about the fact that magic will be a big part of it.

The story I heard about the way Tarot cards came into existence was that at one time, knowledge was seen as power, and the churches were interested in holding all that power. When the libraries of Babylon and Alexandria were burned, the wise men and mystics started looking for a place where they could hide the esoteric knowledge, such as palmistry, astrology, and other symbolic forms; and they decided that a deck of cards was the perfect place, because the church would never think to look for virtue in games of vice.

Man used the Tarot at first for games, and one of the earliest games was called the Game of Life. It was as if knowledge had been entrusted to fools. I think it is worth acknowledging that the wisdom of the wise initiates used vice to produce some loftier results. Many of the things in today's society carry the same idea. TV can be used to produce something mindless or something beautiful. The internet is the same.

So these men designed the Tarot cards and then gave them to the gypsies, who traveled all around so they could disseminate the knowledge hidden within them. Other wise men could easily spot the symbols of the sun and the moon and things like the Wheel of Life. They understood how the numbers worked, and they could keep all the knowledge alive through the cards. The science of colors is included as well.

Some Secrets about Playing Cards

If you look at an ordinary deck of cards, you can see that there are 52 cards . . . and there are 52 weeks in a year. There are four suits, which represent the four seasons, the four elements, as well as the four main classes of people. Clubs represent the working classes and people of the earth. Diamonds represent the money people, Spades represent the warrior class, soldiers, politicians, and so on; and Hearts represent the mystics, the artists, and the people of the church.

Spades also represented personal courage in the face of adversity, inner strength, and integrity; while hearts represented universal love, reaching to God; and embracing mankind, sacrifice, gentleness, mercy, and compassion through which the mystics shed their unwanted attributes. Diamonds represented achievement, ambition, scholarship, lofty ideals, and worthy goals; and clubs, the humbler virtues such as modesty, rejection of earthly power, truthfulness, endurance, and uncomplaining submission to the will of God.

There are 12 court cards, which represent the 12 signs of the zodiac and the 12 solar months; 9 of them are full face and 3 are in profile. The 9 full face cards are the gestation period of the female. There are 13 cards in each suit, which represent the lunar months. If you were to add up the value of all the cards with aces being 1, jacks 11, queens 12, and kings 13, you would have 365, the number of days in a year. These are just some of the secrets in the deck of cards. The Freemasons and Rosicrucians see a lot more.

There are 22 cards in the major arcana, 22 letters in the Hebrew alphabet, and 22 parts in the apocalypse of St John.

Let's look a bit more at the Wheel of Fortune, though, as that is what this chapter is about. The Wheel suggests the advance of civilization, as well as the ups and downs of life, the unexpected twists of affairs.

There is a handle that goes into the center of the Wheel, suggesting that if we want change to happen, we must put some effort into turning the handles. It is by our own efforts that we speed up or slow down our evolution. The Wheel, as it is shown, expresses the idea that the figures are poised and balanced, suggesting that in the world in which we live, a point exists between matter and spirit.

In each of our hearts is a similar point, and this is part of the mystery of our individuality. At any moment we have the ability to turn the balance toward matter and a possible deep abyss, or toward the spirit that will accelerate our return to unity. The teachings of the Tarot suggest that we should not let anything impair the power of our individuality to turn the balance toward the light. There is also the feeling of: "As you sow, so shall you reap."

As a circle, the Wheel stands for wholeness and diversity contained within a unity. The center of the Wheel, which stays still as the outside turns, represents stability at the heart of change. The Wheel might also be the round table of King Arthur. Notice the crown on the figure at the top, which means that to become a king, man must leave the turning Wheel and stand above the ups and downs of material life. When we can find a point of balance between opposing forces, we can establish equilibrium in our lives.

The 10th commandment says: "Thou shall not covet thy neighbor's house, nor wife, nor manservant, nor maidservant nor ox nor his ass, nor anything." And when we have reached 10, the number of completion, there is nothing of another's to covet because coveting denotes separateness.

This is exactly what Sidi teaches us. Here are his words on this:

> *An envious one might be driving and see a person who has a better car and think, "Look at what he has. Why can I not have this? It is not fair." He has envy in his heart. The polite way to handle a situation in which you see something you admire is to say, "Mā shā'a-llāh," which means, "Allāh willed it." Mā shā'a-llāh is said to acknowledge that Allāh gave that person that gift. Be conscious of Allāh. When you see a gift or a talent someone else has, say, "Mā shā'a-llāh." Say, "It is Allāh's will, may Allāh bless him." In this way you will always be grateful for that person, wish him well, and pray for Allāh to bless him."*

There is also the following saying: "No man is a true believer unless he desires for his brother that which he desires for himself." If you look at the success of others and feel envy, jealousy, anger, or any other negative emotion, it will be a barrier to your own wealth. Learn to be happy for others for any success they have and it will open your heart to experience success for yourself.

It is a good example of the personal work you need to do, and this is a key to learning to create wealth from within. Learn to shift your focus from yourself to others. Forget about your personal needs, and think about the needs of others who have even more urgent needs than you do. Think about how you can find a way to fulfill their needs, and maybe even create a product or service to help them.

Most wealthy people are financially successful because there is something they market that helps others, who are willing to pay for it. The higher the demand for what they have, the more valuable it becomes and the greater assets it creates. This could be a service, some type of information, lessons of some kind, a talent, or myriad other things. Great songs have always created strong residual income, so find a song in your heart and share it with the world. Timing is a big factor in success, so don't procrastinate if you have good ideas.

I hope you'll spend some time thinking about the Wheel of Life and its design, and let your own intuition bring up ideas and suggestions that will help you internalize and gain benefit from working with this exercise. The Tarot forces us to think and use our imagination, and I hope the Wheel-of-Life exercises will encourage you to do the same.

Let's get back to our earlier discussion, where we were talking about filling in the different areas of the Wheel.

Help with Filling in the Wheel

When I wish to increase my level of satisfaction in any area, I focus on expanding those weak areas. You'd be surprised how quickly things can improve when you do this, and how fast your level of satisfaction with all the areas of your life can increase.

Here is what I'd do, for example, in the area of money. I would start a new Wheel, which I would call Finances, and I'd divide that into six sections. My sections might be *job satisfaction, pay/cash flow, money management, debt, income sources,* and *savings.* It can be any six areas that you feel are important to you in your financial life. Then do the same thing, drawing the line in the way we did before, then erasing the excess lines and looking at your Wheel.

Let's say that job satisfaction is the lowest level of satisfaction. Then I would make a Wheel for that.

If I get stuck at any point, I take a sheet of paper and draw a line down the center, and on one side I put, "What I like" at the top of one side, and on the other side I put, "What I don't like."

Then I make a list, which might look like this if I had a nine-to-five job where I was just working to earn money.

What I Like	What I Don't Like
I get paid on a regular basis	Not enough pay for my lifestyle
Health insurance benefits	Not enough pay increases
No work to take home	Not enough vacation time
Like my co-workers	Too much conflict with supervisors
Stable Company	Does not further my purpose
Retirement benefits	Worried about lay-offs later

These are just a few examples, but they should give you some ideas about your current reality and what changes you might need to make if you really want to create a magical life. How much of your inner magician, your potential to create something magical, are you really using? What is really holding you back? Is it fear? Is it that you just don't have a clear idea of what you would really like to be doing? What has made you feel stuck in a place where financially you're not satisfied . . . and what do you need to do to change this situation?

Please don't be one of those people who are always blaming their current situation and circumstances for what is wrong in your life. Don't do what I did and play the victim role. Instead, look for those situations that will empower you the most, and if you don't find them, then figure out how to create them yourself. I can't tell you how many times I've had to take charge of a situation and change it so it was something that worked for me. Sometimes I just decide that if I want something to change, I need to make a radical shift to get the momentum I need to effect a change. One thing I *won't* do is allow myself to remain too long in a situation that doesn't feel good to me.

Understanding the Creative Process

One of my favorite authors is Robert Fritz, who has written a number of books on the creative process, and on what we need to do to create lives we love. He says that one of the most important things we must do is clearly identify our current reality. Then we must decide where we want to go, and these two opposites will create a tension. Since the universe will want to have this tension resolved, it will move toward where we focus the most attention.

When I first learned goal setting, it was always about making a list of my goals and looking at them every day. Fritz taught me about the value of being honest about my current reality, setting those goals, and then if those goals involved other people, having a conversation with them about their level of commitment and accountability in moving toward that aim.

Let's say you're married with two teenage children, and one of your goals is to spend more time with your family and take three vacations a year. Since this goal involves other people, it's important that your family members agree to participate. Maybe your wife has a huge project at work and is unable to get away. Maybe one of your kids wants to play tennis and needs to work out with the school team every weekend. Your chance of reaching your goal depends on other people, so it is vital to make sure that they're part of the plan.

In my business, I do a lot of team building. If I want my business to grow 10 to 20 percent next year, I need to either have my team players agree to grow their businesses or go out and find new people who are willing to do so. By establishing my current reality, I can determine if I have other players or not, and by asking for levels of accountability from my teammates, I know whom I can work with who have the same shared goals, which substantially elevates my chances for success.

Let's look at some ways in which the Wheel can help with some of these ideas. If I decide I want to focus some attention on my family and home life, I can then take the Wheel and make six new sections.

On the first Wheel, I put myself, my wife, and then one section for each of my kids, so the Wheel might look like this:

First, I want to look at how I'm doing with each family member, including myself, as far as communicating, and spending quality time, with them. When I put it down in black and white like that, I might see that I'm spending a lot more time with one child than the other, or I might see that I'm not allowing any free time for myself outside of work, or I might see that I hardly have any alone time with my wife.

Then I can take the Wheel and look at six different areas of my family and home life, such as *vacation time, activities, conversation time, playtime, going-out-together time,* and *expanded family time.* That Wheel might look like this:

Let's look at how this might apply to one of my businesses, such as a nonprofit I founded and run. Maybe there are only four main segments I want to look at. I don't always need to have six segments. So first I break it down to the four segments. Maybe they will be *financial, management, marketing,* and *fund raising,* as an example.

Or if I were to do my home-based business, it might be *recruiting, marketing, follow up, mentoring, income growth,* and *learning.* Now the recruiting might be further broken down to include *cold market, warm market, U.S., Europe, Asia,* and so on. I think you get the idea.

Then when I set my goals to increase and expand the places on the Wheel that could use expansion, I already have a good look at my current reality. I can then also make a list of any people I need to communicate with that will be part of the process, to determine their level of desire and accountability. So the wheel allows me to really get into the layers of the different areas of my life and build it from a true and balanced foundation. It allows me to clearly see the weak areas and the strong places, and then to create a more balanced and better-functioning experience. And like everything else in this book, if you don't actually sit down and try it, then you will never know how powerful it can be.

EXERCISE

Start learning to use this tool, by creating a wheel for the six areas
of your life as described in the previous paragraphs: Spiritual,
Financial, Health, Educational, Family and Social. Continue by
trying some of the examples described in this chapter.

_____

_____

_____

_____

_____

_____

_____

_____

_____

_____

_____

_____

_____

_____

_____

_____

_____

_____

_____

_____

Are you searching for sustained balance in your life?
Join me in our 8-week program for in-depth support.
www.MakeYourLifeMagical.com/explore

Chapter 8

.ஃஜ.

The Importance of Gratitude

"Once a person said to a dervish, 'All I ask for is a small dwelling in Paradise.'
The dervish replied, 'If you displayed the same contentment with what you already have in this world, you would have found ultimate bliss.'" — SHEIKH ABDUL QADIR JILLANI, "FAYUZ E YAZDANI"

I hope you took the time to create or refine your purpose statement, and if you didn't, I would encourage you to go back and do it now. Also, I hope you have tried out a number of examples of the Wheel of Life, so you can experience firsthand what a life-changing tool it can be.

I'm going to assume that you've done this now, and move on to some other ideas that will, hopefully, help you attain your dreams. By now you should be more conscious of what your purpose is, which will help you move toward your destiny.

Often we take a road that we think is taking us away from our destiny, only to actually meet our destiny on that very road.

Sometimes something happens that we think is really bad luck, but in the end something sublime comes out of it. Maybe you fall and break your leg on the way to an important meeting and think you really missed out on something, but later you fall in love with and marry your doctor. Or, maybe you get fired from your job but end up securing an even better position that you really love.

Sometimes when we get something other than what we thought we wanted, we find out later that it's exactly what we would have wanted. Yet initially we were probably really disappointed. Try viewing some of the things that don't appear to be turning out the way you wanted or giving you what you thought you wanted, and look deeply, within your heart, and see if you can find the hidden gift.

One thing that makes it easier for me to decide whether something that happens is positive or negative is to ask myself, "Does what happened further my purpose, or not?"

I'm willing to put up with a lot to move along the path that allows me to fulfill my purpose. So even if something appears to be contrary to what I want, I'm careful before turning away from embracing it. When I feel that I don't know something, I can still be grateful for the opportunity to learn something.

This leads me to the next thing, which I believe is absolutely vital to creating abundance in our lives, and that is gratitude. I don't think I have ever read a book I liked about abundance that didn't feature gratitude as an important precursor.

Why would God want to give you more of anything if you haven't said thank you for what you already have?

I find it is just as easy to focus on being grateful as it is to spend time complaining, and it feels so much better. When we're feeling and expressing gratitude, we are focused on positive things, and thus, we tend to *attract* positive things.

For me, it starts in my belief that
everything I have is because God has
provided it for me, and that God is the most
reliable source of fulfillment for all my desires.

And when I feel this authentically in my heart, it creates an overwhelming feeling of gratitude deep inside of me. Proximity to the Divine makes it a lot easier to access the things you want because you are so much closer to the Source, and one of the best ways I know to experience proximity is to let your heart fill with gratitude.

Gratitude is A Beautiful Expression of Love

As I am writing today, I am listening to a webinar with Vic Johnson, who had some great success giving away a book called *Think and Grow Rich.* Today Vic shared a wonderful quote from a book called *The Magic of Thinking Big:* "The size of your success is determined by the size of your belief."

When our belief is strong, it is almost impossible not to feel gratitude, because we know how much we're receiving, and we bathe in a feeling of being blessed. The more grateful we feel and the more gratitude we show, I believe the more we receive. This is because the "attitude of gratitude" draws us closer to the Source of our blessings and brings us into contact with others who live close to the Source and who can help us achieve our dreams.

I also believe that there's no reason to be given more when we haven't been grateful for what we already have. My teacher says that every step we take to move closer to God, God takes many more steps toward *us.* To reach what we want, our hearts have to have a true yearning for it. Keeping gratitude at the forefront helps remind us that we're connected to God, and this connection keeps our yearning alive and well. When we are grateful for many small blessings, then we become open to receiving greater blessings.

When we forget to be grateful, then we open the door to feelings of "not enough," which then leads us away from our Source and into feelings of need. If you think about it, when people love from a place of need, it's not nearly as powerful as those who love from genuine passion, from what they can give, rather than what they can get. As JFK said, "Ask not what your country can do for you, ask what you can do for your country."

**Giving gratitude is like giving love.
The more love you give,
the more the love grows inside you.**

When love is pouring out of us, we usually feel pretty ecstatic, and expressing gratitude feels pretty much the same. Expressing gratitude is one of the best habits you can form, and one of the best ways I know of opening yourself to be ready to accept true abundance. Living from love and in gratitude is one of the most powerful healing methods, and when we're healed, we can then come from a place of wholeness and joy; and people will be attracted to us because joy and love are so charismatic. When we build ourselves and our businesses from such a place, the joy of the process becomes more important than the outcome; and when we can detach from the outcome, we are leaving it in God's hands. He is a better manager than we can ever hope to be.

There is an African proverb that says: "When you pray, move your feet." Gratitude is a wonderful form of prayer, and activity born out of this kind of prayer is usually the most fruitful. Whatever your intentions are, if you really and truly want to see a change, it's important to perform the actions necessary to accomplish your goals. Prayer is powerful but "actions speak louder than words." Have you ever heard the expression "God likes me when I sing, but He loves me when I work"?

Don't Be Afraid to Ask for Help

I have never been afraid to ask for something that I feel I need, and most times I find that others are very happy to help. People enjoy the experience of giving. There were times in my career when I had to actually phone other photographers and have them explain how I could do something technical, as I had never done it before.

For example, one day I was shooting an ad for a hair product in the early days of my career. The client wanted the model to kneel on the floor looking out the window into the sunshine, but I had no idea how to make it look like the sun was shining because it was the end of the day and dark outside. I called my friend Lester Bookbinder, whom I'd met through David Montgomery, another great photographer I would call for help, and he walked me through the whole process, as he had done many times before and did many times after. He explained how I could put a sheet over the window and put a flash outside, and it would give off a very pretty soft light coming into the room, and then I could use another flash inside direct to the hair. He explained how many f-stops of difference I need to make it look right, what speed I should use, and everything else I needed to know. The client was a little concerned that I didn't know how to do this on my own, but I allayed his fears by sharing that *my* problem was to solve all *his* problems, and that was what I was good at. I also told him if I already knew how to do everything that presented itself to me, then my prices would be a whole lot higher than they were. I also said I wasn't shy about asking for help when I needed it because I didn't want to stumble through the shot and make a mess of it.

He was quite happy in the end, especially when I mentioned that it was Lester who was helping us, as he was a big name in photography at the time and took amazing photos. As a result of experiences like that—that is, never being shy about calling people when I wanted to learn something or needed some help, I have always been happy to repay those debts of gratitude by helping others when they reach out to me. I have never forgotten how grateful I was at the time.

Most people are too shy to ask others for help, and that's one of the major reasons why so many people never have anything more than a dream. To manifest your vision, you have to act, unless you know something I don't know. As I mentioned, when I was first trying to move out of photography and work from home, I got involved in multilevel marketing (MLM), and I was mailing a ton of tapes every week to people. Because of the tremendous success the tapes generated, I was getting a lot of calls. I was on the phone all day, and frequently doing three-way calls with new prospects to make them feel we were a team and to get answers to questions I didn't know.

One of the people I was working closely with, Pete Buntman, would be on the phone with me quite a bit. We both worked a lot with another partner, a very successful and well-known networker by the name of Robert Butwin. We were never shy about asking Robert for help as far as bringing people into the business, but often when we called him, his wife would say, "Sorry, guys, Robert is playing golf, or Robert is playing basketball, or Robert took the kids for ice cream."

Now this would get Pete pretty upset, and he would say, "I can't believe how Robert is always out having a great time while we're working 24/7, and he still makes commissions from all we do without a lot of effort." My response was that we should perhaps look at how Robert created so much income with so little effort, and figure out how to manifest in a similar manner.

I hope you understand from this story that neither Pete nor I had any trouble asking people for what we needed. So pay attention to how many of your dreams do not get realized because you are too shy to take action and ask for help.

Later in the book I will write more about gratitude, because it's so important to understand its value if you want to create any kind of wealth in your life.

> **Feeling a lot of gratitude on a constant basis**
> **and expressing thanks to your Creator**
> **in every moment possible is one of the keys**
> **to creating wealth from within.**

If you want wealth of any sort—financial, spiritual, or emotional I believe you must experience gratitude in your heart on a constant basis.

Don't Take Things for Granted

We simply take too much for granted. How many breaths of air have you taken today alone, without ever expressing gratitude for this ability that was given to you by God? Just this morning I woke up with tremendous pain in my right eye, and it was so bad I decided to go to the emergency clinic because it was 6 A.M. on a Saturday and I wouldn't be able to find a doctor anywhere else. On the way there, I was thinking how grateful I was for the ability to see, how grateful I was that my wife got up to go with me, and how grateful I was that there were people who stayed up all night just to help others.

When we got to the clinic, the doctor put a cream in my eye and the pain immediately stopped, but he said I couldn't take home any of this cream because it numbs the eye and I might do some permanent damage if I had it on and forgot and then scratched my eye. He used it because he had to put a dye in my eye to determine if it was scratched or if there was another problem. As grateful as I was for the temporary relief, I have to admit I wasn't feeling great that I couldn't get any. But as I write this, I'm returning to the feeling of gratitude, and I promise you it is relieving the pain in my eye.

If you want to know how lucky you are to be able to have air to breathe, put your head under water for a couple of minutes and you will know right away how grateful you should be.

As with almost everything written here, I want to emphasize that these ideas and principles do not originate with me, but from the spiritual traditions that millions of people follow.

"Let us rise up and be thankful, for if we didn't learn a lot today, at least we learned a little, and if we didn't learn a little, at least we didn't get sick, and if we got sick, at least we didn't die; so, let us all be thankful." — BUDDHA

"Give thanks to the Lord, for He is good, for His steadfast love exists forever." — PSALM 136:1

"Every good gift and every perfect gift is from above, coming down from the Father of lights with whom there is no variation or shadow due to change." — JAMES 1:17

"When you realize there is nothing lacking, the whole world belongs to you." — LAO TZU

"If you concentrate on what you don't have, you will never, ever have enough." — OPRAH WINFREY

"Joy is what happens to us when we allow ourselves to recognize how good things really are." — MARIANNE WILLIAMSON

"Gratitude makes sense of our past, brings peace for today, and creates a vision for tomorrow." — **MELODY BEATTIE**

One of the most repeated expressions for a Muslim is: "Alhamdulillah" which means "Praise to God," which is similar to the Hebrew phrase "Halelu Yah" (Hallelujah).

We shouldn't feel gratitude just because someone does something for us, but because we benefit from what they did or shared. We should also feel gratitude for the blessings we get from being able to do something for someone else. Think about how blessed we are to be able to help others, and to experience the feeling of joy in our heart from sharing something of value with those we care about.

I wanted to bring up the subject of gratitude to raise your awareness of how feeling grateful can radically change things for you. Maybe up till now you've felt that you've been in one gigantic struggle, that things have been always stacked against you, and that you feel really angry at the world and at God because you're so unhappy. I want to remind you that I was in a similar place, as were many thousands of people who turned their lives around through the very same principles you're being exposed to here.

As I shared with you earlier, there was a period of about four years when I felt little or no gratitude, and because of that, I was mired in self-pity and depression until I finally opened up my heart again. Khalil Gibran said that the pain in our heart is just the breaking open of the shell that blocks the full expression of our feelings, which we think protects us from being hurt, but which also locks our sorrow within us.

EXERCISE

Start a gratitude journal. Every day of your life, write one thing you are most grateful for. Today I wrote: "I am so grateful to be able to travel with my teacher and help introduce his teachings to so many people and be able to help them experience the beauty they all have within themselves."

Make a list of things *you* are grateful for and highlight the ten most important items, and then memorize them; and every time you have a challenge or feel sad, repeat those ten things, connecting with your heart as you do so. You might also get into the habit of starting every day by thanking God for those things that you're grateful for. Do this before you get out of bed.

_____

_____

_____

_____

_____

_____

_____

_____

_____

_____

_____

_____

_____

_____

_____

_____

Would you like support to stay in the stream of gratitude?
Join me in our 8-week program for in-depth support.
www.MakeYourLifeMagical.com/explore

Chapter 9

❀

The Power of Love

"Why do you stay in the anteroom? Follow me, my beloved, as I pass through every doorway to the truthroom of the innermost secret. And say always, 'Sing His song with me.' Really, when you sing, do not think you sing, but He, through your tongue." — SIDI MUHAMMAD AL-JAMAL

I would like to take a moment here to acknowledge my four children: Jessica, Jason, Justin, and Tara, because they are without a doubt among the most inspirational people I have ever met; and when I think about love, I think about them a lot. They show me every day and every moment, the Divine potential that exists in every one of us and the power of loving unconditionally. They share their hearts openly, honestly, and courageously. I have never, ever gone a day without feeling their love. I love them totally and completely, and I am blessed to have them in my life.

I love the expression "To have more, you have to be more." I am such a big believer in personal growth. I don't know how many hours I have studied, how many books I have, how many seminars I have attended, how much money I have spent, how much time I have spent learning from others, but I do know that the biggest and most important investments I have made have been in myself. As I have said before: "You can't build a business bigger than yourself."

To reach your dreams and move toward the expression of your

purpose, it is important that you never cease to grow; and as you do so, you can grow every area of your life.

When you act in harmony with Divine principles, things seem to flow and there is little resistance, so when you choose a purpose that is pleasing to God, you will not meet the heavy resistance that can occur when you are off the path or moving away from your natural destiny.

Making a Difference

When choosing a business, I always want to feel that the people involved are moving in the same direction I am. It is really a pleasure for me. And knowing in my heart that there are others feeling the same thing gives me the satisfaction that I am part of a team of people who want to make a difference with their lives. They are into responsible global stewardship. They are into helping others. And all of this is in total alignment with the life purpose I have, so I never feel alone. It is so much easier to get things done when others are there to help you. And because of this alignment, I have had enough success that I am now able to live a much freer lifestyle than I ever could have imagined during the time I was barely surviving.

**In my current business, the vision of the company
is to inspire people to experience wellness
and to create wealth for their life purpose.
I resonate so much with this vision that sharing
this opportunity flows from me effortlessly.**

Another thing that is absolutely vital to building wealth from within and creating success in your material life is the burning desire to do whatever it takes, and doing it with emotional commitment. Every action must be done with love. This was probably the biggest lesson I brought from my other business life, and it remains the fuel that keeps the engine running. I have an absolute passion and never-ending desire to be successful while working from my home. I love working at home, and I love modeling the awesome possibilities of this lifestyle for other people.

I am a big believer in harmony. We need to be in harmony first with the different parts of ourselves. If your left hand is working in opposition to your right hand, things can be difficult.

We want to have alignment. When we run, we want to have all parts of our body in sync. We also want our head and our heart to be enjoying the experience.

"You, yourself, as much as anybody in the entire universe, deserve your love and affection."— BUDDHA

If you are out of tune with yourself, it is hard to help others be in harmony with you. I have worked with a number of different companies. Basically I bring the same skill set to each company; however, I am sometimes much more successful in one company than another. I have found that without exception, the more I am aligned with the mission of a company, the better results I experience. The more I love what I'm doing, the more success I experience and the less I feel the effort.

Athletes can sometimes thrive on one team but not on another. People can have a great relationship with one person and an abrasive one with someone else. Some parents can get along great with one of their kids but not another.

And the root cause of all dissension is blocked love. When our hearts close even a little, conflict starts to rise within us and in relation to others. And our hearts close when we are not in alignment with the principles being expressed in our environment.

The more we grow, the more we learn how to keep our hearts open and avoid conflict. When we are experiencing joy, conflict seems far away. And when in conflict, it is hard to find the joy. So I like to choose environments where I feel in alignment with my surroundings, especially the individuals involved. Too often people find themselves working to further someone else's vision or purpose rather than their own.

I am always happy to work to help someone else reach his or her goal, when at the same time I am doing something to further my own. I have spent the major part of the last ten years helping my teacher Sidi share his teachings and his message, and I have loved every minute of it, because I love the teachings, and I also love helping others. It has been a tremendous vehicle for helping me realize my dreams. Sidi has taught me the value of living a life deeply committed to helping the disadvantaged.

If abundance is what you seek, then once you have determined your purpose, choose goals and activities that are in alignment with the inner vision that is dear to your heart.

As vision does become reality, hold the vision firmly in your heart and keep thanking God for every breath you take that allows you to pursue your dreams. Pour love into everything you do until it becomes a habit.

Recently I watched one of the greatest tennis matches I have ever seen between Rafael Nadal and Novak Djokovic during the Australian Open final. The match lasted almost six hours and took each competitor to the edge of collapse, but it was their passion for tennis, for competing, and for being the best that kept them going. They were both so tired after the match that chairs were brought to them during the awards ceremony because they could barely stand. I was riveted to my TV until 7 in the morning because I was mesmerized by the willpower they both exhibited. It was fantastic to be able to witness firsthand the amount of dedication it takes to be the best at one's sport. It is through sharing moments like these that I've learned that there's no way that I'm willing to accept mediocrity due to a lack of effort.

So choose to be around people who think and feel and work toward the same objectives you do. Choose work that allows you to express who you are and become who you would like to become. Engage in activities that feel like a prayer and that make you feel joyful. Find mentors and teachers who can guide you along the way and help you open your heart. Many times we have moments of inspiration and feel like we catch a glimpse of a connection with the Divine. I would like to encourage you to learn to sustain that connection.

When you reach a point where you feel connected to God, not only in moments of joy, but also in moments to struggle, you will have discovered the real treasure, and this is the secret of abundance.

Mark 12:30 says: "Love the Lord your God with all your heart and all your soul and with all your mind and with all your strength." When you can achieve a feeling of abundance in any part of your life or your being, then it becomes a lot easier to re-create a similar feeling in other areas of your life. Once you have the feeling of hitting a winning forehand, it becomes easier to hit a winning backhand, because you know what it feels like to hit a winner. If you have a successful relationship with a friend, then you know what it feels like, so it should be easier to have a good relationship with someone you're in love with.

We are all one heart, one mind, one body, and one spirit. We all come from one father, Adam, and one mother, Eve, so we are all brothers and sisters. We must collectively take action to move toward this reality if we want wars and conflict to end. And within us we must arrange our thoughts and feelings and actions to be in harmony with the higher spiritual laws that have been gifted to us through all the holy books. We have to be in tune personally so that we do not create discord with others. No one can change another person, but we can all change ourselves.

Take Daily Surveys

Every day I do a kind of personal survey to take note of the parts of my being that I feel are conflicting with where I want to go or who I want to be.

When you really love what you're doing, you can be a lot more patient and accepting of delays in the fulfillment of your goals. It can allow you to have more understanding of the people you're working with, and develop mercy and compassion for their shortcomings as well as your own.

"Love is patient, love is kind. It does not envy, it does not boast, it is not proud. It does not dishonor others, it is not self-seeking, it is not easily angered, it keeps no record of wrongs. Love does not delight

in evil but rejoices with the truth. It always protects, always trusts, always hopes, always perseveres. Love never fails. But where there are prophecies, they will cease; where there are tongues, they will be stilled; where there is knowledge, it will pass away. For we know in part and we prophesy in part, but when completeness comes, what is in part disappears. When I was a child, I talked like a child, I thought like a child, I reasoned like a child. When I became a man, I put the ways of childhood behind me. For now we see only a reflection as in a mirror; then we shall see face to face. Now I know in part; then I shall know fully, even as I am fully known. And now these three remain: faith, hope and love. But the greatest of these is love."
— **1 CORINTHIANS 13:4-13**

I look for things within me that I feel are not in harmony with my higher self. Right now one of my current focuses is to lose another 12 pounds. I know I need to exercise more and take better care of my body, so I am currently creating a plan of action around this goal. To be truthful, I am a little disappointed in myself, because around a year ago I decided I was going to drop over 20 pounds, and I kind of stagnated at a little over the halfway point. I think one of the reasons was that when I was 24 pounds overweight I could really feel the discomfort, but where I am now is easier to accept and doesn't feel so important. As Tony Robbins says, we change because we either run from pain or move toward pleasure, and I am stuck in the middle.

So what am I going to do to go from where I am to where I want to go? I think I will start by following my own advice. I have established my current reality and have accepted that I am the one responsible for my current condition; and if it is going to change, it is up to me. I have my clearly established purpose in life—helping others to help themselves—so I am going to establish goals in harmony with that purpose. I need more energy to do all the things I want to do, and carrying the extra weight is tiring me out. So I am going to give myself goals every 15 days and then input those into my calendar with a reminder every Sunday to keep myself on track.

So I will break everything down into segments. I would do the same thing if my goal were to increase my income by a certain date, or finish this book, or complete any other project. Then I'm going to clearly state my plan in writing and keep that plan in front of me on a daily basis.

So now I'm going to delineate my action steps, especially focused on workouts and exercise. I'm going to commit to one half hour of exercise every other day to be completed within one hour of waking up. Then I'm going to look at what I'm eating and decide what I'm going to focus on eating most often. Instead of focusing on what I will *not* eat, I'm going to choose a menu that I will enjoy following, as I always like to focus on the positive.

I have actually set a plan in motion to complete this book and the web-based program that I am developing along with it by the end of March 2012 as well. I will first decide on a date to finish the writing of this book, get it to an editor, and then start working on the modules. To accomplish this, I must spend about 30 to 60 minutes a day researching the magic portion of each module and practicing the effects, because they take time to learn. I will also start every day by writing and will not do less then five pages a day. (I am just now going through the editing of the book, so I have finished the rough draft. The date is January 31, 2012, so I am a little behind schedule but am planning to make it up. However, I am not doing so well with losing weight, so I am going to put additional focus there.)

This is really how I move forward on almost every single project I have. I first choose something I am passionate about accomplishing, and then set my current reality. I then decide what date I would like to reach my goal by, and then I break it down into bite-size chunks. Doing so immediately makes tasks that seem overwhelming more doable.

Next, I look at accountability. Besides myself, who else can help me finish this project? I need someone to design a cover, and I have already put out feelers for this, planning to have most of what I want by the end of this month. I want to submit this to an editor, so I choose the person I want to send it to and plan to have a proposal and a sample of what I have done so far submitted by

January 2012. (I actually did find an editor with a considerable amount of experience, and she instructed me to basically rewrite and restructure everything, which is what I am now doing.)

I am feeling a lot better with the flow of things as a result of her suggestions. I feel no pressure about any of the tasks I have to do or their deadlines, because I absolutely love doing them. I love the idea of losing those last pounds. I love the idea of getting this book and program out. I love putting everything in black and white in front of me every day so I am reminded of what I want to do. I am having a ball developing new magic routines, and am spending a lot of time practicing. I am also excited to share these effects with everyone in the module. Each effect I am choosing is going to illustrate many of the points in this book.

I want to get back on track here with the subject of love. Here is a teaching from a talk from Sidi about the prophet of love, Jesus:

> *"Jesus understood the human being through his mother. Through her suffering he understood the suffering of all human beings. He was Light, but his body was from the body of his mother and she fed him the food of this world and the love. God gave him Wisdom. Jesus is spirit. He gave completely without self but saw God behind every human being. This is the Spirit. He is you!*
>
> *Jesus gave the people the meaning of the Deep Secret Love. The meaning of the message of Jesus and the meaning of his life—from the moment of his birth—was to put the real life into every person and everything he came into contact with.*
>
> *His words were all the Wisdom of God and how to live in the love and the unity with God, not just as they imagined, but as it really was. He showed the people how, through the love, a person could know God, and this was the first time this deep inside message of the love had been given. He also gave the people the deep inside meaning of the Law through the Essence of the Love.*
>
> *I want all of you to be like Jesus, and see God in every person and in every thing. Jesus, he taught the people, from his message, to see God in every face and for that reason, to give the love to all people; to erase everything from one's soul and one's deep heart and to*

be completely with Allah all the time. This is also the meaning of the name Messiah; to clean oneself from everything that is not for God.

Jesus brought this message to the people and showed them how to live it. The meaning of his love was a love without separation; to love one's fellow men like oneself, which means not to make a separation between him and you but to be in the Unity with him and with all creation. He told the people how to look with the eye of the heart, and through this eye, to see the other as oneself, and to understand and love him."

One of the things I love about Sidi, whose full name is Sidi Shaykh Muhammad al-Jamal ar-Rifai, is that even though he is a Muslim, he understands and talks about Jesus in ways that I have not experienced before. It is his love for Jesus, as with all the Prophets, that makes this happen because it feels as if his heart knows and understands Christ completely.

Follow a Plan

There's a reason why I've been sharing the process I go through, and how I move from the beginning to the end in the creating of things. I believe we all have a gift to share with the world, that inside of each of us is something special that can benefit others, and I want to let you know that a good way to overcome your fears and insecurities is to make a plan and stick to it.

I want you to get the idea that the creative process for me takes discipline and planning, but it is still filled with the power of my love for what I'm doing. I don't know how *others* create, but this is how *I* do it, and I share it because I know it works for me.

Brendon Burchard is an amazing creator, and goes into extraordinary detail during his teachings about what he does when he wants to write a book or create a new program. He is basically teaching people who want to become experts in their field, and as far as I'm concerned, he is absolutely the best right now because he has all the elements in place, including the marketing. I have invested over five figures in the last month alone to learn from him, and this is just the beginning.

The most important thing for me is that I can look forward to doing all these things because I love sharing anything that people will find useful. It is the power of this love that gives me the energy to do everything I've set my mind to. I certainly don't *have* to do it. I am comfortable enough financially now that I could literally do nothing and be fine, but I don't *love* doing nothing. I love keeping active and involved and making a difference in both my life and in that of others.

I've been fortunate to come a lot closer to my other major goals for the year, and am planning to set some pretty audacious goals for the coming year—and a lot of them involve marketing this program. I am excited to be learning so many new things and hope that not only will it help me with the marketing of this program, but with the book my wife is writing as well. And I know it will all help me grow my business, too.

When you help enough people get what they want, you end up with what *you* want.

There are many people who can benefit from these teachings. Sidi wants to build another school in the Holy Land, and we have a university up here in Napa Valley (near San Francisco), where I live, which I'm hoping will grow so his teachings reach more people. I really believe that what I'm in the process of learning is not just for promotion of my own material, but also for the greater good. And because I love teaching and learning so much, I feel that whatever the outcome, 2012 will be a phenomenal year.

Robert Fritz writes about the process of creating as well as anyone, and has made a huge impact on me. He can take something that's difficult to explain and make it something that can be shared and taught. I recommend his great book *The Path of Least Resistance*, which has taught me so much.

Every year the investments I make in my education always seem to pay a huge dividend. When I started, I couldn't spend a lot to do this, but I didn't need to because there were so many books I could read that taught me what I needed to know. Then, as a result of applying those principles, I created a flow of abundance that allowed me to continually learn and grow more.

"The instruction we find in books is like fire. We fetch it from our neighbors, kindle it at home, communicate it to others, and it becomes property of all."— VOLTAIRE

Also, these days, people are teaching and giving away amazing amounts of valuable information for basically nothing. To see how this works, look at Brendon Burchard. You can buy his book *The Millionaire Messenger* on Amazon, and he outlines everything he teaches there. If you look him up online, you can access hours of free training, which is the best there is in his field, as far as I'm concerned. Due to Brendon's generosity, I grew to really like and trust him, so it was an easy decision to want to learn more. I love when people go into detail about every step of a process, and I have never found someone who goes into as much detail as Brendon does, who gives as much, and who comes from such a deep place of service. I resonate with his message and am in harmony with it, and I hope you will seek out people who touch your heart and whom you can learn from, too. Of course, I would be honored if you end up feeling this way about me.

This may sound like an ad for Brendon, but I'm not selling anything here. I'm just sharing information that is helping me transform my life and attain my goals, and I want the same for you. As I've mentioned, my favorite teacher is my spiritual guide, Sidi, and I have spent almost 20 years now learning from him and helping him share his message. All of this is outlined in the book I mentioned earlier, *My Journey to Know the Truth: Healing the Broken Heart*, and I will be sharing a lot of Sidi's teachings in this book and the internet modules that go along with it.

Just wanting something isn't enough. It's so easy to get distracted in today's world, and we end up spending hours either watching TV, playing video games, spending time on Facebook, sending e-mails, texting friends, or doing things that are really more about other people's agendas than our own. I absolutely have to do things every day that I love doing, and which help me reach my goals, or

I will wonder very quickly how I got so far off track. By knowing my own purpose so clearly and knowing that what makes me feel the absolute best is when I choose actions in harmony with that purpose, I tend to do things that add meaning and relevance to my life on a pretty steady basis.

One of the modules of my program, and one of the chapters of this book, is about being the son or daughter of one's moment, meaning to stop procrastinating and do what needs to get done now, and not tomorrow. I'll go into more detail on this topic later.

For 20 years I've lived side by side with Sidi as he has traveled to all the different cities where he has students. I have arranged all his trips, and been kind of a personal assistant and right-hand man. It means that for six months every year, my life is completely dedicated to serving him and helping disseminate his teachings. The rewards have been immense, and I wouldn't trade it for anything. It means that almost every weekend we're traveling somewhere, and since the end result is helping others, it is completely in alignment with what I want to do with my life. I love it because I feel that I'm making a difference.

I earn my living through working with a wellness company that has a very unique business model. They do millions of dollars of media advertising every month, bringing in thousands of customers every week; and people are allowed to purchase shares of the co-op advertising, thus acquiring customers from whom they earn residual income. It has a multitier payout similar to MLM or networking companies, but it is the only organization I know of where one can actually purchase buying customers. So in effect, each person has their own wellness business, but the company handles all the product, ships it out every month, does mailings to all the customers, and then allows people to earn commissions. It's like owning a franchise at a fraction of the cost, with no employees and no rent, which would be the case with a brick-and-mortar establishment.

What I do is look for people who want to earn residual income, especially those who might have some discretionary money put aside, and show them the tremendous benefits of being part of this company. It really feels like very little effort, because I love what I do so much and am happy to share it with others. It helps people with their wellness experience and allows them to reap huge financial benefits without altering their current work habits.

Despite this tremendously difficult financial time in the U.S., many home-based businesses have grown substantially. For example, the company I am with has grown around 50 percent, and my personal business has almost quadrupled in just the past year. I have many friends in the industry who have experienced a lot of growth as well. Residual income has allowed me to do whatever I want, whenever I want, and wherever I want, and this kind of freedom is worth the world to me.

There are a number of things you can do, right here, right now, that can help make a big change in your life or make an already good life better. Set aside some time every day to write down the types of things you want to do. Writing them down and keeping them in front of you increases your awareness of what you want. Think about the many blessings in your life that you can be grateful for. Too often we focus on what we don't have and want, rather than what we have that is already making our lives good. Think about what you would like to have happen in your life in the coming years, and initiate a plan for accomplishing those goals.

EXERCISE

Write down the areas of your life where you're feeling conflicting thoughts and feelings. Note how you think you could approach things in a different way that would help resolve those conflicts, and where and how you could bring more love into these areas.

Make a list of the people you most care about, and set aside time to tell them how much you care about them, how much they mean to you, and how much you love them. Feel the love in your heart and spend time with it. Do not let more than a month go by before speaking to them or writing them. Better yet, do it *now*. Let the people close to you know how you feel about them before it's too late.

_____

_____

_____

_____

_____

_____

_____

_____

_____

_____

_____

_____

_____

_____

_____

Desire to set goals in alignment with your purpose?
Join me in our 8-week program for in-depth support.
www.MakeYourLifeMagical.com/explore

Chapter 10

Tools for Implementing Change

Sometimes it's hard to visualize the future and the opportunities that are presented when a new opportunity enters our lives. Here are some pertinent quotes from some of the brightest, most educated people and well-respected publications in history:

"Consider how hard it is to change yourself and you'll understand what little chance you have in trying to change others."
— **BEN FRANKLIN**

"Well informed people know it is impossible to transmit the voice over wires and that were it possible to do so, the thing would be of no practical value."
— **EDITORIAL IN THE *BOSTON POST*, 1865**

"I think I may say without contradiction that when the Paris Exhibition closes, electric light will close with it, and no more will be heard of it."
— **ERASMUS WILSON, PROFESSOR AT OXFORD UNIVERSITY, 1878**

"There will never be a mass market for motor cars—about 1,000 in Europe—because that is the limit on the number of chauffeurs available!" — **SPOKESMAN FOR DAIMLER-BENZ**

"The average American family hasn't time for television."
— *THE NEW YORK TIMES*, 1939

"I think there is a world market for maybe five computers."
— THOMAS WATSON, CHAIRMAN, IBM, 1949

"Man will never reach the moon regardless of all future scientific advances."
— DR. LEE DE FOREST, INVENTOR OF THE VACUUM TUBE, 1957

"The potential world market for copying machines is 5,000 at most."
— IBM EXECUTIVES TO THE FOUNDERS OF XEROX, 1959

If you want to change your life, you have to listen to your heart and not allow other people's negative beliefs to impact you and make you doubt all the possibilities that are out there for you. Those individuals (some of whom are mentioned above) who went on to be hugely successful probably never listened to the doubters, but rather, followed the paths that they intuitively felt they needed to pursue.

You cannot change everything in your life in one moment, but you *can* change the direction in which you're headed. But how does one go about creating change, and what are the tools that create maximum efficiency? As with everything else, I believe that the way to have a rich and rewarding life is to do everything with free-flowing passion.

When actions come from the heart, they are in harmony with who we are and who we want to be; and because they come from a good place (the heart is the home of God), they also create positive energy. When you love what you're doing, it is easier to detach from the results, because the action itself is rewarding.

I've spent a lot of time wondering what makes some people so successful, while others don't do as well. Two tennis players use the same ball, the same racquet, the same clothes, the same court, the same umpires, and so on; but one tends to win most of the time, and the other does not. When two pitchers play in a game, they both throw the same type of ball, so why is one player sometimes so much more effective than another? There are many companies that market the exact same product. Yet there is always one that rises to the top.

If you want to change, you have to first accept the fact that if you feel there are limits to what is possible for you to accomplish, this is due to your own limited vision.

Many people have an invisible bubble surrounding them that they are unaware of, and they cannot see beyond the shell of this bubble.

One way to burst through that bubble is to be so passionate about someone or something that it creates a powerful force where previous limitations no longer restrict you. As such, you burst through the bubble into a wider place of expansion. Don't confine yourself to a small bubble that you might have constructed to protect you from outside forces, because that bubble will also confine you to being in a type of prison. If you put a shell around your heart to protect yourself from being hurt, this same shell will block the love that wants to flow out of you.

For me, what makes a difference is the quality of passion and integrity that exists during the execution of any action. When there is a lot of love present in each moment, it will help create a very positive outcome. I believe that the difference is on the inside. When there is a window of opportunity, some people just jump ahead and don't let fear stop them. They take action instead of creating excuses.

And this is what we need to do: surrender to the love, and let the love carry us to create momentum. Love helps expand our entire being.

Why I Love Terry Newsome

I often work with a man named Terry Newsome, who has also become a close friend because we both have so much passion for what we do. I grew up using the name Terry, so I resonate with the name. I changed it when I was working as an actor because there was already a Terry Kent. Terry is one of the most brilliant marketers I have ever met. I usually have my recorder on my iPhone ready each time I talk to him. The inspiring ideas emanating from him flow like rapids, so there's no way I could write fast enough to keep up with him.

Terry's level of commitment and passion is an example for everyone interested in being totally committed to whatever they're doing. He has an uncanny ability to take any idea and make it better. And he is one of the most accomplished presenters I know. Also, Terry and I both have a deep spiritual connection with our Creator and rely on that bond.

One of the things Terry has taught me that has been invaluable is how to share suggestions with people in a tactful manner so that they really hear what I have to say without getting defensive. I have a tendency to be a bit too direct for some, especially when I'm trying to offer what I consider constructive criticism. My wife, Elizabeth, is similar to Terry, in that she has an innate sense of how to be sensitive and share information with others in a way that allows their hearts and minds to stay open.

Terry is a great example of someone who gets so much done because he's so passionate and purpose driven. I'm so glad that Michael Ellison had the vision and foresight to see how great Terry is and brought him on as International Sales Director. As I mentioned, my wife and I had the privilege to follow corporate executives through five cities in Australia as they prepared a launch there, and it was amazing to see how hard Terry and the rest of the staff worked each and every day.

The lesson I took from that was that if you're going to hire people, or partner with others in business, make sure they share the same level of enthusiasm and passion that you do, because then you don't have to worry whether they're going to be an integral part of the team or not. I think that most success has its roots in the passion that people have for what they want to accomplish. With great passion comes a deep commitment to follow through on things, and do whatever is necessary to transform a vision into a reality.

The fact that there is someone in the corporate office who is always ready to answer my calls and respond to my questions enables me to come across to my team as a leader who has access to those in the know and who can get things done. I know how busy Terry is and what a load he carries, so I'm careful not to ask him for things I can get done elsewhere. As a result, he trusts that when I call, it's important; and the last thing I want to do is abuse that trust.

Too often in business I see people who don't respect the responsibilities of others, so I want to encourage you to be aware of this as you develop your business relationships. Associate with people who have the same level of work ethic you do, and give people the same level of trust that you ask of them. I hope you're lucky enough to find the Terry Newsomes in *your* business world and develop relationships that are mutually beneficial.

I don't think it is possible to create an organization bigger than ourselves.

We all start with great intentions, but what differs is the level of commitment, and this is usually directly proportionate to the amount of love we feel. As my passion grew, and as I learned more and more about my company and the products involved, the more my love grew; and along with this came passion, dedication, commitment, and all the fuel that comes from a full heart.

My favorite tool is love, and all that love brings. What the love does is connect me to everything.

I've tried applying the same skills I've developed working in other companies before, but never with such outstanding results, because my heart was not in harmony with the overall vision, so my love did not flow so easily. When my love is blocked, I usually encounter some form of resistance, so while building my current business, I felt really open, and all the actions were mostly fun.

When we have a really strong *why,* the *how* just seems to take care of itself. There have been other companies where I was in harmony with the owner's vision, but never so much as where I am now.

Filling Actions with Love

Let me use this philosophy to explain how I would choose a tool, or a path of action. I am someone who absolutely loves the creative process, but I don't enjoy the more mundane tasks.

I have found that I am less effective with action steps that I don't love, so what do I do? I hire someone who does love doing these things.

By working in this manner, I conduct business in a loving way, even if a particular task is not being performed by me personally.

Currently, one part of my business requires each person who acquires customers through our co-op advertising program to connect with these customers and educate them as to how to use the products in order to maximize their wellness experience. I love attracting the business builders more than talking to the customers, so I've hired someone who *does* love to do that, and she makes all the calls for me. In fact, she loves doing this so much that she has now trained a team of people to call customers for people who, like me, are either too busy doing something else or just don't want to make the calls. She now has a number of clients and a growing business.

This has worked out perfectly for me, because I can now approach a number of people who are interested in having a business that is well run, helps people, and generates income, but is hands-off for them. It also fulfills the moral responsibility I have toward the company, which expects us to take care of our people. I also believe I can be more useful to the company in this way by helping it grow and spreading its message of wellness to others.

One of the things that I really value highly is *time freedom,* so I always try to delegate. And when I do decide to perform a task, I do it with full integrity, am totally present in each moment, care more about the other person than myself, and help others feel connected and part of the process—in short, to be the best that I can be.

By making every action like a prayer, our entire life becomes a life of prayer.

Isn't this what we all want? I believe that if you want something, then you should give it away, or put a little differently, be the person you want to attract into your life.

Once you have written out a purpose statement and have deeply understood *why* you are doing something, it becomes easier to choose tools that are in harmony with your purpose and figure out the *how*.

When you take actions that are fun for you and that you feel good about, the results usually reflect this attitude.

This is one of the reasons why some people might excel at something even when they're not particularly gifted, while the gifted ones might not do as well. No matter how gifted people are in any area, if they don't enjoy what they're doing, chances are they'll lose their enthusiasm; whereas those who are driven by passion will be relentless in their pursuit of excellence.

Have you ever watched the kind of person who is always busy and yet never seems to get a lot done, and then watch a person with purpose accomplish massive results in a short amount of time?

I prefer quality to quantity, and I believe that quality action is a lot more efficient. Similarly, I believe that quality people are easier to work with than large groups of people who do little. That is why it is said that 80 percent of the work is done by 20 percent of the people. I have also come to learn that the success of these individuals is usually due to the fact that they all did a lot of little things rather than one extraordinary thing.

When I built my business, every day I would do many small things that at the end of the day amounted to a lot, and I did this over and over again each day. I truly believe that a lot of people could have done what I did. That is why it's said that in today's world, there are a lot of ordinary people making extraordinary incomes. There are so many opportunities for the self-motivated person willing to assume personal responsibility.

Just like many others, there were moments when I had some fear, but I never let the fear hold me back.

Instead, I would always change my focus to something more

positive. Everyone in my company had the same tools to work with that I did. The systems that I used I explained in detail on my website for people to access for free. The way I talked to people and the words I used are similar to what I've learned from others who were successful, and I just modeled what they did. The websites and the information packets were something that each of us could have used. Many people simply waited because they wanted to see if it worked for others first. I built my own website, but everyone else could do the same if they wished. Not every window of opportunity stays open forever.

There are red lights and green lights in our world, and if we don't move during the green lights, then we will find ourselves waiting during the next red light.

Windows of Opportunity

In our lives, the windows of opportunity do not always operate with the same regularity as traffic lights, so when it's time to move, we have to be aware that the window is open and we must take the action steps that are necessary.

If vision is to become reality, then thought must be turned into action.

For example, if a lot of talented people hadn't taken action and created the technology behind laptop computers, I probably wouldn't have been able to write this book as quickly as I did. If it were still just a thought in someone's mind, I would have had to use a different tool to express myself. No tool has great value unless you use it. The hammer as an idea does not carry the same force to build a house as the manifestation and *use* of the hammer. You can't sit on the *idea* of a chair; someone has to make it. When love and passion are added into the equation, the same object becomes a much more powerful tool.

Let's return to the baseball for a minute. In the hands of the proper person, the ball can become a vehicle for enormous personal growth and transformation. Not too many years ago, a young pitcher on the Los Angeles Dodgers by the name of Orel Hershiser got into "the zone," as athletes call it. Inning after inning he stayed concentrated and focused, and ended up breaking the record for most consecutive innings pitched without giving up a run. He then went on to lead his team to a World Series. During this run to become a world champion, there were many moments when the other teams had small windows of opportunity, but at these times, Orel would always bear down and come up with a great pitch. He wasn't a lot better than anyone else on the field, but the small difference that *was* there accumulated to make a huge difference in the end.

One thing that happened is that Orel's ability to stay focused leveraged out into the rest of the players. As the team made it through each phase of the playoffs, each individual member started to believe more and more that a world championship was really possible. As Orel remained a dominating force with his ability to throw a baseball, his and their futures changed dramatically. Orel Hershiser became a world champion and a millionaire due to his ability to use the baseball as an effective tool.

Now, ever since I was a boy, this tool was available to me to build a life in baseball if I so desired, but even though I loved the sport, I never developed my abilities the way Orel Hershiser did. It wasn't one pitch that made the events that transpired so extraordinary, but rather the thousands upon thousands of pitches that he threw during his life. Similarly, there wasn't *one* phone call that built my business, but *thousands* of calls.

Persistence and consistence are keys to success in every endeavor, as well as actually taking action rather than merely thinking about the possibilities.

During the breakup of my marriage, my wife told me that she had met someone else and that it totally surprised her, and that it felt like her heart stopped. For a long time I thought about this and came to realize that the reason this occurred was because of enough accumulated moments of disconnection between us that we didn't even consciously notice. There were probably countless windows of opportunity that we were offered to save our marriage that we weren't even aware of, but it felt easier to ignore them. That is why not doing something can alter your life as radically as doing something different.

Maybe because I was so involved with so many other things, I was not really totally present with my wife, and because *she* was involved with so many things, the same was true in reverse. We had probably just gotten lulled to sleep by this disconnection without paying much attention to it. Then she connected with someone who was more focused on her and the things she was interested in, and it woke up something within her that had gone to sleep, so to speak. Of course, this was difficult to deal with at the time, for both of us, especially since I was too close to the situation and had no understanding of how this could have happened. It was only through my profound connection with Sidi and his teachings that I learned some things to help me eventually understand why and how this could have occurred. All of these lessons will, hopefully, prevent me from making the same mistakes in my *new* marriage.

In the same way that it took many calls to build my business, and many small but persistent recurring action steps, the repetition of small, seemingly unimportant moments of disconnection might have caused the dissolution of my marriage. So it's important to not only look at what you're doing on a daily basis, but also at what you're *not* doing.

What are the things that you're repeating each day that are preventing you from where you want to go? Maybe you're spending too much time surfing the web, or watching TV, or just hanging out with people who aren't helping you grow in the way you want. It's easy to get lulled to sleep with these kinds of things, so be careful about how you spend each moment.

To Act or Not to Act

Choosing to take action or not take action can create powerful outcomes. Doing the opposite of what you're doing can help effect change quickly. When I really want to create rapid change in my life, I look at what I'm doing and then do the exact opposite. Maybe my business is stagnating because I'm not really focused on it, so I will decide to make my work my main focus for a while.

That's exactly what I did in October of 2010. My business had stayed pretty much the same for the previous seven years because I was busy doing other things, but that month I decided to refocus on building the business again, and over that next year I more than quadrupled my income. Had I chosen not to make a radical change, I'm sure I wouldn't have realized that same level of same success.

If Gandhi hadn't chosen nonviolence as a tool of freedom in India, there would have been a totally different outcome and message. Nonviolence became a powerful tool of liberation because he chose to use it and to take action. And it was the exact opposite of the violent actions being perpetrated by the British at that time. There was no *one* monumental action that Gandhi took that freed India, but rather, the consistency and persistence of steadfastly refusing to give up his dream.

I understand that not every opposing action works to counteract negative forces; otherwise, goodhearted people would have eradicated evil from the earth by now; but I know that for me, a quick path to change is choosing to do the opposite of what I'm currently doing that's not working. These days, for example, if I'm overtired from lack of sleep, sleeping more helps. If I'm gaining weight due to a sedentary lifestyle, I exercise a lot more.

When you know what you need to do to change and then don't do it, it's because you're simply not committed enough to making that change. So if you're stuck and really unhappy, make a list of actions that you're currently doing, and then a list of those actions that represent the opposite, and you might find some clues to moving forward.

One of the challenges people have when choosing tools to change their lives is that sometimes they select certain avenues that worked for someone else, but which won't really benefit *them*. (In my case, working out every day is an example. I just don't like to do it.) So many people are used to doing things that they don't love just to put food on the table, and so used to working for others and doing what they're told to do, that when they're free to build their own business and choose to do something they love, they don't even recognize that this freedom exists. Most people I know who make a living doing something they love would absolutely refuse to make a living doing something else. It's not the money that drives them, but the love of their chosen occupation or path.

I don't think that through all his teenage years, Orel Hershiser thought very much about how rich he would become as a result of his ability to throw a baseball, but I bet in his mind's eye and in his heart, he'd "thrown" hundreds of pitches that led to a World Series. He had a passion for playing baseball, and that passion is what led to his enormous success.

One of the things I've learned is that a lot of people in the sphere of influence of the person wanting to change resist it because they're uncomfortable with the unknown. They worry about what will happen, and try to pass on this worry to the person desiring to change. For example, someone might think that if one's spouse changes and grows, their relationship won't be with the same person anymore; or if their child becomes successful, the family unit will be altered.

Worrying about something that hasn't happened is like paying interest on money you haven't borrowed.

Imagine what a different world it would be if Jesus had let the resistance of other people block the changes he was bringing about. Someone once said to me how great it was that Jesus took 12 illiterate people and built one of the largest networks in the world. Now I don't know if they were all illiterate, but the comment stuck with me because it was the faith and belief in what he was teaching that touched the hearts of just a few people in the beginning.

So if *you* want to build something, develop a network of people who also believe in your vision.

Creating Tribes

In the seminars I attend given by top marketers, I've learned that this is how most of them started. First they developed a small core group of people who were attracted to what they had to share; and from that core group, they developed a *large* base of supporters.

Once we discover our purpose, the next step is to determine what action steps we can take that are in alignment with that purpose, and which are also things that we enjoy doing. Author and entrepreneur Seth Godin gave a great talk on **TED.com** about how movements start because people have a cause. (TED is a nonprofit devoted to "Ideas Worth Spreading." It started out in 1984 as a conference bringing together people from three worlds: Technology, Entertainment, and Design.) When people share the same passion for a cause, you don't have to sell them on the idea . . . because they have already sold themselves.

During my seminars, when I teach people how to connect with their purpose, I ask them if there are causes they're supporting. I start the process by having attendees write down their talents and their best qualities, because when it comes time to take action, I can help them select action steps that will be fun for them. People get involved in causes because it has meaning for them; they are passionate about wanting to effect positive change, and about connecting to people they can relate to. If I know that someone has a passion for skiing, I will help him find action steps to connect with others who share this passion; and if someone else tells me she has a passion for cooking, I'm not going to suggest that she try to connect with people on ski lifts.

When people choose action steps that feel good, they usually will undertake them joyously and effortlessly.

Joyous, effortless action almost always produces better results. People's hobbies and talents are usually good indicators of where they like to play, and the more they feel as if work is play, the more successful they'll be. And when they can act collectively rather than individually, they're going to have a more satisfying experience overall.

Every time you choose an action that you perform in a joyful manner, there is a vibration that accompanies this action that adds more power to it.

Think of how you accept things in your own life. Recently my wife and I ate in a restaurant where my daughter is a server. She has such a wonderful, happy manner about her because she loves working there, and it makes eating in that establishment a joyous occasion—not just for us, but for everyone she serves. I would go back there just because I enjoy her energy so much, even if she wasn't my daughter. In the same manner, when you go to a restaurant with poor service, no matter how good the food is, if the experience is not fun, you probably won't return. I have the same uplifting feelings when I'm around my other daughter and watch her interact with horses. She has an absolute passion for those animals, and it is a joy to be around her when she's with them.

When I speak to people in the business world, whether it involves speaking to them about certain opportunities or about my nonprofit efforts, I am so full of energy, optimism, and a sense of well-being that people don't want to resist my offers, suggestions, or help. They can sense my love, passion, and commitment.

Whatever tool I use is infused with positive energy.

Because there is no doubt in my being about the validity of what I'm doing, and because I believe in myself, I usually get good results. So it's not a physical tool that counts, as much as what is in my heart.

Positive energy attracts positive energy, so when we learn more about energy fields, we realize that when we meet someone, there's a lot of unspoken communication going on.

The Reticular Activating System

Humans possess something called a "reticular activating system," which works as a kind of filter. When you feel that something is important in your life, information relevant to that particular project, idea, or passion is allowed through this filter. For example, when a couple is preparing to have a baby, it seems that everyone they meet is going through the same thing; when you're interested in pregnant women, you'll notice them, whereas someone else might pass ten pregnant women without a second thought. When you buy a certain car, you start to see that car all over the place. When you have a beloved bulldog, you'll notice that breed all the time, whereas others won't give them a passing glance.

I love seeking to know God, so I'm aware when I run into others seeking the same thing. I love helping people who want to work from home, creating predictable, sustainable long-term income—so I notice those who talk about hating their jobs, who are looking for work, or who wish to start their own business. Because I love tennis, I am aware of who's winning a certain match, while you might not be familiar with any of the players because you have no interest in that sport.

When I took photos for a living, all my energy and focus was narrowed down to a small, isolated area visible through the viewing hole. I was so focused on what was happening in that hole, so aware of what was happening in the focused area of my intent that I was oblivious to what was going on around me. I was filtering out things that weren't relevant to me. Yet I could sense the movement of the sun; I could feel everything in the surrounding area that might improve the quality of the photo I was creating. I was aware of subtle shifts of light and the movement of the clouds, although I couldn't see them in the small viewing area.

Our reticular activating system filters out a lot of unnecessary information so that our minds don't overload. It protects us from an already existing assault on our senses. Sidi knows how to work with this concept to help us focus on things that are valuable to us. He opens our awareness, and guides us to see and hear things that we might have missed before. This is one of the ways in which our veils can be lifted. Through an intense focus of energy, we can penetrate into deeper layers of perception, and gain an understanding that might otherwise escape us.

As Sidi teaches, the value of spiritual practice is that it strengthens us, so we can stand strong in the face of storms, and continue to examine our situation. Our spiritual strength is evident in the way we deal with adversity. It isn't hard to stand strong while all is going well, but we're truly tested when we have to make decisions in times of adversity. Adversity strengthens us and helps us to build character and other skills with which to overcome challenges; and as we learn to do so, then others are given courage as well.

Right Livelihood

A long time ago, I lost my younger brother in an accident; and when I went to my parents, I realized that I was more or less impotent when it came to helping them deal with their immense pain. No amount of money or success (this was during the time I was doing very well as a fashion photographer) was able to give me insights on how to help them. I actually ended up renting my studio to someone and moving to India to try to find some meaning in my life. The following is how I wrote about this in *Walking in Awareness:*

> I want to share a story with you. I have had another big loss in my life. This was when my younger brother died in an accident. When I went to meet my parents to try to deal with this challenge, I realized that there was no material thing that I had, that could help to ease their pain and their suffering. I felt so spiritually inadequate that I couldn't comfort them and that I couldn't help them with their pain that I went back to Europe. I completely left the photography business, and I went to India to look for different teachings and different masters. On one of these quests I was in a little village, in the foothills of the Himalayas, and I was on my way to have a meeting with a teacher that I revered. We stopped in town and it was pretty sophisticated because it had a restaurant, and the restaurant actually had a covered outhouse, so that was really, really sophisticated. I went out to the outhouse and I was happy because I was in the woods but there was actually a cover. When I went inside it was almost blissful because in the hole in the ground right next to it there were all these magazines and newspapers, so I didn't have to use leaves. So I'm sitting there and I'm contemplating the universe as we all do, and I take some of these papers and I crumple them up to make them soft. Something (I don't know what it was) made me want to open the pages. I opened them and what did I find myself gazing at? I saw a double page photograph that I personally had taken in *Elle* magazine, now a piece of toilet paper in India. Do you know how that made me feel about right livelihood?

It is so important that each of us discovers how to make our work feel like we are making a contribution of value. This doesn't always mean we need to change jobs, but it often means that we have to change our viewpoint and attitude about our work. It is important to know who we are really working for and whose dream we are helping to realize. If every action we take is like a prayer, if everything we do, we do for God, then we can start to feel as if we are living a life of service. Sidi says that if we see everyone as a Divine creation, we are always serving God rather then some individual. Sharing all I have learned adds a deep, deep value to my life because I know I'm changing people's lives. Not that that my photography didn't make a contribution, but it wasn't the contribution that I intended making. I feel much more empowered to come out and teach people how to get in alignment with their purpose.

I think one of our biggest fears is to lead a life that doesn't have meaning. To lead a meaningless life or to not lead the life that we think we're destined to lead is a very, very painful thing for almost everybody.

One time after coming back from India, I visited a private zoo in England. I walked into a cage with a large puma, and the big cat seemed very quiet and friendly. At one point, he put his front paws on my shoulders from behind. I felt okay, and wasn't experiencing any fear at that time. However, one of his claws got caught in the clasp of a leather necklace I was wearing and I got a little nervous. Because the person with me couldn't get the claw unstuck, I felt my fear rising; and as my fear rose, the puma started this rather loud growl. For a moment I was really scared, and in that moment, the cat almost howled. I had said nothing, but he sensed my fear right away.

When we meet others, a lot of unspoken energetic communication occurs, and in subtle ways. We know when we meet a loving person; and when we are loving ourselves, we feel compatibility immediately. Watch kids get together who don't know each other on the first day of school, and undoubtedly all the troublemakers will gravitate toward each other. Watch adults do the same thing. Because we have an inner sense that talks to us, when we are in touch with ourselves, we're able to use these powers of discernment in a positive way.

I believe that we have the same energetic intuition with respect to inanimate objects. When we eat food that has been prepared in a loving way, even if we're not consciously aware as we're eating it, I believe that it digests better. So if you send a sales CD or any other tool to a prospective customer, internally this person will have a reaction that is sometimes more important than the external one. Our unconscious responses are powerful because they guide us in ways that we're often not consciously aware of, and we do things without really knowing why.

If one day someone decides to send bulk mail in a less impersonal way, addressing the envelope with lovingly careful handwriting, I think people will have a harder time throwing the envelope away unread.

When we are totally committed and present in every action we take, when we commit to excellence with every fiber of our being in the performance of that action and that action is filled with love, then every moment is capable of producing an amazing outcome. This is a key to creating wealth in your life—not just financial wealth, but abundance in all areas.

EXERCISE

Make a list of the most important actions you perform on a daily basis, and evaluate them on a scale of 1 to 10. Determine how much love and excellence you put into those activities. Take note of the actions that are *not* being productive and see if you can find an action that would change the momentum, taking you from where you are to where you want to go.

Would you like to change the direction your life is heading?
Join me in our 8-week program for in-depth support.
www.MakeYourLifeMagical.com/explore

Chapter 11

Relationships

Something else that determines the quality of our lives is the quality of our relationships—not just our relationships with people, but those with God, money, nature, and everything that exists. Without people we can't have relationships, and the quality of our relationships is going to be determined by the quality of people we attract to us. In turn, the quality of people we attract into our lives is a reflection of who we are and who we want to be. If we want to attract loving people, we should start by being loving ourselves.

Along these lines, D.H. Lawrence wrote a beautiful poem called "Search for Love" that goes like this:

Those that go

searching for love

never find love.

They only make manifest

their own lovelessness.

Only the loving find love,

and they never have to seek for it.

The best way I know of to find a good partner is to *be* a good partner. This is based on the principle that the love you give is the love you get, and this is yet again another teaching from Sidi, as well as so many others on a spiritual path. When I'm with him, he reflects back to me not only my own potential, but I can also see the greatness that human beings can aspire to. I can taste the Divine through his heart, and the unconditional love that he emits to every human being is something I aspire to and how I want to express myself. Sidi's ability to embrace everyone and everything without judgment or separation shows me that it's possible for a person in human form to live and walk in total awareness.

Experiencing this in a real and tangible manner is, for me, more powerful than reading about it. To be accepted in such a way and to be able to experience this unconditional love shows me that I can express the same type of love to my friends and family.

My experience has taught me that people treat those in their work lives in the same manner they treat individuals in their private lives. In *Conversations with God,* by Neale Donald Walsch, he mentions how we must actually act out intent to directly experience a feeling. Once the thought or feeling of loving others gets acted out and manifests in loving ways, the reality is experienced firsthand. Otherwise, it's just a concept.

I often *intend* to do more things with my kids, but many times I get caught up in something and I procrastinate. I think about them all the time, and I am always full of very loving thoughts and great intentions, so in my mind I'm a good father and take great care of them. The reality is that I could do a lot more with them and be a lot more present, rather than just having good intentions.

This same tendency can be seen in my relationship with those I work with. I think about them a lot, am very grateful to have them in my life, yet I don't actually spend time doing things with them because I'm always busy doing something else. I can rationalize by saying that this helps create strong, individual leaders who don't get co-dependent, but that isn't the point.

**The point is that it takes more than good intentions
to make a vision become a reality.
Action steps need to be taken.**

During those years of struggle with the darkness within me, I became an expert at feeling sorry for myself. Looking back, I can see now how the attitudes I kept choosing created the atmosphere in which I lived. Change seemed impossible because I didn't know how to change my *attitude.*

Due to a seemingly casual encounter that my ex-wife, Nathalie, had in a market one day, I ended up working with a shaman and healer named Martine Practel. I don't remember exactly how it happened but after Nathalie gave me his number, I found myself sitting in Martine's home, which precipitated dramatic changes in my life. Martine, besides becoming one of my closest friends, had a profound effect on my spiritual life and thus the rest of my existence. One thing I learned is that it isn't only the encounter that matters, but whether or not some action is taken. Wayne Gretzky, the hockey player, once said, "I missed every shot I never took." We can't expect to score a lot of goals if we never attempt a shot in the first place.

We need action in addition to thought to manifest something concrete.

The same weaknesses that I exhibit in my personal life are reflected in my business, and vice versa. The strengths that I have in my personal life are also the strengths of my business. That's why I submit that you cannot have a business bigger than you are. If you want to manage a large organization, you need to expand your possibilities so that you can encompass the hearts of all those involved.

Building a large team can stretch us in many ways, and the more we're able to handle, the more we will be given. There are so many stories of people who won a lottery, or who inherited a lot of money, who weren't adequately prepared to handle it, and whose lives were ultimately destroyed. Look at the number of rock stars who have died so young due to their inability to deal with fame and fortune. The inner work we do is crucial to being able to assimilate all the benefits that networking can bring to us, and as we expand inwardly, we can also expand outwardly.

Relationships are not about obligations; they're about opportunities. When we are with other people, we have an opportunity to experience ourselves in relation to these individuals. Sidi shared a saying with me that goes like this: "I was a hidden treasure that longed to be known, so I drew all of the creation out of myself in order to know Myself." So even God uses relationships to know Himself. He created something out of Himself to be able to look at and experience Himself.

Our life is made up of all kinds of relationships. The quality of our health is determined by how one part of our body relates to another. When one part becomes dysfunctional, other parts are severely affected. If we lose our sight, our hearing improves; if one muscle grows weak, we compensate by developing another muscle.

Our Relationship with Money

Our relationship with money is one of those issues that most people find tremendously challenging. When we want to receive something from a relationship, it's easy to give in to the temptation to conduct oneself without integrity, and nowhere does this show up more frequently than in financial matters.

As with everything, love is the doorway to triumphing over money issues. I have learned to truly love all that money can do for me—especially what it allows me to do for others. I feel no guilt or shame over making a lot of money, because in my heart I know I only want it so I can have more to give. The time freedom I have because of residual income allows me to do a tremendous amount of work supporting Sidi, and thus help thousands of other people. Be clear here—it isn't money itself I love; it's what money can do for me and others.

I want to share a story that really helped me understand a lot about my relationship with money. I was in Reno, Nevada, for a weekend masters seminar, and Richard Brooke from the wellness company Oxyfresh was talking about how people usually have an intention or goal that is quite a bit larger than their internal expectations. That is, people will express outwardly that they'd like to make $5,000 a month, but internally they really only truly believe they'll make $1,000; and the way he shared this with me was so powerful that

I would like to share it with you, too, because I realized that there was a lot of truth in what he said.

First, Richard asked us to write down a figure that we would like to be making per month a year from that day, and for these purposes, let's say we wrote down $10,000. He then asked us to choose an amount that we were absolutely *sure* we'd make—so sure that we would bet our lives and our homes on it.

Now please realize that this was just an exercise, and that we weren't actually being threatened with having to lose something precious, but we all played along with the premise. So let's say we originally put down $10,000, but because we really wanted to be absolutely sure that we didn't lose our lives and homes, we put down $4,000.

The point here is that the $6,000 difference had a lot of importance. When I did this exercise and looked at the discrepancy between the two amounts, I had an interesting realization. When I intended to make $10,000 but only really expected $4,000, this latter amount is what my internal voice was telling me I was going to make. So if I ended up making $5,000 that month, I could either choose to be unhappy because I'd made less than I wanted to, or I could be happy that I made $1,000 more than I thought I would. I also realized that I knew exactly how I'd spend the $4,000, but didn't really know how I would spend the additional $6,000 if I were fortunate enough to make that additional amount.

The point I'm trying to make is that we let a lot of dissatisfaction creep into our lives because we compare results with dreams rather than realities. After I did this exercise, I acknowledged that throughout my life I had always made good money, but I had never really made more than I thought I needed. So I was constantly caught in that endless struggle at the end of the month of trying to make ends meet. Even when my income doubled, I still *spent* everything.

What I realized as a result of this exercise, and in my subsequent conversation with Richard, was that if I wanted to increase my income, I really needed to make more "real" the use I would have for the intended income.

So following his advice, I decided to write a one- to two-page story of what my life would be like when I was earning the intended income. The story started in the morning when I woke up and was walking out to the mailbox to get my check. I described what I felt like, where I lived, and the feeling I had when I opened the envelope. I then described walking back into the house, going into my beautiful workspace, feeling great, sharing the check with those working with me, and then letting them take over the responsibilities of paying off all the monthly expenditures.

I paid myself first, putting away 10 percent to use for fun, then another 10 percent for tithing. By the time taxes were paid and bills were caught up on, I still had some money left over, so I carefully allocated it to things that had value for me.

I loved that feeling of having complete financial freedom, so I spent the rest of the time writing a detailed version of what my day felt like. It has not even been a month since I did this, and already things have occurred that have helped me increase my income significantly. By simply making the income difference more realistic, I expanded the possibility of acquiring it; and as it became real in my thoughts, it manifested in my life.

Just as every object was a thought in someone's mind before it became a reality, and just as this text was a thought in my mind before I brought it to creation, the more tangible something is in the mind, the more tangible it becomes in the real world. So by actually creating on paper a life for this extra income, I believe I drew it out of creation and into manifestation.

Similarly, when you truly connect with people in your life and discover what their dreams are, you can help them manifest their desires by sharing these concepts with them. These individuals will feel that you really care about them because you share their dream. Once you help them really understand and feel the *why*, the *how* will happen by itself, because once they are acting in harmony with their highest aspirations, they will live each moment with fuller integrity. Each decision will be easy to make because they will choose the path that will help them fulfill their purpose. And because they will be acting with purpose, they will be acting from their heart, and with much more passion. What they're doing will feel so good that they'll detach from the result, and then the field of unlimited possibility will be open to them.

I believe that it's important to always focus most on what you want money for rather than how much you want to make. Many people set the goal of making more money, but that goal is impossible to attain because no matter how much one makes, there is always the feeling that it isn't enough.

I think it's very difficult for most people to feel good about being passionate about money, but it's easy to feel good about being passionate about helping others. Our souls are deeply nourished when we can offer help to those less fortunate. I can think of numerous people I know who have deep wounds with respect to money because their families had a lot of it, just as I know people who have issues because they've struggled financially all their lives.

Some people who inherit money feel deep down that they didn't really do anything worthwhile to earn this wealth so they struggle with low self-esteem, and the wealth can end up being an albatross around their necks. Many of them have never had to work, so they never develop a passion for anything, and often spend their time turning to drugs or alcohol to numb their feelings of inadequacy.

Money used properly can be a tremendous tool for personal transformation and growth, and I've seen this happen over and over again. Look at Bono from U2 and how he has not only used his money, but also his fame, to contribute to numerous causes all over the world. I often hear people talk negatively about Bill Gates because they think Microsoft is a big, controlling entity that monopolizes certain sectors of society at the expense of smaller companies, but I am personally inspired by all the charities that Gates supports and the examples he has set.

Just because someone makes a lot of money and runs a huge business that dominates an industry doesn't mean he can't be a source of responsible global stewardship and make a huge difference in the world. I was stunned to recently learn that it was Bill Gates who loaned Steven Jobs the money to resurrect Apple. And it was a loan in the millions of dollars.

Deep in the heart of most of us is a desire to contribute to the lives of those we love, as well as those who are in need. It is a basic human desire, because it reflects how our Creator cares for *us*.

Money is a symbol that we use to negotiate our way through many exchanges. It allows us to learn about honor, integrity, mercy, and compassion; and it teaches us to be fair, and resist the temptation to be unethical in our material lives.

The Soul of Money

After I'd finished writing the first draft of this book, I read a book written by Lynne Twist called *The Soul of Money,* and I loved it so much I wanted to share some of it with you. It is one of the best books I've ever read about our relationship, or lack of it, with money. People will always gravitate in large numbers to any person who is able to solve their major life dilemmas; and as far as I'm concerned, I hope that Lynne receives whatever rewards she yearns for, because she has truly created an awesome gift for humanity with respect to the way she clarifies money issues in such an effective manner.

As I read over what I wrote about people with money often having just as many problems as those without, I remembered that Lynne had written about this quite succinctly. So I want to share a few passages from her book:

> *But their money and the lifestyle of privilege also cut them off from the richness of ordinary everyday life, the more normal and healthy give-and-take of relationships and useful work, the best of the human experience. Often their wealth distorted their relationship with money and only widened the gap between their soulful life and their interactions around money. Sexual abuse, psychological abuse, addictions, alcoholism, abandonment, and brutality are part of the dysfunctional world that hides behind the walled communities, mansions, and darkened car windows. Hurtful rejections, custody suits, legal battles for the purpose of attaining more and more money harden family members and shut them down from each other. The access to money and power at high levels can amplify these situations and make them even more lethal and unbearably cruel.*

Mother Teresa's admonition and my subsequent fund-raising work with the very wealthy taught me that, surprisingly, wealth is no protection from human suffering. I would come to learn that people with excess wealth—not all of them, but many—struggle in lives disconnected from the qualities of the soul. They live trapped in a prison of privilege in which material comforts are plentiful, but spiritual and emotional deprivation are real and painful. In that prison they lose touch with the values of the heart. They can become the manifestation of money's darkest side. For some, wealth only serves as a weapon that expands their capacity to do harm.

Can you feel the power of this kind of thinking and realize the intensity of belief and commitment that lies inside someone who would write something like this? The beauty of a heart that would commit to not just making a dent in people's hunger issues but instead chooses to eradicate it entirely? And she doesn't do this because she *thinks* it's possible, but because her belief system tells her that she *knows* it's possible.

What would *your* life be like if you chose to champion a cause that was bigger than you are?

Wow! This woman expresses my feelings and thoughts in such a beautiful manner. I sit here thinking, *Who am I to be writing about wealth when someone can write as well as she can and from such a deep place in her heart?* I hope that any of you readers who are interested in learning more about your relationship with money will read this book, study it, and share it with as many people as possible.

And if it wasn't enough that everything Lynne shared here was a corroboration of what I was trying to express, my wife and I went to see the George Clooney movie called *The Descendants*. At the beginning of the movie, Clooney's character is talking about how even though Hawaii is like a paradise, people there can still experience sorrow and pain, and the story goes on to show that all the wealth in the world can't protect you from difficult emotional experiences.

As far as I'm concerned, the ultimate tool or resource for overcoming life's challenges lies in our hearts, and in our power to love and connect with God on a more constant basis. Then, through rigorous spiritual disciplines, we can strengthen ourselves so that we can stand strong in the onslaught of life's challenges.

Here is more from Lynne:

> *When you know with certainty that things can be not just different but entirely resolved, you engage in the work in a more fundamental way. You don't wonder "if." You determine "how to."*

What if you apply this to yourself? Don't you know with certainty that you can change, that things can be different? All you have to do is figure out the "how to." And as you read this book you should certainly come to see that if you actually *do* what I've shared here, then change is inevitable.

It has worked for me and thousands of others, and as I have said over and over, all I've done here is take other people's knowledge and have shared it in a way that is a beneficial road map for all.

Lynne continues with questions you can ask yourself:

> *Who do I need to be to fulfill on the commitment I've made? What kind of human being do I need to forge myself into to make this happen? What resources do I need to be willing to bring to bear in myself and my colleagues and in my world?*

Does it seem like mere coincidence that so many messages share the same truths and that you are drawing them to you at this time?

Lynne says:

> *When you discard your own pettiness, center yourself in integrity, and reach into your soul for your greatness, it is always there.*

I want you to use the gifts that God has given you to help yourself live the life you were born to live. And in your heart I am sure that you want this as well.

Experience Your Greatness

You can experience your greatness by giving as well, and it doesn't always have to be money. Money is a tool, and there are many tools that can make a huge impact on people, and which will also help you personally. Many people will appreciate just having your time, or some guidance, or some emotional support. You can volunteer at a soup kitchen, you can clean out the clutter in your life and give it to those who can use it, you can look into your heart and see where you're holding back in sharing love with your primary relationships, and you can feed someone's heart by giving more of yourself. There's no limit to your potential, and all you have to do to change things in your life is to start *today* to actually do some things differently.

I could actually quote even more from this book because I feel it has so much useful information, and I could also put in more of Sidi's teachings as well as those from so many of the people I have been blessed to come across because they have taught me so much, but I've mentioned the names and shared many sources, and now it is up to you if you really want to change. Please actually go out and do something with all this information. Remember that a donkey with a load of books on its back is still a donkey. And if you're already happy with where you are and are now in a place where you want to help others, then please feel free to draw on these resources and share them with other seekers. These are the teachings that I personally endorse because they've helped me create so much abundance in my life, and as I will keep saying over and over, I believe that this abundance came through "creating wealth from within."

Personal Relationships

In our personal relationships, unless we grow into multifaceted individuals, our relationships will stagnate. The more we grow personally and the more we learn to nourish ourselves, the more we can nourish others. And the more we reach out to help others, the more we help ourselves and the more we grow.

Early in my career as a photographer, I had a lot of difficulty giving directions to models in a studio setting. One night after a session when the studio was empty, I went out on a set with just a white paper as a backdrop and tried to work out a few poses. I really felt uncomfortable, and from that day on I had a lot more patience with, and understanding for, the models when I put them in similar situations.

The same goes for my organization now. I like to personally try everything that I suggest to others so that I can empathize with all the challenges they might encounter. The best way to build something is to choose an action that you're passionate about, and the more passion you have, the less resistance you will experience.

This is also true in our personal lives. The more passion we bring to our relationships, the more excitement there will be, and the energy will flow through us. For me, the most important relationship in my life is with God. This is the basis on which I build everything, and it is here that I find the qualities that I like to express—when I am alone and when I am with others.

We might have different bodies, but we are all created from the same essence, and this essence is forever around us, embracing us, and permeating our very beings. If we are to find peace in our lives, it will benefit us to act in harmony with this essence. Some call this essence God, others call it some other name. If we are to live as an extension of our Creator, then we should love in the same way, with the same unconditional love—loving everyone and everything without separation of any kind.

If we are all part of the same emotion, every time I hurt you, I am also hurting myself. Every time I deceive you, I deceive myself. As we are all one heart, everything I feel, you feel. As we grow in awareness and expand our consciousness, we are able to know this in a more tangible way. We are connected to every person who makes a breakthrough of any kind because we all swim in the same ocean of love. And when someone suffers, we are also part of this suffering. The masters of this world are able to love both the fire and the garden with the same equanimity because they know they are of the same essence.

When Gandhi showed the world the power of nonviolence, we all felt this power with him; and as hundreds of thousands of people felt free, we tasted freedom. We cannot separate ourselves from the truth of this unity. We can forget it, and we can remain unconscious to this knowing, but the truth still stays the truth.

By ignoring something, you are certainly able to diminish its hold over you, but you can't stop time by ignoring it. When you go to sleep, you still wake up later.

Our most important relationship is the one we have with ourselves, and with our source of creation. Whatever feelings we have about ourselves will be the same as those we have about others. And when we have faith in our own divinity, we are able to experience this divinity in others.

When we trust ourselves, we are able to trust others.

When my life appeared to fall apart, I questioned my faith. I asked many questions of God, but I couldn't hear any answers and my heart seemed unable to experience love. I would pray and feel disconnected. Whatever I tried didn't feel good, and I lived in fear. I no longer trusted myself, so I was unable to trust others. I was obsessed with my problems, and I constantly regarded myself as a victim. I had spent my life learning how to focus energy, so I was very good at playing the victim role.

As a photographer, I would often shut out the world around me except for what I saw through a small aperture in my camera. I became so good at blocking out the rest of the world that I would drive others nuts because I wouldn't hear them talking to me while I was focused on the limited world I saw through the viewfinder. So while I was focused on my role as a victim, I wasn't seeing or experiencing the opportunities that were coming my way. New relationships with great potential came and went, and my heart was in pain because I wasn't allowing my love to flow.

Because our natural condition is a loving one, when we do not love, we feel pain. By staying consciously aware of the source of our love, we are able to access this love; and when we are loving, there is less fear, and where there is less fear, there is usually less pain.

When we are able to love ourselves and embrace our darkness, we are then able to be with others in a compassionate way because we are more likely to love them and be able to embrace *their* darkness as well.

I have found that I have a great ability to attract people into my life who mirror my own thoughts and feelings. When I communicate with others in the business world, it becomes easier for me to see myself in others. I have certain tendencies which, if left unchecked, would look exactly like some of the qualities of people whom I meet and am at odds with.

I know a number of individuals who expect great results but don't really put in a lot of effort. Some complain about how much they work, and others don't like doing ordinary things that take a lot of time. I can identify with each of these people because through their hearts, I can feel my own. There were times in my career as a photographer when I hated to have to make appointments and show my portfolio to people, and there were times when I hated calling people back after I'd seen them. Almost every challenge others confront when they're working for themselves I've also had to face in my life and career.

These issues are universal, so as I clear them up, it shows others that they can do so as well. As they see and feel that my own faith works, the faith and belief of others gets stronger.

Once there's a crack in the container that holds the love, it's an opening for the erosion of faith. I think that everyone at some time or another experiences doubt—about themselves, their abilities, and the work they're doing. I have certainly experienced this myself. Keeping focused at all times is a challenge for everyone I've ever met, and when doubt creeps into our hearts, we can get way off track if we're not careful.

I've heard many successful entrepreneurs state that it's not a good idea to put all one's eggs in the proverbial basket, so I can appreciate that people can have different viewpoints, and different ways of going about things. Some people excel when they stay singularly focused on doing one thing. Other people excel with diversity. The only rule here is that there *are* no rules. I know many people who constantly look for new conquests, and others who strive for perfection in one area. There is no right or wrong.

Clear, focused attention has a lot of power.

As for me, I enjoy experiencing focused energy, when I receive it and when I'm the one sharing it. Relationships grow closer when each person is able to be totally present for the other; and when we're fortunate enough to share moments like these with loved ones, our need to have more people in our lives diminishes. That's why so many new lovers like to be alone. They wish to experience the whole of creation with and through each other.

When I'm with my four kids, totally present, I don't wonder what it would be like to have more kids around. At those times, it's as if they are my whole world. What happens is that the experience is so joyous that we seem to attract others into our energy field.

Imagine that you only have *one* person in your life, which is something that just about all of us have experienced at one time or another, if only for a short while. If you were to completely focus all your love and attention on that relationship, and completely nourish this other person and honor them 100 percent (and this might mean leaving them a lot of space), chances are that the wonderful vibration of this relationship would attract others to you. At the same time, if you developed a frustrating relationship with this person, you would probably attract more of the same. By loving, we attract more love. By being free and powerful ourselves, we attract free and powerful people into our lives.

As we all grow through the archetypal patterns of relationships, and as we learn more about ourselves in relation to each other, we make it easier for all those who follow.

All our cells are connected, all our thoughts are connected, all our feelings are connected within ourselves, and as my energy reaches out to embrace yours, *we* are connected. Two people sharing a lot of intimate time together become a collective force.

When your energy melts with someone to co-create a business or to just share an event or a life, everything appears magnified. I remember the feeling of having dozens of people all focused on creating a great photograph, and how we were all connected through the process. Their success became mine, and I felt as if I were a part of their lives, too.

Daryl Kollman, the founder and president of a company I was once involved with, said that his distributors were his arms and his legs. He was experiencing these people as extensions of himself. Managers or coaches of a team can experience the same thing: the players are extensions of their energy, and while the players are out on the field, they're acting out their ideas.

We're all an extension of Divine energy, and we're all connected to each other through our Source. As one of us grows, the whole collective ocean of our consciousness expands, and we are able to experience this expansion. When all the strings of a guitar are strummed, only the most trained ear can differentiate the sound of each individual string. Out of the entire symphony of thoughts created by humanity, some thoughts reach out more than others, but we are all part of this creation.

While I was going through the breakup of my marriage, I was experiencing massive pain, and I've come to understand that it wasn't just *my* pain I was experiencing, but the collective pain of all my brothers throughout the world going through similar situations. As I tried to convince my wife that there was a better way, I felt great resistance, and I was experiencing the collective resistance of all the women everywhere who felt the need to start new lives and who didn't want to stay in their marriages.

As we experience our issues through our relationships, it's important that we not think of ourselves as being alone. Sometimes what we feel is our connection to the total pool of energy in which we live. If we learn to rejoice in the success of our friends rather than be envious, we will be acknowledging our own capacity for success.

There exists an enormous reservoir of love out of which we were all created and to which we are able to return when we remember the path we're on. It is from being in this pool that we know that love is unlimited, that it is always there for us, and that the more we drink from it, the more we contribute to it. This is the source of all abundance of any sort, and the spiritual laws that govern one aspect of our lives works in sync with all the other aspects as well.

When someone or something is in a relationship that is harmonious with universal laws, there is no limit to what can be accomplished. Divine energy is a totally inexhaustible source of nutrition for body, mind, and soul; and as long we collectively respect this concept, love and support will always be available when needed.

Respect for Others

If you learn to respect each person and thing in your life as an aspect of the Divine, your relationships will flourish, and *you* will flourish. There is no limit to how many people you can touch with your love. Only conditional love has limits, but if you open yourself to experience *un*conditional love, you will also open yourself to unconditional growth.

We have learned conditional love from other humans, because at no time does Divine energy come to us in a conditional manner. True spirit has no bounds and knows no limits. One of the biggest gifts we can give ourselves as well as others is to share our love; and as we open our hearts, the hearts of all others will open.

Global transformation starts with personal transformation, and when we are nourished with love, we grow quickly. We can then share this with others and grow together. Not only is our relationship with ourselves and others of vital importance if we want to grow a big business, for example, but our relationship to the earth and all this implies plays a key part in our growth process.

As a result of all the information that is now available about responsible global stewardship, I have grown in awareness to a greater extent. I have come to accept that our lives are determined as much by what we *choose* to do as by what we choose *not* to do.

By not taking certain action steps in my personal life concerning the well being of our planet, I was not living in harmony with the spiritual laws I so respect. By not living in harmony with these laws, I was stunting my own growth; and my relationship with our planet was not nearly as meaningful as it could have been. As I paid more attention to what was going on in my world, though, I realized that the more responsibility I assumed about caring for the planet, the more I felt nourished by it; and the more I felt connected to Earth, the environment, and God.

When I feel more connected to my Creator, the quality of my entire life improves, as does the efficiency with which I do business. Expectations are a source of disappointment, and I prefer to undercommit and overperform, as it feels better to me.

We all have love inside of us, even though there are some of us who have challenges when it comes to feeling and expressing this love. Right livelihood is something that can be totally transformational in our search for inner excellence, and our relationship with our work is as vital as our relationship with our spouse. Depending on our level of commitment and involvement with either, we can feel more or less fulfilled.

I have always felt totally fulfilled in relation to my children, and that's because I fully invest my heart with them. I have never felt that I had to sacrifice anything for my kids. They have been a constant joy in my life, always giving me a wonderful feeling that adds immeasurably to my existence.

Total Engagement

Someone's higher self is always going to know when your higher self is not fully engaged. When I got involved with my current company, I engaged myself 100 percent, and everyone I met could feel it. When you meet couples who are deeply connected and totally engaged, it's quite mesmerizing. It often makes people feel that they'd like to have an expression of love that is similar. And when people sense that you're fully engaged and passionate about every aspect of your work, they feel the same way.

I saw a T-shirt in the Albuquerque airport one day while waiting for my luggage that said:

"The most valuable possession you can own is an open heart. The most powerful weapon you can be is an instrument of peace."
— CARLOS SANTANA

I feel that there's a Divine presence that is the Source of absolutely everything, and exists in everything, and I want to exist in a place where this Presence, which permeates all, is obvious to everyone. By opening our hearts and letting the love flow freely, we are in constant communication with this Divine energy, which supports not only the individual but also the entire world. Just like the ocean exists in every drop that makes it up, the Divine exists in every heart that makes up our world.

Love knows no limits, and through knowing love, we can taste the Divine, because once we have the experience of accepting, we can make the step to accept other things greater than ourselves. We don't need to be limited by our rational minds, but can attain knowledge via the heart, which is the path of the great mystics.

This feeling of completeness creates a joyful feeling of exhilaration, and when action springs forth from this condition, it is usually very productive. When I first started sharing health products, I focused primarily on how they had helped *my* life, so I drew people similar to myself to me.

Now that I'm in a more joyous state, I seem to draw *happier* people to me. What I desire now is to attract those who haven't lost their yearning for enlightenment, and who want to make a difference in the world. People want their lives to have meaning, they want to leave a legacy of having made a difference, they want to feel that their lives have some value—in *their* eyes and in the eyes of others. It is through serving others that we can feel a connection with God and have a sense of being more than just a statistic.

By reaching out and helping others, we satisfy one of our greatest needs: the need to feel connected. With all the divorces occurring worldwide, families aren't staying together as they did in the old days, and as people spend more and more time in front of their computers, they experience friendship through social media in lieu of physical connection—and I am as much to blame as anyone. I'm still working hard on being present for those I draw into my life. Sometimes because I'm doing so many things at once, I feel that I'm not available for some of the people who might need more information and commitment from me.

I look deeper now when I enter into a new relationship with people, and if I feel any resistance from either their side or mine, I become more careful about making any commitments. I want to spend most of my time with people who have open hearts and open minds, because these people seem to be more connected to Divine energy, and I find these to be the most enlightening and empowering relationships. I am now attracted to people who want to do things for themselves, and who truly wish to co-create rather than having others do things for them. I still love helping people and am committed to always doing so, so I have come to the realization that the more I help strong people, the greater number of lives will be touched in a positive way.

Overcoming Fear

One of the biggest fears I've encountered in many people I've met is that they're afraid to share their ideas with those who are currently more successful than they are. Naturally, it takes time and effort to start a new business or any other new endeavor, so some are hesitant to talk to successful people about what they're trying to do, thinking that they have to wait until they're successful themselves to do so. They have no resistance to sharing with those making less, but have genuine fears about going to more successful people with their opportunity. However, I've found that people who share their dreams with powerful personalities bring so many great ideas into fruition. So I suggest that you release your fear in this area; and ask for help, advice and support from successful men and women when you need it.

If I write a great movie script, it is doubtful that a local taxi driver is going to know how to raise the money to produce it. I did say "doubtful," not impossible. So I would look first to connecting with a successful producer. Many successful people find it very fulfilling to be able to help others still struggling, and if you don't have the courage to walk through your fear, you're actually depriving *them* of the opportunity to help. We all have fears, but if you're passionate enough, you can walk through the fear and experience what is waiting on the other side. It is the passion that will allow you this grace.

One of my business mentors, Rick Tonita, sent me this e-mail on my 60th birthday:

"I did a dissertation on Fortune 500 companies a few years back and found that over 85% of those companies were started by people 60 years or older who had been bankrupt at least twice in their lives."

So it's never to late to start over. I am now 70 years old and feel as if my life is being completely renewed. I am writing this book, which I believe will bring a lot of change into my life and into my wife's life. She is starting to write her own book as well. We're both thinking about going out on speaking engagements because we're passionate about sharing our message. I welcome change, and hope you do, too.

As we reach out to embrace the Divine in all that we do, we find that we're on a journey that has no end and knows no limits. When you live each moment in its fullness, not expecting any particular outcome, and being totally committed with all of your being, then you have the opportunity to experience the true mystery and wonder of life.

More from Sidi

Following are some excerpts from some of Sidi's teachings relating to being connected in relationships; This one is called the *Beloveds of Allah:*

I want to speak about the prophets and the father of the light and how all the prophets lived with their wives. Listen with the ear of your heart, my sons and my daughters, to hear what I say because this is a very important subject. This is from the order of God to speak to you about how to live with a husband and wife as beloveds of God.

I have given you many subjects before to help you to know yourself, to find the key to open the hidden treasure inside you. After you have walked in the way and lifted the veils of darkness to see the light of God, He brings you a step higher to see Him in the face of your beloved. The understanding of God and all that His love means to you is completed by the sharing of the deep secret love with another because it is putting the essence of all the teachings, all the books, all the sciences, and all that God has given to you into manifestation through the love you share with your beloved. Everything before has been a preparation for seeing the light of God in the eye of your beloved. You have cut through many stones in your way for the world is full of darkness and troubles and many things have come before you. But it is necessary to erase everything and to leave your past behind, to come to your beloved with a clean heart in order to live in the heart of God. He wants to show you the true picture of Himself in the face of your beloved, and it is necessary to be careful with those whom God gives us to care about because they are really the jewel. Their hearts are pure and clean and through them you can see the true image of God. You share a love whose depths cannot be fathomed because it is the love of God. His secret is in the love. It is important for you to care for your beloved as if you were caring for God, and to speak to your beloved as if you were speaking to God. At every moment you stand facing God and God is your Beloved.

You must be polite with your beloved and give your whole self to this love. Sometimes God manifests through your beloved as the jamal (beauty), and sometimes as jalal (severity). He who cannot accept both is not in the unity, because He is manifesting what He wants you to see of Himself. Give the love to your beloved, and it will change the darkness to the light, the jalal to a garden of love. Care for your beloved. Make each word and action contain only the love of God and His polite. Understand what God wants from you in every minute. What He wants is for you to be the father and the mother, sister and brother, wife and husband to your beloved, to be everything at any time. Do not search for your beloved in any other place because he holds all the qualities of God. And you also are the beloved of God. There is no separation between you because you both carry the soul of God. He does not make a difference between her and him, and she does not make a difference between him and her. They are one. There are no numbers in the truth. From the picture I have given you, and from the religion of your soul, the soul of God and of the guide, send mercy to your beloved because in this giving you are sending mercy for yourself.

Life in the marriage of beloveds is for each to be holy, and to care about one another. This marriage is like a holy tree whose roots grow deep into the earth, and the earth is the heart of God. How do you nourish this tree? You nourish it by giving it love and clean water—water that has been cleansed of all the troubles of this world. It is necessary for the tree to grow strong in order to give shade to all the lovers of God who are beneath it. When nourished, her roots will grow deep into the earth, becoming all the qualities of God, covering the universe with His essence. This is the Tree of Life and it is necessary for it to be nourished with the love of God. Then it will give the holiest of fruits with His permission and have the sweetest flowers, because it comes from one source.

Surround her with love and clean water. How do you do this? By helping each other, in the way, to remove all obstacles that come before you, and letting nothing stand in the way of this love. The heart of your beloved is like a glass, and it is necessary to take care of it so that it will not break. When it breaks, you have broken yourself; you have misused its care. Then God will take you from His garden.

The heart of a beloved is a jewel, and there are responsibilities for caring for this heart. Your time together as beloveds has three parts: The first part is to yourself, the second to your wife or husband, and the third part for your children. From all this you can give to your mother, father, sisters and brothers. All of these parts are for God. If you walk straight and you give your whole self for the love of God, He will give you a life of happiness and peace. What more could you want?

The husband is like the father of the universe but first he begins in the home. His example is like the earth, which anyone can walk upon and take what they want. Its soil is the ground of love. He stands strong as the source of love and understanding in the family, and behind the strength is all the mercy of Allah. God has made him a captain of a ship to provide for the family. His wife can come to him at any time, and he gives her the love and the caring of God. He is the support and strength of the family, maintaining the home in balance.

The way of every prophet has been to help his wife, not making a difference between him and her. She is his equal. The Father of the Light, our Prophet Muhammad, may Allah bless him and send him peace, helped his wife with everything. He cleaned, cooked, sewed, brought water from the well, coal for the fire, and played with his children at home. This was the way of every prophet.

God says, "Know that your wife is your mirror, and through her reflection you can see yourself. If she remains in your heart, you can see Me through the eye of your heart, but only if you care for this heart and send her love."

Yes, my son, when your work is finished, and if she has not finished it is necessary to help with what is needed. The responsibility of a husband is great. He must provide love where love is needed, and help without being asked; keep peace in the family, and know that there is no kingship in being a captain. The wife is not a servant for her husband, nor the husband for the wife—both are slaves for Allah. If God is your beloved, then you are slaves for each other. If you treat her as a jewel and appreciate everything that is done as if it were coming from the Hand of God, then she will be happy and not turn outside. She will keep the home as a loving garden.

The wife is the mother. Not only are her family her children, all the world are her children. She is a fountain of love, showering the world with her water. Its source is a deep spring flowing directly from God. She has the love to give without asking anything in return and without holding anything back, because her giving has no end. She knows that the caring for her family is the expression of her love for God, and anyone can come to her at any time. She gives patience and understanding without end. Her home is kept as a place of beauty, and food is prepared as if her Lord were a guest for dinner. She is the most precious of jewels; she must only open the jewel inside her. The jewel is hidden within in the deepest valley, holding all the wisdom and the love of God. If she reaches this valley, she will know the meaning of the love she gives.

When she speaks with her husband, she must know that she is speaking with God, and that every word is a prayer. It is the same for him because everyone is the face of God. If anyone is not polite with this reflection, then he is not polite with God. If a husband feels that his home is a garden with a loving wife, then he will not turn outside; he will feel peace and happiness in his heart.

It is necessary for every child born from this holy marriage to see only light from the beginning and to grow up in a happy home full of love. Teach him the meaning of courtesy; teach him politeness towards his mother and father, and do not leave him to follow his own impulse, but guide him in everything. If he is left to follow his own impulses, he will feel the troubles of the darkness. God will ask both the parents why the child was left on his own. It is also from this message to not give the child, after he or she has grown up, to anyone who is not from the family of God. Others do not know the meaning of politeness in the same way.

In the religion of God, the woman is like a jewel, and it is necessary for the man to drink from the cup of her wine, because its essence is the deep secret love of God.

My sons and daughters, if you knew what God has given to you, you would not do or say anything to break the heart of your beloved. The key to living a life with a beloved is to give each other what each needs. I am sure that if everyone does all that I have said, he will live this day in the garden, and feel peace in any place and in any religion. This message knows no difference between people or religion. There is no life like this life because you live all the time with God, and pray all your time with God.

I send my voice to all the world and carry everyone in my heart. La ilaha'ilallah. (There is no God but one God.)

— From *Conversations in the Zawiyah*

I think you can see from this teaching that to apply these kinds of truths to your daily life, you must feel truly connected to God, your partner, and your family. When you *give* love to them, that is also what you would like to have *from* them. As you open your heart in giving, you create a pathway for them to enter into your innermost being.

EXERCISE

Make a list of the most important relationships you would like to work on. You can write down names of people, groups, things, or whatever comes to your mind. Your list might look like this: *spouse, kids, family, boss, employees, money, garden, a cause, education,* etc. When this is done, place a number next to each item based on your level of commitment, with 10 being high and 1 being low. Then write down the action steps you can take to raise those lower numbers.

_____

_____

_____

_____

_____

_____

_____

_____

_____

_____

_____

_____

_____

_____

Do you desire harmonious, loving relationships?
Join me in our 8-week program for in-depth support.
www.MakeYourLifeMagical.com/explore

Chapter 12

Personal and Professional Growth

"The way you are to others is how God will be to you." — UNKNOWN

How do you get from where you are to where you want to go? This is an often-asked question, with as many answers as there are ways to go about it. In most of the areas we've explored a bit, there are spiritual truths that guide the way, and even though the action steps might differ, the inner laws remain constant. What works in one field will work in another; truth is truth and love is love, and it doesn't matter if the outside picture remains the same. So step one can once again be to give thanks. Expressing gratitude is always appropriate, so if you ever feel lost, start by giving thanks. Be grateful that you recognize you're lost, because many people are, but have no idea that this is the case. And remember that it's not uncommon to be fearful about going from where you are to where you want to be, because in a sense, you're going from the known to the unknown.

Change Through Shock

Sometimes change is brought about by a tremendous shock, and within every shock there is a revelation; the greater the shock, the greater the revelation. I think that the greatest shock I ever experienced was the accidental death of my brother, Wick. The precious nature of life was brought home in one sudden thundering lightning bolt. My heart, head, and spirit were stretched and expanded in ways I had never dreamed possible. I learned how limiting most of my belief systems were, and I learned that I no longer could accept things at face value just because entire societies believed them to be true.

When I went through my divorce, just because almost everyone I met would say that it was undoubtedly for the best, I still couldn't accept it because it didn't feel as if it served me at the time; and it certainly didn't seem like the situation would take me where I wanted to go. When Wick died, I was hard pressed to experience this event as a positive thing that was serving the higher good. All I could feel at the time was profound emotional pain—some of it mine, and some of it on behalf of the other people involved.

Because I'm terribly impatient in most ways, having the patience to wade through moments of transition is sometimes really difficult. It's hard for me to stay totally present, because I tend to either go back in my thoughts to what I knew, or project forward to what I think might happen. I do this when I speak at times, and I also do it when I read, by jumping to the end of a book or report. I used to get impatient when I played tennis matches, just wanting to get to the end—either the win *or* the loss. In short, I was always rushing. What I learned was that all of this was based in a feeling of lack, in a fear that if, for example, I didn't eat fast enough, the food might disappear.

I could argue till I'm blue in the face that I only rush because I want to get to the next experience, but deep inside I know that when you do something to come out of the present, it's because there's a lack of belief somewhere that *every moment contains a miracle, and every experience contains the world.* If you don't believe this, then you're coming from lack, because you're saying that something is missing in that experience. To totally relax, and fully trust that every moment contains the fullness of the Divine—which lacks nothing—don't allow a space for fear to exist.

Fear and worry are part of a mind that doesn't feel the totality of its connection with the Divine.

When I'm in the presence of spiritual masters, I always notice how they're always in the moment. Each and every second, they are present and loving, not projecting into the future, not getting hung up in the past.

Sidi says that we need to be the *sons and daughters of our moments*; and when you learn to live like this, totally focused, totally present, totally involved with where you are, never procrastinating, then you start to live in constant connection with the Creative Power. This Power is the Source of all, and the more you connect to this Force, the more you can access It . . . and when you can access It at will, then all things become possible.

Goal Setting

Goal setting was not taught to me when I went to school, and I attended what were considered the elite schools in the States. I feel that most of what I've learned of great value I absorbed through my *own* pursuits. Not only that, but my four kids have taught me more about life than the best school teachers I ever had.

I do accept that I might be more ready to open up and learn now than before, but what I've learned from my kids has served me in every part of my life. I've seen what happens when you can leave enough space for someone to truly be themselves, and I have seen how this manifests in a powerful exhibition of creative uniqueness.

I constantly allow my kids the space to lead the lives that they want to, rather than those *I* might want them to live. Naturally I put in my two cents, but I think I give them a lot of latitude. I hated being told by adults that I had to do something and that they knew best because they were older, and I don't ever want to be responsible for creating this feeling in someone else. I've had to put a lot of effort in this area, and it hasn't always been easy.

We have the choice to either reproduce patterns of behavior similar to those we were raised with, or decide to do the opposite. I am not in agreement with people who say they can't help behaving in a certain way because they were just modeling what they were taught by their parents.

We have free will, and that means that in every moment we're given the choice to be who we want to be.

When we sometimes choose the lesser path, we are the ones who suffer the most, because lesser choices separate us from a feeling of oneness, which causes us to miss opportunities where we can fully express ourselves.

I had to work to change the patterns of behavior that weren't working for me anymore. That is, they weren't helping me progress along the path of enlightenment. True, everything we do eventually propels us into perfect creation, but as I said earlier, I have always been fueled, in part, by my impatience.

As I mentioned previously, I spent some time with a shaman, Martine Practel. We became friends and would go horseback riding together, and he would be in touch with all of the nature that surrounded him, no matter where he was. From this practice, he extracted profound wisdom. Sidi does the same thing. They both get so much out of every moment because they put so much *into* every moment. They live fully engaged with their surroundings.

We have to learn when we enter into relationships, even fleeting ones, to look deeply into every moment if we are to appreciate the many gifts the Divine offers us, including the many opportunities for personal growth. Expansion is expansion, and when we expand in one area, we expand in others. We need to know how to allow the space to be empty so that pure energy fills it, and if the space is taken by the energy of the ego, we will only attract *more* ego. Ego is limited, whereas the Divine is infinite.

"There is a huge difference between someone who says, 'I have failed three times,' and someone who says, 'I am a failure.'"
— S.I. HAYAKAWA

Look at the sport of baseball as an example. Every time a batter swings and misses, he doesn't look at this as a failure, but simply a miss. Even when he strikes out, he isn't going to view himself as a failure; and if he does, he'll develop a very negative attitude. One thing's for sure: if he doesn't swing at all, he won't get *any* hits.

When I share an opportunity with someone, I don't count the misses, because they're not what I want to focus on. I would gladly be subject to heaps of rejection (in fact, I have) to have the organization I do now. So all I need do is repeat the same thing over again, and I will surely see better results. So what if it takes two or three or five times as long? Where else will I find a similar opportunity?

It isn't by focusing on failure that we create success. And because something doesn't work, it doesn't mean that we're failures.

Education and Success

Somewhere along the line in today's world, people have accepted without enough questioning that their value in the eyes of others is measured by their "scores." It starts in school, doesn't it? Suzie got 100 on her final exam . . . isn't she a good girl? Johnny didn't pass his test, so we're keeping him back a grade. There's a stigma that goes along with not getting a passing grade that does massive damage to a child's psyche.

Most parents don't know how to love unconditionally. Unconditional love is a component of the Divine, so the child who hasn't been guided to maintain a Divine connection will depend on human love for nourishment. When this love is tainted with judgment, as is most human love, the child feels more and more isolated. I don't imagine that the God I love will love me less if I fail some exam somewhere. Yet what parent doesn't feel full of pride when their child is an honor student?

I know many people, and I mean many, who failed lots of exams, just as I know many who had straight A's. I do not accept the contention that those who got A's are living more productive or fulfilled lives today than the others. Too many artists, sports personalities, adventurers, and other creative people didn't do well in the system; and they were strong enough so that the system couldn't snuff out their fires. So many children today have their wills broken by a barrage of constant criticism.

I remember a few years back I asked someone from my past how some of the kids I grew up with were doing, and she didn't have a whole lot of positive things to say about the kids who'd been the honor students. Competition has its value, but it also leaves a lot of bodies strewn across the playing field. Look at the vocabulary. We *lost,* they *beat* us, you *goofed,* you *failed,* we got *clobbered,* they *killed* us, are just a few of the terms we're subjected to. They sure don't nourish me. How about you?

Today's work world has helped more previous failures find success than ever before. You don't have t be a genius to earn big money; you can be creative or persevering. Some of the old-fashioned qualities work better, such as honesty, a loving heart, simplicity, the ability to listen and share, patience, and integrity, to name just a few.

People everywhere are realizing that they've been duped into thinking that the only way to be successful is to go to college for four years, just the way we were taught that eating meat and dairy products was necessary for good health. We all know now that those billion-dollar industries served the government, which allowed them to get into our schools and show us all those charts, even if they didn't reflect the truth. It certainly was economically viable, and those industries are known to have made large political contributions. I wonder how many billions of dollars are tied up in our education system? I would hate to think that money had anything to do with making hundreds of thousands of young kids hate learning because it's taught in such a competitive manner.

I've read about and visited some schools that no longer give grades. One school in Sudbury, Massachusetts, didn't report a single case of attention deficit disorder (ADD) in the almost 20-year history of the school. Could the fact that they never forced a kid to read have anything to do with this? How many millions are made because parents are told that attention problems are due to a chemical imbalance that can be handled by drugs? Look at your own life. Aren't those who take responsibility for their lives the successful ones? These are the people it's wise to emulate. Today, four years of college or initials after your name are *not* things that ensure success. There are many successful people who might have had less school than you have. And you can do the same thing they did. If you don't know anyone like this, look around and go to some seminars. There are books and articles showing that 10,000 hours of effort put into something is enough for someone to be a master, so let's imagine four years of doing something you love, eight hours a day, seven days a week, and that would end up being about 10,000 hours of time invested.

I think that one of the best ways to become a master at something is to meet as many other masters as you can. Instead of being jealous of their success, do what Tony Robbins and many others say to do, which is to model yourself after these people. Watch them, listen to them, and take the best of what they have to offer. Then assimilate it, and move on to another individual. Look for the common threads of success, and there are many. Appreciate the ways in which these successful individuals reflect consistency and persistence, and feel the power of their vision. Seek out coaches and mentors who have done what *you* want to do, and listen to what they say. Investing in a mentor can be a lot less expensive than four years of college.

I want to be clear here. I'm not telling anyone not to go to college. It just depends on what you want to do with your life. College is a tremendous platform for the right people and the right professions, and two individuals in the same profession might have a completely different experience and outcome. But a college degree does not *guarantee* a successful business life, nor is spending 10,000 hours doing something.

It is not only by watching champions in your chosen field that you can learn, but also through observing champions in any field.

I was taught that the way to hit a home run is to keep your eye on the ball, swing straight, and follow through. That can translate to keeping your eye on your goal, acting with integrity, and following through on your prospects. Because something is basically *simple* doesn't always translate to *easy*.

I heard a joke today in a film, which goes like this: *What can you sit on, sleep on, and brush your teeth with?* The answer was: *a chair, a bed, and a toothbrush.* The point here is that we don't see the obvious, and our minds tend to complicate things. We take something that we're simply sharing because we're passionate about it, and because money enters into the equation, we end up with an internal dialogue that tends to sabotage us.

Think about all the times you've shared something just because you wanted people to know about it and you weren't getting any money for it. Wasn't it easy to share it? You usually call your best friends to share an experience with them, and you don't focus on any particular outcome. I just shared an idea with you about attending seminars as a way to educate and inspire yourself. I'm not reaping any financial benefits from sharing that with you. The idea is simple to share, and easy.

Imagine, though, that I was getting a commission from everyone who goes to those seminars. I would have to make sure that you mentioned my name when you called in, and you would know that I was making some money as a result of recommending the seminars to you. This seems to bring up a lot of complications for people, especially where their friends are involved.

Sexual energy creates a similar complication. Men and women who have been friends will find that if one person has romantic feelings that are not reciprocated, it can create challenges in the relationship. When we try to share love in any form with those we love, there are feelings of rejection when the love is not reciprocated. These feelings of rejection come from years of patterns we develop by creating expectations.

When we share anything with the expectation of a certain outcome, we immediately set ourselves up for challenges. What happens when we hold the idea of an outcome is that we cannot be totally present because a small part of us is already engaged in the future. The problem is that you can't *do* something in the future. Try to pick this book up in one minute. You can't do it unless you wait for 60 seconds. And just holding the thought is going to interfere with this moment.

Next time you share an opportunity with a friend, detach from the financial aspect. How would you share this opportunity if money wasn't involved? What would it feel like, and how would you explain it differently? What would your heart experience, and what would you be thinking?

Detach from Results

I used to have major challenges with charging money for my services, and in some cases I still do. When people would hire me to take photos, I would constantly give more than was requested because I was uncomfortable with how much money I was being paid. But as I became more comfortable, the biggest difference was that I stopped trying so hard and actually started to enjoy myself while taking photos. And when I enjoy what I do, I tend to do it better.

The more I detach from the result, the more I seem to have fun with the experience.

The more I want what is good for the other person, the better the experience is. What's best for me is when I just perform the action or share an experience and don't get involved with the outcome. This is true whether I'm introducing products or telling a friend about a film I saw or a book I read. I used to get really upset when I liked something that someone else didn't like, and I would take it personally. Because my ego was involved, my self-esteem would suffer when people didn't like what I did or said or thought.

I think that if people can figure out a comfortable way to share their products or services with their friends without worrying, they'll have a key to opening a part of themselves. Not only will their businesses improve, but their relationships as well. Wouldn't you rather buy products you actually have a need for from a friend than a stranger? Wouldn't you feel good about supporting some of your friends financially if you could?

You know what your intention is when you introduce your dream to someone else, and if you know in your heart that you believe in what you're doing, you should have the inner strength to avoid letting other people's negative thoughts bring you down. The more you connect your feelings to your own set of values, and the more you allow your life to be determined by your own integrity, the less others can pull you off course.

It's not the doubters in your life who are going to take care of you if you don't follow your dreams; it's not the people who don't trust you now that will be there later, either. Try talking with complete honesty to your friends when some sort of money issue bothers you. Share that you want them to get involved but feel awkward about the financial aspect, and ask them how they feel about it.

EXERCISE

Choose three instances where you've shared something with someone you care about and felt really excited to do so. Maybe it was a film you saw or a book you read. Take note of those feelings, and the next time you're sharing something with someone for professional reasons, see how close you come to that same feeling. Do you really believe in what you're doing?

_____

_____

_____

_____

_____

_____

_____

_____

_____

_____

_____

_____

_____

Would you like to experience every moment as a Miracle?
Join me in our 8-week program for in-depth support.
www.MakeYourLifeMagical.com/explore

Chapter 13

.⁕.

Hope

"What is true of the individual will be tomorrow true of the whole nation if individuals will but refuse to lose heart and hope."
—GHANDI

There are few things that fuel the human heart as fully as hope. My life felt like it was renewed when hope came alive. It was like being reborn. The energy that was available to me through hope nourished my spirit.

When one part of my being is nourished or challenged, there is a ripple effect; so when my spirit feels uplifted, my body reaps the benefits. When I am stressed spiritually, my body is as well. When I laugh, the chemical balance in my body is altered, and when I am physically challenged, my emotional body is taxed.

So just as we are all connected to each other, the different aspects of ourselves are also connected; and what affects one part, affects many.

Every moment of existence contains the total truth.

God is in everything, the Source of everything and the Container of everything; with God everything is possible. Every moment of our lives has within it the potential to bring total change and transformation to ourselves or to those we touch. Within the heart of this Divine potential exists the seed of unlimited possibility and

165

the total freedom to become who we want to become. This is what hope is about.

The first time I traveled to India, I made a couple of short films, one that was about daily activity as a form of prayer. The film showed how particular gestures, such as those used for ablutions, were repeated in various activities. Certain movements of sacred rituals, like those used in yoga, were remarkably similar to some normal gestures used during the performance of simple daily tasks.

A friend of mind at the time, Louis Malle, was also making a series of documentary films about India. Louis was a very talented French filmmaker with worldwide recognition, so he was getting a lot of assistance from the Indian tourist board and the government All kinds of information and knowledge were imparted to him, making him privy to profound experiences and insights, which affected him deeply.

I remember a discussion we had one day on the subject of hope. He'd made one short film on the new housing developments for the poor in Calcutta. He told me that one would think this was a really great thing—that is, the government subsidizing housing for the disadvantaged, but unfortunately, the more apartment buildings that were being built, the greater the problem became. This was because for every 500 people that were given a place to live, 1,500 would show up, hoping that they could find housing, too. Hope for a better life was a scarce commodity in the rural areas around Calcutta, so when people were given an opportunity, they flocked to it.

This was the time of the Bangladesh crisis, and the government of India was apparently spending over one million dollars a day to give the refugees bread and water. I visited a camp there and saw five to ten families huddled together under huge drainpipes. This was the first time in my life I'd really witnessed anything like this, and it was disturbing.

Our guide went on to tell me that even though this was one of the model camps (the others were off limits to the press and public), and even though the average age of the refugees was only around 30, over 80 percent of these people would die within two years due to disease and malnutrition. That visit has stayed in my consciousness for years now, and is one of the reasons I'm so happy to be involved with my nonprofit organization, as it gives me the opportunity to really do something about situations like this.

Just like too much of any one of our qualities can transform into something negative, the same can be true of hope. It might be difficult to believe that too much hope could be problematic, but that's what happened in India, and I've since seen other situations quite similar.

However, if someone finds a solution to this kind of challenge through the power of networking, the whole world will be able to share in this knowledge. Many of us involved in the network marketing industry hold the vision that providing a way to make a living is vital to overcoming poverty. It's more important to give someone self-esteem and the ability to earn money than simply giving them food and housing. This is not to downplay the generosity of those who help others in this way, but is simply to say that there's more than one way to give.

I've said repeatedly that what we do is not as important as who we *are* while we do it. In other words, what is in our hearts and minds as we do something deeply affects the quality of the action. And we always have the choice to choose our reaction.

Plug into Hope

This morning a friend called me up who's dealing with a challenging issue. The man she's living with seems unable to release the feelings he has for another woman, and his heart is closed for the moment, so he is unable to share his love with her. This is making her angry and frustrated. The man is someone who has a very contradictory nature. I know this because I used to be this way myself. I think I mentioned this not long ago. If my friend says something's white, he'll take the opposing viewpoint.

When my friend told me about the situation, I could feel her pain, and it reminded me of my own when I was living with Nathalie after the breakdown of our marriage. I was so angry and judgmental about everything, and was constantly blaming her (just as my friend was blaming this man), that it never felt good for my wife to be in my presence. So I pushed away what I thought I wanted, just as my friend was doing.

I advised that she try to use this as an opportunity to love unconditionally, and thus, even if the relationship didn't end up working, she might become more enlightened. So every time he did something to annoy her, I suggested she could say to herself, "Great, another chance for me to grow." She laughed at this, but I could feel a renewed sense of hope emanating from her.

When things aren't moving along as you'd like while you're building a relationship, your business, or your life in general, always look for what you can do to plug into hope. Remember how you felt when the project or relationship started, when you were so enthusiastic, and this time hold on to that dream.

Look what happened to all the people from the '60s who let the dream-stealers rob them of their dreams. How many of them went on to fulfill those dreams? And then look at the people who *didn't* let their dreams die, who hung in there, and finally got what they wanted. Hope is worth more than anything, and when I look for people to work with me now, I always make sure they still have the ability to dream. When these individuals are motivated from within, when they view any opportunity as a path to reach their loftiest dreams and live their highest ideals, I don't need to constantly motivate them through financial-incentive tactics because they value their dream more than they value money.

Money is an energy form to assist us in realizing things, and I love it for this reason; but it is what we can accomplish with money and not the paper itself that merits consideration.

Making a Difference

We are all here on Earth for a reason. We each have a unique gift that makes us special. One of the greatest things that can happen to us in this life is to be able to work at something we love that is in harmony with our purpose. When our work hours are spent making a life rather than a living, and when we take action fueled by passion rather than necessity, we live a more fulfilled existence. I believe that it is everyone's dream to live in this manner.

The biggest fear people have in today's world, spoken or unspoken, is that we're leading lives without meaning. The reason most of us aren't facing this openly is that it's very traumatic to look at the possibility that we're not living up to our potential, especially if we have no idea how to remedy the situation.

I believe that most of us are drawn to the experience of change, yet we let our fears hold us back. Shocks, such as the one I experienced with the breakup of my marriage, usually force some kind of change; but for the most part, people aren't necessarily going through any sort of crisis, so life just continues on, one day at a time. There were probably countless wake-up calls that preceded the actual shock of Nathalie turning her attention to someone else, but I didn't recognize them.

We all want to make a difference with our lives; we all want to be part of global change and transformation. But we can't help change the world if we don't know how to change ourselves. From a business standpoint, there has been a continual challenge in modern society of finding jobs that are service oriented and also pay well, and which don't require years of study and various degrees in order to work in these fields.

There are many businesses today that have met this challenge head-on and have emerged victorious. And there are thousands of people now living their dreams as a result of being involved with one of these newly formed positions, many of them working in home-based businesses. This means that they're doing something they believe has value and earning a substantial income at the same time, which allows them to grow spiritually, mentally, and financially. Let's look at some of the reasons why and how change is a form of spiritual growth.

Change as a Form of Spiritual Growth

There are those who say that the greatest human need is the need to feel connected. Working with other people fulfills this need—

connecting people of all races, colors, and creeds where everyone has an equal opportunity. When we learn to work cooperatively with others instead of in competition, we create hope. When someone is successful in our chosen field, it shows the world that success is possible and builds hope in the hearts of others. So many new businesses and new technologies are being developed today, and until one person creates success, a lot of people don't always believe that this new path will work. That's why it's so important for all of us to hold on to our dreams, and not give in to frustration or discouragement.

In network marketing, there's no steady paycheck. Our success is truly up to us, so we learn a lot about personal responsibility. When we work hard and are successful, we reap the benefits rather than an employer, and this increases our sense of self-esteem and increases our level of hope for a better future.

In the past, when I worked with inner-city ex-gang members from South Central Los Angeles, a young man named Casper, wrote: "I was raised by the streets of Los Angeles where no one wants to hire me. I know of no other place on this earth that has given me the gift of a legal business opportunity." To be able to share an opportunity with people like Casper has opened doors to places in my consciousness I never accessed before.

Today, what is happening through success in businesses where people work for themselves is redistribution of the wealth of the world into the hands of caring individuals. This is pure free enterprise and a way of doing business that honors each participant. It is the perfect place to live out the purpose of helping others achieve success. Nothing creates spiritual growth more than opening the heart, and as we help others grow, our hearts cannot help but open more.

**The quality of our lives is determined
by the quality of our choices,
and when we make positive choices,
we end up with positive lives.**

When we work for ourselves, we are living *our* destiny and not someone else's. Once we accept that we have the power to be whatever we want and become something more than we are, we are no longer someone else's tool for achieving *their* dream. Instead, we are responsible for achieving our own greatness, which is the way it should be.

I must say this again: you cannot have an organization bigger than you. You have to grow in order to expand any dream. When you work for yourself, you learn how to honor all different kinds of people, how to understand and appreciate the uniqueness in each of them, and how to give them what they want rather than what you *think* they should have. You learn about patience and developing the skills of a leader, and about not asking of others what you're unwilling to do yourself.

If you want to create wealth for yourself by starting your own business, it's important to understand that cash flows to you when you're part of something that solves a big problem, such as alleviating some type of pain or discomfort, or simply providing a solution to a life challenge. You must fill a big need; or help people experience fun, pleasure, or relief—that is, something from which they benefit.

Wealth comes to those who are able to solve people's most urgent needs. If you want different results, then *do* something different, and learn to *be* someone different.

There are a lot of ordinary people doing extraordinary things. One of these extraordinary things is creating a team of powerful leaders who are spiritually sound, and who build their businesses by helping others realize their dreams. There are many people today who understand that they can serve God and live in integrity, maintaining their highest ideals without compromising their noblest truths. They see that they cannot only create financial freedom for themselves, but others as well, and they can enrich their lives and thousands of others by sharing the process. They can be proud of who they are and what they do, and know that by pursuing their dreams, they will be fulfilling the reason we are here on Earth . . .

which is to experience personal development and spiritual growth. Hope is kept alive by taking action when opportunities present themselves.

EXERCISE

Write down a statement describing what you would truly love to be doing every day if finances were not involved. If you *are* doing what you love, then write down a statement of gratitude for being so blessed. If you're not doing what you want, then write what you feel you have to change in order to achieve that dream.

_____

_____

_____

_____

_____

_____

_____

_____

_____

_____

_____

_____

_____

_____

_____

_____

Take your next steps to grow your life "bigger."
Join me in our 8-week program for in-depth support.
www.MakeYourLifeMagical.com/explore

Chapter 14

Right Action

"Always aim at complete harmony of thought and word and deed. Always aim at purifying your thoughts and everything will be well."
— **GANDHI**

We all possess an ability that when properly used, can unlock the mystery of how to succeed in anything we undertake, yet most of us use very little of this ability, for a variety of reasons.

With this ability, we can recognize numerous windows of opportunities we might otherwise miss, potentially great prospects that could slip by unnoticed—including meeting a future spouse before we even know his or her name. Developing this ability allows us to understand where our lives are blocked, and know ahead of time whether something will work for our higher good or not.

Sound interesting? Figured out yet what it is? If you haven't, it's because you're not using it; and if you have, it means you are. The answer is *intuition.*

We are born with our intuition intact, but because we let other people's perceptions cloud our own, little by little we stop trusting our natural instincts. We all know in our hearts what's best for us, but accessing this information without letting the mind get in the way necessitates staying connected to our feelings, and not many of us seem to be able to do this with any sort of consistency.

Intuition is one of those things that rests in the *being* side of our nature and not the *doing,* and because the majority of the world seems more comfortable acknowledging the doing more than the being, too many overlook the value and potential of developing and trusting our intuitive abilities. Most people in the world want things to be tangible for them to be able to appreciate them, and people seem to have a love-hate relationship with the inner life. They confuse natural intuition with psychic ability because they get uncomfortable with things they can't understand. This lack of understanding creates all forms of prejudice; and because it is based in fear, it doesn't serve anyone well.

When people don't understand something, it makes them nervous; and when they get nervous, they become fearful, and then the fear produces dysfunction of all sorts. If people all over the world understood each other better, we'd all experience less discomfort, strife, and feelings of separateness.

We have to feel free to question ourselves. Basically, we all hold within us the answer to every question we could possibly have. If we think of life as a process of uncovering or remembering what we already know rather than going out to find new knowledge, we will be heading in the right direction.

At any point in our lives, in every moment of our existence, we have the capability to tap into the universal energy flow, to accept our connection with pure, Divine being. Because God knows everything, and because God *is* everything, we just have to let go of anything that blocks us from experiencing this unconditional love. So all knowledge is available to us at all times. When we learn something through study, it is from mankind, and we are repeating something that someone else is sharing; whereas when we access the knowledge that's deep in the heart of our Infinite Knowing, it's from a nonhuman source. That's why meditation is so important.

Meditation is the book of life—a place where we can go to find universal knowledge, where we can tap into the large ocean of wisdom and experience unity with everything. When we experience a unified state of being with even one other person, our hearts rest in a blissful state of peace that transcends ordinary daily living.

Our minds cease to question, the chatter dies down, and the heart opens up and expands as it melds with the heart of another. In these moments, there are no questions and no explanations are needed because we are connected to universal understanding. We know that everything is possible, and nothing else matters but this feeling of oneness.

The great leaders and mystics are those who experienced this sensation often and knew how to access this state on a regular basis. Gandhi knew that he could not be separated from a single person or from any part of humanity, and he lived his life accordingly. He knew the heart of every untouchable because it was *his* heart, and he understood that there was no personal freedom until *every* heart felt free. My experience of Sidi is similar. He is so totally committed to the poor and those who are suffering that it seems that there is never a moment when he is not holding them in his heart.

I conducted a seminar in the San Diego area several years ago and took the time to visit the temple and grounds in the coastal city of Encinitas, where Paramahansa Yogananda spent time and where his Self-Realization Fellowship maintains a center. I was looking through the bookstore there, wanting to carry home a tangible form of memory, and opened the daily calendar, which they call *Inner Reflections.* In it are wonderful quotes from one of the world's greatest spiritual masters, and I was attracted to one that said: "Before the searchlight of Divine love, everything is revealed."

Basically, Yogananda stated in nine words what it has taken me thousands to express. The great masters have a way of focusing their energy so as to make their points with remarkable clarity. This comes from the fact that their hearts are so connected to the heart of the Divine. Since they know love in such a complete way, they *become* love, and we are blessed to be able to experience this state of being through them.

Focused Thoughts

Through meditation we learn how to focus our thoughts, and we have already seen that focused energy has power. Once we're able to experience the difference between thoughts that lack love and are fear based, and those that make us feel we are one with the universal flow of energy, then we're able to consciously choose between these two thought-forms. As we exist more and more in a positive state of mind, our physical bodies benefit as well. So, we are creators and subjects simultaneously. Through the direct action of our will and imagination, we can transform who we are into who we want to be. Plants and animals don't have this ability of self-modification. We can influence them, but left to their own devices, they will usually revert back to their original tendencies.

As we progress mentally and spiritually, we also need to learn how to transform the physical into a container for higher thought-forms. Recently I was feeling sickness in my body, and in the past few years, this has been a very rare occurrence. So I did some inner exploration to determine what was happening to me mentally, emotionally, and spiritually that allowed the space for this to happen.

As my body battled with my malady, I felt the existence of a number of negative thought patterns, and I struggled more than usual to stay focused on the positive.

My body was sore, I had a bad cough, and was feeling slightly feverish. I was aware that I was struggling to stay positive, and that it was certainly taking a lot more effort to resist negative thoughts than usual. I was convinced that all the toxins in my body were having a very direct influence on my thinking and feelings. Consequently, I stayed off the phone, removed myself from challenging situations as much as possible, and really looked within. I was feeling less expansive, less generous, less decisive, and less loving. But I realized at the time that this was a huge gift, for it put me back in touch with a different reality than I was used to experiencing.

I haven't worried much for a long time, and I've found myself worrying a bit lately, so I have a wonderful playing field to see if I can practice what I share with others and really make it work. I can look at the worry and truly experience it as a negative state of being. I appreciate that it's useful for pointing out areas of concern, though, so I'm working on constantly bringing my mind around to focus on solutions. When I worry, I feel cut off from the Divine; I feel weak and separated from the more positive side of my being. I notice that when possibly stressful situations occur, I'm more sensitive emotionally and less detached. I now appreciate that good health is one of our greatest gifts, and I am going to be careful about taking it for granted.

Healthy Choices

I know that I have to stop procrastinating about exercising more, and I need to make the intention to do it, focus on that goal, and then take action steps. I believe that we can improve our abilities by imagining hitting the perfect golf or tennis shot, but I don't think that we can imagine increased physical stamina or an elevated heart rate. We need to actually engage in some aerobic activity. Good health plays such a vital role in our ability to deal with stress and be good at what we do. A lot of people, myself included, spend hours in sedentary activity, especially on the phone, so physical activity brings about balance.

As I mentioned previously, I am an independent distributor for a company that promotes vibrant health, so I want to be a reflection of what I promote. I believe that the products I distribute do help the body achieve a higher vibratory state of well-being, and that this state is conducive to self-improvement, but there are other things I must do if I am to optimize my potential. As important as exercising is, it is equally as important to know how to *still* the body and rest. Learning how to maximize sleep and relaxation time is vital to our well-being, just as meditation is beneficial for stilling the mind during waking hours.

Good health is a combination of many things, and since there are so many books on this topic, I won't dwell on it here. However, I urge you to be careful when you start exploring this field because there are a lot of different paths to choose from. Pay attention to how you feel and to what feels intuitively right to you, and don't accept everything you read as gospel. That also goes for the material in *this* book: take what you like and discard the rest.

Your personal health and wellness program will probably reflect a bit of one person's ideas and a bit of another. Be sure to nourish all parts of your being—your spiritual body as well as your physical, mental, and emotional one. I've chosen to learn as much about each area as possible so that I can assume personal responsibility for my wellness. I like to eat superfoods, which are a more recent science within the field of nutrition. I like alternative medicines rather than prescription drugs, and I prefer to explore new ideas in the field of education.

Similarly, I delved into all the different religions before choosing to focus on one, and I researched various businesses before choosing my current one when I wanted to make a change. You can perform due diligence and make your *own* choices.

More and more, I'm learning to trust where my heart leads me. I want to be a person who lives from a feeling place in my heart rather than just from my mind. We all are exposed to similar situations in life, but the difference lies in how we respond to various situations, consciously or not.

As more and more people start working for themselves and building their own businesses as a vehicle for financial freedom, others experience the potential. Every single breakthrough is a breakthrough for all of humanity. Our thoughts are known to have an effect on the chemical balance in our bloodstream. Through meditation and visualization, we are able to send different messages to our cells. Just as every moment holds the potential for our lives, every cell holds a similar potential. One unhealthy cell will create another, while every healthy cell will help keep another healthy, so every message we send a cell is important.

The more conscious we are, the more we can assume responsibility for ourselves; and once we know how to pay attention, the more we are free to decide if we want to or not. For example, once we know how to make money, we are free to decide whether this is important to us or not; but if we don't know how, the choice is no longer ours. When we are comfortable driving a big car or small car, we can make a conscious choice of which one to drive; but if we feel fearful about driving a big car, the choice to drive a small car is not coming from an empowered place. We can justify it by saying we're using less gas, and thus, are helping the environment, but we still have been led to a choice by fear.

Create More Options to Choose From

That is why I like experimenting with different techniques in business. I can then choose from what I want to do rather than being forced to do something in a particular way because it's all I know *how* to do. When I first started out as a photographer, I only knew how to take photos in natural light, so that was all I did. Later I learned how to use strobe lights and flash, so I could then choose between these methods. Still later I learned about using studio lighting, and then how to light an interior space, so I had more techniques to choose from. I learned about different types of film and cameras, and as I grew more and more technically proficient, I had more choices with respect to creating images. As such, I felt less and less limited.

Look at all the periods Picasso went through. Eventually, when he stood in front of a canvas, he had a foundation for unlimited potential, because he had so many choices available to him.

**Our lives are like empty canvases,
and we're free to create whatever we want.
The more we develop ourselves,
the more choices we have.**

When I look at my future, I realize that over the years I've developed a lot of skills that I can live by, resulting from doing things I truly loved. For years I was a professional magician, and spent many wonderful hours honing my skills. I am confident that I could earn a living performing magic today. I have already made a living from photography; and I am currently involved in both direct sales marketing and network marketing, and have developed my skills as a writer and seminar leader. I am also learning about the process of marketing one's expertise in multiple areas.

What I'm trying to convey here is that I've created a lot of options for myself, and all of them are things I love to do. I've done well renovating houses and reselling them as well, so when one type of income stream falls off, I feel that I can turn to something else. Too often people limit their options because they don't take action early enough. I know that I always have the option to work for someone else, but this limits time freedom, which is worth more than money to me. The ability to spend my time how I want really excites me.

I encourage *you* to look deeply at your hobbies and your passions and focus on what it would be like if you could do things you love every day of your life. I know that many of you reading a book like this may already be living in such a manner, but for those of you who aren't, now is the time to start.

Procrastination does more to keep people from their true destiny than almost any force on Earth.

We all have abilities, we all have unique gifts, and we all have the capacity to live richer and fuller lives. Too many people fail to understand their own power and so, fall under the spell of another individual's power. When we fully accept that we have the potential to live as fully realized divine beings, our choices become unlimited.

With this realization, of course, comes the responsibility that we have to live in accordance with our realization. There are certain choices that will no longer be available to us, such as doing things that are out of integrity, but there is still no limit to the number of choices that exist. The more we grow, the more choices there are, because there are more things we can do, and more that we're capable of.

I like to go inside myself and imagine on a continual basis what my life would feel like if I were living out more of my potential. I constantly question how open I am to change, and how willing I am to let go of attachments. I look closely at what it would be like to have a stronger physical body and a more aware spiritual sense. There are still times when I'm unsure of what to do, and I still experience fear over some things. Because I don't *often* feel fearful, though, I thank God for all of my opportunities. I am able to look at areas I haven't delved into for a while, and I can sense when I've made progress and where I need work.

Before my life fell apart, when I was always feeling blessed and happy, I almost couldn't imagine what others felt when they suffered. I wondered if I was too detached from humanity, and questioned whether I was a totally selfish person, because I had such a hard time understanding why others allowed negative feelings to dominate their lives. But when I was so deeply humbled, I learned from the very core of my being what it feels like to live in a state of emotional pain and despair. I may still feel moments of arrogance because I'm blessed with a wonderful life, but I can detach from those feelings now and ask for forgiveness because I don't like the feeling. My ego still feels pride, something else I want to quell. So I thank God for giving me the grace to *recognize* pride and arrogance, and the strength to overcome these emotions.

The mind doesn't really care whether you feel happy or sad, and can really only hold one thought at a time. It's far more empowering to hold a positive thought than a negative one.

We manifest what we expect, so if your life is not where you want it to be, then look at the thoughts that are dominating your life at this moment, and realize that one of the most important discoveries about life is that you can *change* those thoughts. No one can *make* you think something for very long if you don't want to. One of the things I learned as I studied and practiced magic is that I could actually lead people to think what I wanted them to momentarily, which was basically getting them to suspend belief in the impossible. For me, this became something transformational, because I would see a trick performed by someone and have no idea how it was done. It seemed to be truly impossible, but then I realized that it was only a mystery as long as it remained unexplained.

Much of life is like this. When we come to understand the spiritual laws that govern the universe, we realize that the seemingly impossible becomes possible. I might eat something in a restaurant and have no idea how it was made, while my son and son-in-law, who are both chefs, would have no trouble understanding, and be able to make it themselves.

Great spiritual masters know what to do every moment of their lives because they understand the mechanisms underneath what appear to be mysteries to the less initiated. They can make decisions leading to positive outcomes because they know ahead of time what will happen in various situations—just as chefs know the outcome when they mix certain ingredients together, or a musician knows what a song will sound like if certain notes are merged in one piece.

I am now writing my fourth book, so I have an idea what the outcome will be, but when I wrote my first one, I had no idea what the process was going to be like. And now, after so many years studying and practicing spiritual laws, I have a sense of how my life is going to proceed, because I've come to trust that when certain laws are obeyed, certain outcomes will occur. But it took me 50 years to get to a point where I even realized I had to reevaluate my life and possibly change the way I thought if I wanted to have better results.

If we're not content, we can either change our beliefs in order to find happiness, or we can distort reality to fit our beliefs and stay where we are.

I hope by sharing my thoughts and challenges so openly that you can feel what's in my heart. I don't want to paint a false idea for you—that is, that once you reach a certain stage everything in your life will be sunshine and roses. I'm sure that in the end it will be, but I still walk in my humanity.

For too many years we've all been taught that we grow up, fall in love, make a six-figure income, and then live happily ever after. We're taught that when we accept God in our lives, everything will be perfect. What I found is that when we accept God, the real work begins, because now we have the tools to face the darkness. So instead of everything becoming rose colored overnight, all of a sudden we're thrown into the big battle—the one with the ego. When we completely accept God, we can finally let go of the ego, but the ego doesn't like this one bit, so it struggles for its very life.

I want my children to know that love involves pain, that enlightenment involves suffering, but that both pain and suffering can be a part of us and that we can learn to embrace them. I want them to know that challenges keep coming our way so that we can ascend to higher states of consciousness, and that we can learn to embrace all of life, not just a few parts of it.

EXERCISE

Write a one-page essay detailing what an ideal day would look like, feel like, who you'd encounter, and what work would you'd be doing. Start out with how you'd wake up, where you'd be; and what the sights, sounds, and smells would look and feel like. Talk about your financial, physical, and emotional state; really express your true feelings. Have fun with this!

_____

_____

_____

_____

_____

_____

_____

_____

_____

_____

_____

_____

Are you ready to manifest through right action?
Join me in our 8-week program for in-depth support.
www.MakeYourLifeMagical.com/explore

Chapter 15

A Positive Attitude

"A pessimist sees the difficulty in every opportunity; an optimist sees the opportunity in every difficulty."— **SIR WINSTON CHURCHILL**

I love people who have a positive attitude. It is one of the most charismatic things about them. I just love it when they radiate energy, well-being, happiness, enthusiasm, and qualities that reflect that they're enjoying themselves. There's nothing more draining for me than being around negative energy and people who continually exist in a victim mode.

I feel terrible when I think about those years when I was like that. I know now that I'm compensating by serving as an inspiration, because I went from such a negative place to one of power. Most of those who knew me have to figure that if *I* did it, they can, too, because I was really feeling sorry for myself back then.

When I encounter this energy now in others, I feel a lot of compassion, and know that they're going to remain in that state until they decide to change. I know that *I* needed to wait until I was ready; I had to completely experience my process, which was an integral part of my journey.

What truly inspired me to change were those individuals who encouraged me to transform my pain into passion, and to let go of the thought patterns that no longer served me. So when I perceive this energy in others, I try to do the same thing. If, after a while, I feel that there's nothing I can do, I tend to withdraw and wait.

This kind of occurrence is very familiar to those of us who work for ourselves, because when you work with a lot of people who have stepped outside the normal work force, a certain number of individuals are bound to be going through some strong emotional traumas. The kinds of people drawn to this lifestyle are those who deeply yearn for personal growth. They want to control their own lives and accept personal responsibility, and they want to live their lives as creative spirits. They want to rid themselves of erroneous thinking, and instead, apply conscious self-direction.

This transition takes time, and we need to honor those who come to us for support with this endeavor. I believe that it's by fully honoring what each individual wants at any given moment that we can create enduring connections from the heart. If we always, without hesitation, choose to allow others to live their lives as they wish, we will not only create strong business partners, but lifelong friends as well.

But I suggest that you never let your own personal agenda get in the way of someone else's life. This is quite difficult for me to do with my children. I would love it if they worked in home-based enterprises, just as I would love it if everyone in my organization worked as hard as I did. The financial rewards would be much greater for everyone, myself included, yet few seem willing to do what's really necessary. Everyone would like to make more money, but not everyone is willing to do what's necessary to achieve that aim.

So I've learned to not only accept that others have different paths and rhythms, but to bless them, and release any ideas about what *should* or *could* happen.

I do feel that a lot of people allow themselves to give up quicker than I would, but I don't have as much judgment about this as I did in years past. I do realize that I love to help people, but don't want to do more for them than they're willing to do for themselves.

We tend to want for others what we've tasted for ourselves, so we let our energies seep over into others' lives. This is wonderful when these individuals pick up on that energy and run with it, but when we end up supporting their efforts so much that we replace their contributions with our own, we run into eventual burnout.

What works well for me is to use my energy to help instill a burning desire in others that matches mine. Then they'll run on their own fuel rather than mine, and develop a sense of self-empowerment and overall confidence in their own abilities.

Transformation

I've been blessed with some great mentors, especially in the home-based business and self-employment arena. Thanks to programs and hands-on seminars conducted by top leaders in the personal growth and business areas, I've been able to experience many different ways in which I can work in this industry. The principles I apply in my current business are no different than those I used as a photographer, or even when writing this book. Persistence, consistence, passion for what I do, and faith that everything will turn out as it should, are but a few of the traits that are applicable. Sometimes we hear the same truth in a different way, or we hear the same thing ten times and we finally get it.

Prayer is like this. Over a lifetime of accumulated prayer, we are transformed. It's true that one genuine, heartfelt prayer holds as much potential as 1,000 repeated prayers that come from a sense of obligation; but then, of course, 1,000 truly heartfelt prayers would have an even *greater* potential. When I first started to learn to pray, it was the same as learning anything else. I had to learn the words, then memorize them, then say them on a continual basis. Then I could relax a bit and didn't have to think about what I was saying, so I could put more feeling into what I was doing. The more feeling I put into it, the better I felt, and the more I received.

The thing to realize is that if you don't go after what you want, then you most likely will never get it. If you don't move *toward* something, then you will always stay right where you are.

When I work these days, I try to put a conscious amount of feeling into what I'm doing. The more I pay attention, the more aware I am, and the more clues I get as to how I can best serve the person I am with. One totally focused call can easily accomplish what ten uncommitted calls might do. Quality always works better for me than quantity. One small moment of truth can be fully nourishing and last for a long time.

It's important to not get too immersed in the safety of your routine. If you want to change your life, live from your passion, and do things you really love, there is risk involved. However, the risk of staying where you are and not living fully is about as big a risk as one can take, because you might end up with massive regret down the road. All risk really means is that you might lose some of what you have, but if what you have isn't making you happy, then it's not really a risk.

When we love, we risk experiencing pain, but is that pain greater than the pain of living without love? When we cry, we risk appearing soft or sentimental to others; and when we laugh, we might appear foolhardy, but do you really want to live without laughing or crying?

When I first learned to swim, I risked going underwater and getting a mouthful of chlorine. When I first played baseball, I risked striking out. When I first played tennis, I risked being beaten badly on the court, especially when I wanted to play better players so that I could be challenged more.

To be a success at something, we have to go through a certain amount of risk if we wish to improve, so it's far better to embrace and love the process rather than fear it, because loving something feels so much better. Here is another chart I found on the Internet that shows what happens when we step out of our comfort zone.

Don't Listen to Negative Voices

When we start out in life, our parents may have told us that we couldn't do this or that. For example, so many of my teachers said that I couldn't write the way I did, but I've done fine writing in my own way. Those I've shared my writings with tell me that their lives have been transformed by my thoughts, advice, and reflections, so I'm quite happy doing what I love rather than worrying whether it conforms to anyone else's opinion of how it should be done. As Abe Lincoln said, if you try to please too many people, you end up with mediocrity. Many artists have said that they'd rather be either really good or really bad, but not mediocre.

Don't listen to those who challenge your positive belief system, and don't listen to your own internal dialogue when it tries to attack your belief in yourself. Do you remember when there was a high jumper, Dick Fosbury, who was doing back flips over the bar and was told by everyone that he was doing it wrong? He ended up setting records with his "Fosbury Flop," and now scores of other jumpers emulate what he did.

New ways of looking at old paradigms change the world. Wouldn't it be great if we could look at the way the world is being run and find a better way? As I write this, the Middle East is in crisis, Europe is in crisis, the U.S. is in crisis . . . in fact, most of the world is in crisis, so let us pray that some people will come up with new visions and new methods that will get things back on track

The same goes for your life. You need to view it through a new lens and see what you'd like to change. Look at how you'd like your life to be, rather than letting others determine that for you.

Start to confront your fears, and look at the voices holding you back. Are they yours or those of others? The more you start to address your fears and overcome them, the more you'll realize that the difference between those who are successful and those who are not is the extent to which they overcome their fears.

Financial freedom is a tremendous boon to our lives. As such, a large part of our internal dialogue and worry relates to financial matters. When we learn how to create abundance in our lives and not worry so much about money, our energy is freed up and we can focus our attention on other concerns. Financial freedom allows people to do things out of passion and desire rather than just for a paycheck. What holds most of us back is that we're scared of change, yet if we don't ever change anything, we're going to simply maintain the status quo.

EXERCISE

Write down the change in your life that you would most like to make. Choose a date when you'd like to accomplish this change, and then write down the five most important things you have to do in order to effect that transformation. Make note of precise areas where you can adopt a more positive attitude along the way.

_____

_____

_____

_____

_____

_____

_____

_____

_____

_____

_____

_____

_____

_____

_____

_____

_____

_____

_____

_____

_____

Are you ready to view life through a new lens?
Join me in our 8-week program for in-depth support.
www.MakeYourLifeMagical.com/explore

Chapter 16

.❀.

More on Gratitude

"A person however learned and qualified in his life's work in whom gratitude is absent, is devoid of that beauty of character which makes personality fragrant." — **HAZRAT INAYAT KHAN**

I like to think of every day as a new beginning. Every moment has within its potential the possibility of a life-changing event. Every morning when we wake up we experience a rebirth. The whole field of unlimited possibilities is before us, and we are continually given the chance to change our attitude and thus change our lives. We are given the choice to live with love, or live in fear.

After not feeling well for a while, my body is now starting to repair, and I feel renewed energy. With this energy comes hope. I am grateful for the last few weeks because I see more clearly how easy it is to give in to others' fears. I can see how disconnected this makes me feel, and how small. I believe that my body is recharging itself, and similarly, my thought processes are becoming more positive.

As I'm writing this, I'm on my way to Boston with Sidi to give some teachings. My body feels tired, but my spirit is strong. Spending the entire day on planes and in airports really allows me to experience the world. (As an aside, given all the people who travel and the great popularity of natural foods today, I would think that someone would start a chain of healthy restaurants in airports and sports arenas. It's almost impossible to eat a healthy meal in any of these places, although it has gotten better and better with time.)

I bought a little book one time in the San Francisco airport featuring a quote from Henry Wadsworth Longfellow that said: "The talent of success is nothing more than doing what you can do well, and doing well whatever you do." The more I grow in awareness, the more I appreciate the freshness of each moment and the inherent opportunity to do everything well.

Living every moment as if it is our last certainly helps us become more aware of how we spend our time, and makes us more selective in our choices. Because I tend to rush things, which helps me get a lot done, I don't know if I do them as well as I could. I wonder as I write this book if spending more time on it would be better. I don't even take the time to reread what I've written, but I go with my feelings, and I'd rather write than read right now. When I do reread a few pages, I can't even remember writing what I've read; I can hardly remember having those thoughts. Life is truly miraculous.

When Does Fear Start to Go Away?

The first step to overcoming our fears is to learn to trust in God. We fear so many things because we're unsure of what's going to happen. When we feel our Divine connection more fully, we know in our hearts that everything will be okay, because everything God creates is perfect. If we're lacking in some area, we find that we have the wherewithal to deal with this lack, and that is part of our journey. If we feel something and don't express it, if the energy is strong, it will manifest itself eventually. So much of violence is anger expressing itself—anger that was never understood and never expressed—so it lies, repressed, seething, and festering—in the dark areas of our consciousness seeking to be heard and felt.

All energy seeks expression of some sort; and powerful energy, like love, will seek expression relentlessly. Truth is also relentless. As we grow older, if we pay attention, it should be easier to sense the patterns that tend to repeat themselves in our lives. From these patterns we can gain a sense of what we fear and what we've come to this planet to understand. As I've shared with you, some of the things I feel I'm here to learn are to be patient, release judgment, love unconditionally, honor others in relationships, trust others as well as myself, and co-create. These are just a few of the main issues.

I also need to learn how to receive. I'm someone who has found it easier to give than receive, and when someone gives me something, I feel a need to give something back. This can tend to diminish the pleasure of those who want to experience the joy of giving, so I'm working on this issue.

Because I've been blessed with material abundance, I frequently hear others ask, "What can I give someone who has everything?" Well, giving isn't only about offering material gifts; rather, it's a way of expressing love. I know *I* love to give things to people, and I know how much love I feel when given the opportunity to do so.

As I travel around the country, I receive many gifts from people, and this has been a blessing because I don't really know some of these individuals well at all, and chances are I won't see them again soon, if ever. So I have to learn to just accept their gifts without feeling I have to give something back. Some of these gifts are books, and more often than not, they offer some valuable piece of information that I've been looking for, consciously or unconsciously.

As I become more enlightened in the areas where I have fear, it feels like a new me is being born and renewed all the time. Similarly, I'm always surprised each spring when all the perennials that I haven't seen for some time sprout up in my garden. Potential isn't visible to every eye, yet it exists. Can you see the oak tree in the acorn when you pick it up? Masters see potential in each one of us and are able to guide us in allowing it to unfold.

Something else I'm working on is how to share constructive criticism in a tactful and loving way. I want to know how to share my heart in a way that doesn't come off as preaching.

This past weekend in Boston, as is the case with other places I've traveled to with Sidi, there were many hearts seeking truth. Often there are people who do not have the opportunity to meet with Sidi one-on-one, so they approach *me* with their questions. Sometimes an answer comes to me that comes from pure intuition. Sometimes I find that I respond to questions in a way that feels harsh to the recipient, and it hurts my heart to share their pain.

However, Sidi has said much stronger things to myself and others, yet he does so with so much love that to the person receiving the information, it feels like a soft embrace. So I'm going to work on being more loving as I share my thoughts with others, and develop this aspect of my being until it feels better in my heart. There are a number of times that Sidi will share something with me, and it *does* feel harsh and abrupt, and I have to deal with my feelings around that, too. I have to decide whether I feel hurt because of who said it, how it was said, or whether it's just that the truth is painful to hear.

I really love traveling with Sidi and supporting his teachings, as I believe that it's important to feel that we're doing something with our lives that will exist long after we're gone. We all yearn to make a contribution, to feel that we're doing something that will make a difference. I know I keep repeating this concept, but it's worthy of repetition.

During a seminar years ago, a participant mentioned that he'd done an exercise that really moved him, which was to write his own epitaph. It's probably a good idea for all of us to get in touch with our mortality, because this acknowledgment can greatly impact us. It's a good way to remember to live each moment fully, and be totally present with ourselves and others. I know that I tend to spend too much time *doing* and not enough time just *being*, and this is one area where I seek more balance in my life.

My children have given me so much. One night many years ago I went into their rooms to turn off the lights because they tended to fall asleep with them on. As I looked at their sleeping faces, my heart was overwhelmed with love and affection. As I gazed down at them, my heart opened to the experience of unconditional love, and I have recalled this sensation many times in my life. Watching them sleep that night, there was such an outpouring of love from my heart as I drank from their essence. I experienced all the emotion that I tend to hold back in so many other moments, and I thought about my mom and dad, wondering if they ever watched me sleep and felt the same way.

I know that there are many people who have supported me in numerous ways, and I don't thank them enough. I realize that if I did that, I would have a much deeper connection with each one. In my business, there are thousands of people in my organization who make a contribution to my life whom I don't even know and have never thanked. Last year when I accepted a trophy for having reached a particular milestone, I *did* get a chance to express my gratitude, but not all the people were there, and so many were probably unaware of my grateful feelings.

I am now endeavoring to remedy this situation. I am sharing with everyone I can these days how much I appreciate them. My heart feels good about this. I love having a plan of action. I'm going to start mentioning people I care about in my videos, and hopefully they'll reach some of those I'm thanking. I really like this idea: gratitude, gratitude, gratitude! It makes me feel great just to think about it.

Express gratitude to those you love and appreciate every day.

Never Give Up!

I've been reading a wonderful book by Og Mandino called *Secrets for Success and Happiness*, which is kind of like a diary; and he talks about his life, his books, his travels, his talks, and his thoughts. He mentions a moment when Winston Churchill stood up, looked over an audience for a few minutes, and then said, "Never, never, never, never give up," and then sat back down again.

Og wrote a book called *The Twelfth Angel,* in which the little hero of the book said the same thing. Og has inspired so many millions of people with his books and talks, and he is such a wonderful crusader for hope. I am putting on my goals list the desire to share an embrace with this man, who touches my heart so deeply.

It seems that who I am today has been formed by reading books by many people very similar to Og. I have absorbed so many thoughts from so many great people that I have truly been blessed. Every person who lives a part of their greatness helps countless others do the same.

For example, any of us who make a success out of a home-based business or who work for ourselves creates hope for countless others. That means that there will be fewer empty houses for kids to come home to after school, more families will be able to spend time together, more people will be able to live their dreams, and more individuals will take the chance to explore their greatness. For every one of us who can make a living staying at home, countless thousands of others will have more choices to make in their lives, and will have the opportunity to improve the quality of their time here on Earth.

Every time even one person has the courage to follow his or her dreams, the positive thought of this possibility floats out into the universal consciousness and congeals with other like thoughts. As these congealed thoughts grow and accumulate, it becomes easier for others to access this consciousness and experience something similar.

As more and more people work for themselves and earn a living while helping others, they will grow spiritually; and the whole world will witness that people can actually make a living doing something they love, and also do it with integrity.

And, as increasingly more people set an example of living in harmony with their purpose, others will know that they can do that, too. We don't have to climb over each other; in fact, in the field I'm in, the only way to succeed is to help *others* succeed. A big check usually signifies that a lot of people have been helped because we took the time to share something of value with someone else.

I find it remarkable that so many people who have affected my life have no idea of the impact they've made on me, both positively and negatively. Imagine the millions of people who've had their hearts touched by Og Mandino, and he has only had the opportunity to meet a handful of them. How many people have had their lives turned around because of something he wrote down or said that transformed their pain into hope? Think about Gandhi and Mother Teresa and all the others who have so impacted our world. We need to give thanks to these individuals who have graced the earth with their presence and who have influenced others in such a positive way.

At times, the greatest gifts come to us in ways that are hard to accept. It's not always the saints or leaders of the world who teach us our most significant lessons; sometimes it's a small, often unnoticed moment that changes our destiny forever.

At times, we make choices that only years later we realize have had a huge impact on our lives. The choices I'm making today might be planting seeds that I will only see evidence of years from now, but if I live each moment with the understanding that it *could* possibly impact the rest of my life in a monumental fashion, I'm going to start paying more attention to everything I do, and am going to walk in awareness every second of every day.

Years ago I remember trying to upgrade my seat on a flight from San Francisco to Denver and was unable to do so. I was feeling a bit bummed out because it's a lot easier to write in first class than economy. When the table is down in economy and the person in front of me leans back, it's really hard to write on a laptop because my arms are so cramped. This time, however, I was given an exit seat, which offers almost as much space as first class, which made it much easier to write. I was thrilled that I didn't get first class, because this experience taught me that I can book an economy seat from now on as long as I request an exit row, have as much space as I would in first class, but pay much less. Had I gotten my requested upgrade, I wouldn't have learned this lesson. So it seems that I was blessed in spite of myself.

This is a good lesson for all those who are disappointed about not getting something they think they want. Often, people get something even better if they're accepting and patient.

I often wonder how much procrastination plays in my life and how many opportunities pass me by. It's so easy to let certain things slip. There are times when I know that persistence is important. I also know it's important to back off from time to time. But what is crucial if you have a dream is to never, never, never give up!

My heart feels so full today, and I'm excited about all the things I want to do. I am so happy to be alive. I'm going to be sure to keep pouring this love into all my activities.

EXERCISE

Make a list of people you want to express gratitude to over the next ten days. Some of these individuals might not even be aware that they've made a positive impact on you. Some of them might be your early teachers or coaches, friends from school, co-workers, neighbors, or just those who momentarily touched your life. If possible, communicate with these people via e-mail, phone, snail mail, or in person to express your gratitude. Doing so can change your life as well as theirs.

_____

_____

_____

_____

_____

_____

_____

_____

_____

_____

_____

_____

_____

Are you ready to live in harmony with your life purpose?
Join me in our 8-week program for in-depth support.
www.MakeYourLifeMagical.com/explore

Chapter 17

General Thoughts

Andra life is an opportunity for expression, and we can choose what we want to express in each moment. As I look at my world, I see millions upon millions of different expressions, each one chosen consciously or unconsciously by those around me. From their clothes to the way they walk, from the way they wear their hair to the expressions on their faces, everyone sends out messages about themselves. How many of us love enough, and how many *feel* loved enough? There are so few people smiling, and if you think about the miracle we all are, it's hard not to smile. But how often do we pause to reflect on that miracle? We are all like an individual sun in a universe of people, and like the sun that shines upon our planet, our radiance has the potential to illuminate everything around us. We also can be like the moon, and reflect back people's radiance to them.

Choose to express a positive attitude in each moment of your life.

My heart wants to know the difference between the ordinary and the extraordinary. Sometimes *extra* isn't necessarily one big difference, but rather, a lot of little things. Our attitude is one thing that definitely makes a difference. Another is that we have a choice as to how to react to everything. We don't have to accept letting our past rule our present, nor do we have to accept letting fear about the future ruin our current life. Our attitudes determine whether *we* run our lives or if our lives run us. The choice is ours.

There's an old saying that says that those who think they can, *can;* and those who think they can't are right, they *can't*. I think back to that day when I stood in front of a workshop and put my goals up on a flip chart to use as an example, and discovered what a priority writing a book was. I never doubted that I could do it; I just sat down and started writing. I hope I can remember what day that was, and what seminar, because I believe that moment was an awakening for me. At the time, it seemed like so many other moments. I would love to remember what the rest of my goals were, but I didn't save the sheet. I think with all I have planned to do this month, I will have to make another sheet because I have so many goals that I wish to attain.

I am now 100 percent convinced of the value of prioritizing our goals. There's no way I would have completed that first book without that exercise. What amazes me is that I don't remember giving myself a deadline for the attainment of that goal. I think I wrote down a date when I wanted to start it, and I wouldn't be surprised if I finished the book before that date. I leave behind the flip charts I use at workshops and usually never look back, because most of the time those sheets are about *other* people's goals.

At this time, I want to share a bit about my plans for bringing this book and the membership program to fruition.

Building a Team

I've been reviewing some of the chapters of this book lately, and these writings have so filled my heart that there has been little room for doing or focusing on anything else. I know I should be focusing even more on my marketing efforts, and I've purchased some courses on how to prepare a book launch. I've decided that first I'm going to finish writing the book by the end of January 2012, and then I'm going to spend half of every day going through the courses and developing a plan.

I've found some great videos made by Lou Bortone that I really love, and he is another resource I highly recommend if you ever want to develop a product of your own, or want something special for your website. You will find a list of many people I recommend at www.MakeYourLifeMagical.com in the resources section. I also have chosen Marilyn Hager to design the interior of this book. The cover was created by Thomas Breher from some ideas that Rick Robbins created for a site for me a year or so ago. Thomas has done some great design work for me, as has Marilyn. I have started the website for the project, and the header was adapted by Rick from the older website I just mentioned. Also, Marilyn's husband, Andrew Adleman, has been building the site. Andrew and Marilyn have worked with me for years, and I am truly grateful for their friendship and the high quality of their work.

I've also been talking with people about representing me as a speaker, have bought some programs about niche marketing to learn how to generate leads through marketing personal-growth programs, and have been looking for a partner to actually implement those programs. And I've been studying how to build a membership site for the modules that will go along with this book. I am sharing this to illustrate that there's a lot that goes into developing a product, but that everyone reading this can do it if they proceed step by step and reach out to others to get help. I will definitely be partnering with someone who will work with me closely to bring this product to fruition and to help manage everything involved in it, and I plan to share generously with that person from the revenue that will result, whatever that may be.

I have also acquired a number of social media courses that I plan to take, as I strongly believe that this is one of the best ways to build a great list. I have offered some of the content of this book for free in the form of an eBook to attract people as well. You might have been one of the people who downloaded *The Art of Abundance*, and as a result, decided to read *this* book. So these are just some of the things I'm doing as I continue to write.

Jeff Walker and Brendon Burchard have amazing courses on constructing a blueprint for launching a product, and I highly recommend their work. I am also getting a lot of phenomenal information from a book by Michael Port called *Book Yourself Solid,* and am seriously considering his coaching and mentoring program. I feel that I might have more of a chance for personal interaction with him than with some of the other coaches. There are so many talented and extraordinarily generous people who truly want to make a difference in the world through helping others live their dreams. I feel a definite bond with these people because I know what it feels like to be successful, and to truly desire to help others experience similar success.

My instincts tell me that something is going to happen that is going to show me another new direction. I can feel it, but don't have a clear picture of what it will be. I trust that when I'm ready, it will reveal itself. From where and through whom, I don't know; and really, it doesn't matter. I'm already thanking the universe that it *is* happening. I can feel that I'm going to find a rhythm of life that is quieter than what I have now. It doesn't feel as if I will do less, but I will do it with less and less struggle and with more and more fun. I believe everything will come to me at the perfect time and place.

P.S. Since I finished the book I have signed on to work in a small group with Frank Kern who has been sharing some truly outstanding teachings on how to market the program I have been creating, and I bought a course called Make Market Launch, created by Mike Koenig and Pam Hendrickson. I am also working one on one with Pam, who helped Tony Robbins for over 18 years, and am just getting ready to fly to spend some time with both of them in San Diego.

I am a big believer in getting coaching and mentoring to learn how to be the best I can be in the different areas of my life.

After travelling side by side with Sidi for over 20 years I know that I could never have learned everything just from his books, and the opportunity to sit with people who can take me deeper into understanding their teachings and how to implement them has been an invaluable part of my life.

I invite you to be a part of our thriving community of successful people, creating more magic in their lives. This elite group of like minded people will participate in our extended program and I look forward to you joining us as well. Full program details are available at www.MakeYourLifeMagical.com

Other People's Opinions

At Christmastime, family members gave my wife and myself tickets to Cirque du Soleil so we could go there with my granddaughter and her parents, and on the ride there, we were listening to a teleseminar for prospective authors. The presenter, Carol Kline, was talking about what stops people from writing, and she was sharing that people just self-edit too much in a quest to be perfect. She then mentioned a book she'd read where the author had talked about "exhilarating imperfection," and my wife and I both had a good laugh.

It's so important for us to step out of our comfort zones if we want to create something and not worry what other people think—that is, not wait until something feels perfect, or talk ourselves out of producing something meaningful. If we want to stand out from the crowd, then we shouldn't worry what the crowd *thinks*. We should do whatever we do because we need to express what's within us, and not because we worry about someone else's opinion. That old saying "What others think of me is none of my business" is very applicable!

Creativity and Passion

As we watched the Cirque du Soleil show, I was struck by what an amazing group of creative people make up the cast and crew. There was an amazing level of intensity and creativity filling almost every moment of the production. It was clear that each scene went under extraordinary scrutiny until it reached the high standards that the troupe is known for. Every moment of music, lighting, dancing, and self-expression was absolutely mesmerizing. Those artists are truly the sons and daughters of their moments.

We saw the show at the Oracle arena in Oakland, California, which seats around 20,000 people. I have to admit I was somewhat disappointed to see that Cirque had replaced the more intimate tent atmospheres where they usually perform their shows and where every person in the audience can feel a connection with the artists. In huge arenas like the one in Oakland, this feeling was lost, and with it a lot of the magic. I understand that more money is made in one night like that than in a week in a tent, but for me, the sacrifice was immense.

I see this occurring in so many situations, and it happened to me in my photography career. When I took my best photos, it was for magazines, at a tiny fraction of what I could make doing commercial work; and I know of very few photographers who could shoot commercial photos anywhere nearly as good as their editorial photos. I think all of us want to be remembered for the beauty of what we create more than how much money we make, just as we will be remembered and loved more for what we do for others than what we do for ourselves.

I understand the necessity to make money, but when is enough really enough? The Cirque makes millions probably every week, if not every day, with all the different ensembles everywhere. And this commercialization of the arts is slowly eroding our culture. It's yet another example of the moral decay we see happening worldwide, where big businesses are putting the dollar ahead of their integrity. I believe we need more emphasis on the arts, as they represent our culture. I am gratified to see the amazing displays of human ingenuity, creativity, and artistry exemplified by organizations such as the Cirque du Soleil, but I would love to see them stay in their original venues, "under the tent."

In any case, since some of the great joys of my life can be found in the moments I share with my wife and kids, sitting in that arena watching the show with my family filled my heart with love, and I made a promise to myself to see that we congregate in that way more often.

What I felt as I watched the show was how I need to focus more of every day in being totally committed to what I want to do, and get better at things by putting even more passion into my endeavors. Each of the Cirque artists probably had to overcome terrific competition to be able to get their roles, and have to stay on top of their game every moment of every performance because there are so many people just waiting to seize their jobs. It must have taken thousands of hours of practice to perfect their skill sets, and to any of you who have ever tried to be really good at something, I'm sure you realize the hours and hours of practice required . . . and much of that time you might be wishing you were doing something else.

And how many times instead of eating what you might really crave, have you made the decision to adhere to a special diet in order to hone your body to be the best it can be? This is why passion is so important, because if you don't love what you're doing, it's just too difficult to maintain the discipline necessary in a world full of distractions and temptations.

There's no one sitting over my shoulder telling me that instead of sitting in the living room and watching TV, I have to sit here and write. As I work, it is now approaching 1 A.M., but I'm writing because that's what I want to do. I love sharing my thoughts, because in my heart there's a prayer that somewhere someone's life might be changed or influenced as a result of what I've written here . . . just as my life was changed and influenced by those who shared *their* hearts and minds on paper.

Back to the Cirque experience . . . after the show, I was talking to my wife, wondering if there were people in the audience who would be inspired and possibly have their lives altered by the experience they'd just had. Maybe a young person fell in love with the acrobats and a seed was planted in his or her spirit, or maybe someone else was inspired by the one-legged dancer and realized that there are chances to overcome all kinds of limitations, or maybe someone heard the violin music and started to think about pursuing that musical path. I wonder if something was going on in the spirit of my little five-year-old granddaughter, and if she was dreaming about being in a show like this when she grows up.

What I came away with more than anything else was that all of those involved in the show would not accept mediocrity in any way, shape, or form. It reminded me that I would continue to elevate my "game," and not allow myself to accept anything less than my best as I move forward with this, or any other, project.

The Danger of Too Much Comfort

I'm easily drawn into complacency as a result of having a good income, and even though many of you might think it's easier to create from the comfort of financial security, I can assure you that for me this wasn't always the case.

When I was in my early 20s and living in New York, I was working in the theater. I was in a play directed by Peter Bogdanovich, and the lead actor was Sandy Baron. Sandy and I became friends, and I remember one day when I was on the subway with him, he was talking about growing up and sharing his bedroom with all his brothers, and how motivated he was to be a success so he could have his own place. He said how lucky I was to have grown up in an upper-class family with material comforts, and how he wished he'd had that opportunity.

I looked at him and said, "Sandy, you have the lead in the play, and I have a much smaller part. Are you sure your past didn't give you the upper hand?"

It's true that if you want your life to change, you have to change yourself. If you think trying hard, and being persistent and consistent with your efforts is difficult, then try doing nothing and see how hard it is to live with *those* results. Here's a wonderful poem from the ancient poet Hamiz. It can provide you with some positive thoughts for reflection.

One day the sun admitted,
I am just a shadow.
I wish I could show you
the Infinite Incandescence
that has cast
my brilliant image!
I wish I could show you
when you are lonely
or in darkness,
the Astonishing Light
OF YOUR OWN BEING

I hope that as you read this book and reflect on some of the ideas here, you'll start to feel the awakening of that "inner magician" within you and come to realize that you have so much unrealized potential. If I can help fan the sparks that are smoldering within you and allow you to feel a deeper connection with your true and luminous nature, then I will be so very happy, but this will only happen if you *take action*. As Michael Port teaches in his work, *Book Yourself Solid,* just gathering in a lot of information is like taking in too much food:

> *Consuming too much just makes you fat. You have to limit your input and increase output. I have gotten to a point in my life where there is so much information coming into my life that if I don't limit taking it all in I won't have any time left to actually create something with what I have already learned. I have started so many programs I have bought from information I received over the Internet, but I haven't actually finished many of them. . . . . It takes a lot more fortitude to finish something than it does to start it.*

When I read *Conversations with God*, there was a message about God talking to us through the songs we hear, the books we read, and the sound of the wind, and so on. I pay attention to a lot of things as they show up in my life, always trying to see what messages I'm supposed to act on. I know I most likely miss a lot, but I've written down things as they appear, such as a book someone recommends, a movie that comes up in conversation, a song someone has heard . . . and I've found that sometimes the thing mentioned is just a door to something that made an even greater impression on me.

Recently I had this type of experience. It's an example of learning something important and receiving a gift from someone or something that we didn't initially feel attracted to in the least. Often what I've learned is that it's possible to detach the message from the messenger if we're willing to swallow the ego.

This is what happened, and it changed the direction of this book…

The Message and Not the Messenger Is Important

While researching niche programs, I came across one I'd bought over a year ago by Jeff Vacek and Ken Preuss called *Info Revolution.* I only found out about it because they'd sent out an invitation to attend a seminar they were putting on in San Francisco that was valued at $3,000, but as I had their program, I could go for free.

So I signed up and brought my wife along as my guest. Before I went, I e-mailed the organizers and asked if this was going to be another one of those seminars with a ton of guest speakers all promoting a program for people to buy, and they assured me that this wouldn't be the case. This was to be a purely informational seminar on how to use the program.

The speakers did start out going over how to use their program, but then later in the day, a speaker named JT Foxx was introduced. He started talking about the importance of coaching and mentoring, which is something I strongly believe in. JT was a young and obviously very smart person, but wasn't really someone I gravitated to. He spent most of the time talking about all the people he knew and how much money he'd made, and how clever he was. Both my wife and I were struck by how many times he contradicted himself, and were really turned off by how he talked down to anyone who asked a question or made a comment.

To put it bluntly, we both felt he lacked integrity, and we had trouble believing in anything he said in the end. I assumed this was a result of his age and immaturity. He was undeniably bright and creative, which made it even sadder, but I believe that one day he will attract a situation to himself that will open the doors to another way of being.

The reason I'm writing this is because at one point I got really upset when JT was rather insulting to a young woman in the audience who I could see was visibly saddened by his treatment.

A few minutes later, he asked if anyone in the room had a product they were getting ready to market, and I raised my hand, as my book was almost done and I was about to embark on the modules. JT asked me what the product was, and I said that I'd written a book called *Make Your Life Magical*, and at the time, the subtitle was *Awaken Your Inner Magician*. He asked me what it was about and who my target audience was, and I said that it was about creating abundance through developing our spiritual nature. His response was less than positive, and he was rather rude in the way he told me that there was really no market for this kind of product. I mentioned that I planned to include some really great people such as Bob Proctor, Mark Hoverson, Jonathan Budd, and so on; and he replied that the personal-growth industry was really in trouble and that even Tony Robbins was in big trouble and was coming to him to help turn his business around. He said my project would never work with this kind of a title, and that I had to direct my efforts toward those interested in wealth rather than spiritual work. If I wanted to make money with a product, it had to have an audience that would want what I had and who would spend money for that information.

There's a classic marketing parable about someone with the best location and the best hamburger in town, but if they don't have a hungry audience, they won't have a thriving business. So what JT was saying was that it doesn't matter how great your product is if people aren't hungry for it. And I have to admit that he was right, even though it was truly hard for me to acknowledge this at the time. Instead, I said that the money didn't really matter to me, which was true, and that was when he chimed in about Tony Robbins being in trouble, which I still have a hard time believing. A few minutes later, we broke for lunch and I went directly to the young woman he'd been rude to and asked her if I could buy her lunch. I then spent the next half hour telling her how she didn't have to buy into JT's criticism.

Let me just briefly share a bit more, because I know there was a great lesson for me in all of this, and I hope for you as well. JT had told a story about how he wanted to purchase a URL that was for sale because he was going to be meeting with Steve Wozniak, one of the Apple founders, and he wanted to impress him with his acquisition of this URL. He then mentioned that the person who owned it was asking thousands of dollars for it, so he called this man and asked what URLs he had for sale. When the man mentioned the one he wanted, he remarked that it was really overpriced and that he'd never buy it at anywhere near that price, and went on to buy a couple of really inexpensive sites that he didn't care about one way or the other. And then at the last minute, JT convinced the guy to throw in the site he really wanted for a really low price, and if I remembered the exact amount, I'd tell you, but it was probably around 100 bucks, if that much.

JT bragged about how clever his manipulation was and what a sharp negotiator he'd been. This was minutes after mentioning that he'd wandered into his bank a few days before to get some checks and was told that the manager wanted to see him, and he couldn't imagine why. He then said the manager asked him if he realized how much he had, and he said no, he didn't know, and the manager informed him that he had over a million dollars in cash and he wanted JT to do something with the money other than just leaving it in the bank without interest. I think everyone in the room thought the story was totally fabricated just so JT could show off how much he had. He had already shared several such stories meant to impress everyone, but which weren't totally credible.

At this point, the young woman I mentioned earlier raised her hand and asked him how he felt about taking advantage of someone in such a way, and asked if he felt this was done with integrity, and that was when he really tried to make her feel small. I felt that he diminished himself even further by making *her* feel bad, and he then went on to explain that she would never be successful in business because she was unable to act in such a manner. He maintained that this was how business was done in America these days, and I sat there thinking how right he was about that. I'm sure all the people he reveres are those who head the large corporations that have stolen all the money from the lower classes, led to all the foreclosures, caused so many businesses to fail and banks to collapse, and have contributed to so much moral decay. I loved the fact that this young woman had the courage to speak out, and wish that a lot of other people in this country would do the same, and stop voting people into office who allow these kinds of things to go unpunished.

Now my original reaction, after spending most of my adult life with people interested in developing their spiritual lives, was to be pretty angry and upset, thinking that JT didn't know what he was talking about. This was compounded by not trusting him due to all the conflicting information he'd already shared. This was during the morning of the second day, just before lunch, and my wife had decided to go home, as she really couldn't listen to him anymore. My immediate reaction was to get in a big argument with him, but I decided to let it go, as I didn't want to make a scene and create a totally negative space.

As I mentioned, I invited the young woman to lunch; and she turned out to be bright, sensitive, intuitive, and totally dedicated to living her life in alignment with the truth. I praised her, did everything I could to help her feel better, and then decided to go home and be with my wife, rather then return to the seminar and say out loud all the things that were in my heart. This was really out of respect for Jeff and Ken, who I felt were very sincere.

On the way home, though, I was steaming. I called my wife and told her I'd left, and as I got on the highway and started driving home, I was sorry I hadn't stayed. I do know that when I'm angry, I often say things that I regret later, and I also don't think clearly when I'm angry. I was really about to turn around and go back, but the traffic going the other way was bumper to bumper, so I decided that I'd just go home, and if the next day I felt it was still important, I would drive back to the conference and speak out. Before I left, I did go up to a couple of people who worked with Ken and Jeff and told them what I thought, and I knew I could always write an e-mail, which I still might do.

But then an amazing thing happened. I don't remember the exact moment, because it was during the time I was half awake in bed that night, but I started thinking about the subtitle of my book, *Awaken Your Inner Magician*. A close friend, Dr. John Laird, who's also a student of Sidi's, had shared with me that he didn't think that the subtitle really explained what the book was about, and it had always bothered me a bit because I respect his advice a lot, but didn't want to change the subtitle because I liked the idea so much.

So I was lying in bed, still fuming about JT and regretting not telling him to his face what I thought about him, when the phrase "Creating

Wealth from Within" came to me, which as I write this now, is the subtitle I've chosen. I also considered "Creating Abundance from Within" but the conversation with JT was still dancing around in my brain. I started to acknowledge that as angry as I was with him, and as much I hated to admit it, he'd actually given me what was starting to feel like a *huge* gift. I now believe that my project is going to have a much larger audience, and thus, *help* so many more people. I had resisted the word *wealth* because of my own attitude about it as it's usually understood, and I realized that this was really an awesome lesson for me.

I immediately got up and wrote down the subtitle so I wouldn't forget it, because it felt so right. And then I went back to bed and slept like a baby. When I woke up, I toyed with the idea of going back to the conference, which was a good hour's drive, just to share what had happened because I thought that it was so interesting. But I opted to stay at home and look through what I'd written to see how I could incorporate this idea into the book without rewriting most of it.

After going through a number of the chapters, I realized that this direction was actually going to make the book and program much more useful, and that I had already written an immense amount about it, so there would be very little to change. In my heart, there's no difference between wealth and abundance, as real wealth is a lot more than just money. In fact, if I had to choose between the spiritual wealth and integrity of the young woman, and JT's financial wealth, I would choose the spirit of that lady every day of the week. That could well be because I don't *need* his money, and I'm glad that I don't have to compromise my integrity in any way.

A couple of other things about that weekend are interesting as well. At some point either Ken or Jeff, and I think it was Ken, mentioned a book called *The Soul of Money*, by Lynne Twist, and I liked the title so much I went to Amazon and bought the Kindle version and downloaded it immediately. It would have been really easy to miss this recommendation and not have had the opportunity to read her book, but as I've mentioned, I keep an eye out for just this sort of thing, and I'm really glad I did— in fact, I fell so in love with this book that I included many quotes in the chapter on relationships.

When I woke up from my peaceful sleep, I started reading Lynne's book on my Kindle, and I was immediately impressed with everything she talked about. I saw that it was really quite similar to what I was writing, only expressed so much better. I'm a little more than halfway through the book as I write this, and I hope you will read the book, too, as it imparts one of the most positive and enlightening messages about money that I've ever read. I immediately went on the web, found Lynne's organization, and left a long message about wanting to meet with her. It happens she lives in San Francisco and comes to the Marin area, where I live, to see one of her children periodically. I extended an invitation to her to be one of the resident experts for all things financial in this book, and now I will wait to see if I get a response. She is very much in demand, so I can understand if she doesn't get back to me right away, but I really feel in my heart that there's something destined to happen in relation to a collaboration of some sort. She's spent a lot of her life raising money for the poor and hungry as well. Maybe the connection is meant to be between her and my wife—I really don't know. But I do know that this is something I needed to act upon.

Letting Go of My Anger

So let me sum up what I learned from all this and why I've spent so much time going into all these details. After reading *The Soul of Money* so soon after JT's comments, it felt as if the universe was confirming that he was right in pointing me to direct more focus to wealth building, and that in this way my book would end up helping more people. It showed me that I still had a lot of ego to let go of, and that I had to release the need to be right. It also revealed to me that sometimes a truth can come to us in a form that might not be to our liking, and that we don't have to like or approve of others to learn from them. I realized that I had a lot of judgment I needed to let go of, and that I shouldn't let anger get in the way of my creativity. I wonder now if I missed even more revelations by leaving the seminar early.

The Buddha said, "You will not be punished *for* your anger, you will be punished *by* your anger." And how true this is. Anger makes me feel really horrible and I know when I feel this way, it's a sign that I have disconnected from Divine energy and have gotten caught up in my ego. As I reflect back now, I feel that in the end everything occurred in the perfect way, because the place it took me to feels really good now. I remember how I felt as I drove home from the seminar and how upset I was. There were so many imaginary conversations running through my mind between JT and me, and they were all negative and accusatory. And I recall how bad these conversations made me feel and how hard it was to fall asleep because of all my petty feelings about the situation. And then I compared that to how I felt after the fact, and how much gratitude I was able to express to everyone involved. The entire experience contributed to a much-needed change in perception.

I can now see that it's vitally important to focus on the creation of what I want to create—in this case, a book and membership program that will help people, and not who is doing what. In other words, if I want my product to be great, I should be open to learning from people and taking their suggestions even if I have to swallow my pride to do so.

In the process of creation, we have to often set aside our egos and try to avoid controlling things too much. In our spiritual lives, we shouldn't confuse the creation with the creator. People just like us, people who had an idea and then managed to bring it into fruition, have created a lot of what is around us. Our homes, clothes, cars, and jobs were all just thoughts in someone's mind before they manifested. If you're reading this book and have gotten this far, I would imagine that you're like me, and would love to create something that is useful to people. But to do so, you have to take action. You can start by doing the exercises at the end of each chapter. And you can join the membership site, where you can find a mastermind group and find partners to hold you accountable. You can also receive ongoing mentoring from me and the other experts who will be sharing their teachings each month. That is, you can start a business and be in it *for* yourself, but not *by* yourself.

When we can create safe learning environments we can allow ourselves to be vulnerable and not feel the need to protect ourselves with a lot of excuses. When actions are not completed, instead of blaming others, as a team we can evaluate what happened and decide what adjustments need to be made in order to move forward. Through this method, we can do what we call "manage at the extremities." What this means is that we look at where the energy is blocked and collectively focus on how to unblock whatever is stuck. When we all use the same system to build our teams, anyone on the team is able to help someone else figure out how to keep creativity alive and moving forward.

I believe that anyone with the burning desire to use my system to create an organization with me, has the dedication to work a reasonable amount of time each week, and is also willing to hold him- or herself accountable, will be able to arrive at the desired result. The reason I don't specify an amount of time is because some people can do more in an hour than someone else can do in a day.

What to Look for in a Business Partner

There are three important things I like to see in those I work with, and which they must bring to the table. They must have a burning desire, a strong work ethic, and be coachable. It doesn't matter how great a system I share with them if they don't possess these three traits, because they're not things I can *give* anyone else. They have to be developed from within by each individual.

I want to share something else that I feel is of major importance. I used to believe that goal setting was one of the most crucial things that people could do with their lives. I taught in my seminars, and wrote a lot in *Walking in Awareness* as well as in this book, about how to determine what our purpose is in life, how to express this in about a dozen words, and then choose goals that are in alignment with one's purpose. But one of the things I've learned is that just writing down goals is not enough in and of itself. Without a burning desire in our hearts to change or improve something in our lives, goals will not take us where we want to go.

I feel that you must be willing to do whatever it takes, for however long it takes, with as much energy as it takes, until the desired result is attained. Without a complete and absorbing passion in your heart, you might just give up and drop out of the process before you've achieved your dream.

I want every person I'm working with on any team I'm a part of to know exactly what my personal goals are, and what the desired end result of whatever project we're working on is. Everyone should also be aware of their own 30-, 60- and 90-day plan, plus their own desired result; and then we can all work together using the same or similar structural tension charts. We can connect on a regular basis to look at our results, and make whatever corrections are necessary to keep us all on course. When one of my partners invites someone new to the team, all team members can then make sure that the new person understands the commitment and actions we expect from the new participant.

Rick Tonita shared with me that 97 percent of people responded positively when asked if they would like to be invited to join a high-performance team and be mentored to success. Everything that Rick shares with me has always been scientifically validated and field-tested. He is someone who is truly passionate about research.

Surrounded by Gifts

Before I change the subject and veer too far away from my experience at the seminar, I want to share one more lesson I learned. I imagine that neither the young woman I mentioned nor JT ever thought for a second about what an impact the whole situation would have on someone like me. And it awakens me to the realization of how powerful an impact we can have on someone's life without even realizing it.

We can hurt others by unconsciously walking down the street past them with a sour expression on our face. Those individuals might feel that we're scowling at them and feel hurt or angry, when in reality, we had no idea that this was the case...in reality, we never even noticed them. Or, we could say something to people that could plant seeds within their hearts that might change their lives in a positive way.

Is it not such a big stretch to think that maybe the fact that Ken or Jeff mentioning the book *The Soul of Money* could have been heard by someone in addition to me who wrote down the title, bought the book, and then became totally passionate about helping the disadvantaged, or volunteering at a worthy organization, or who simply went on to live a more productive and fulfilling result as a result of that one mention? What I'm trying to show you here is that God offers gifts in every second that can be transformational, and it all can start just by living in awareness and then taking action when opportunities present themselves.

It would have been easy for me to find numerous reasons why I shouldn't have gone to the seminar that weekend. After all, there were many NFL playoff games I could have stayed home and watched while I caught up on my writing. It would have been easy to avoid taking notes and fail to write down the name of that book. It makes me wonder how many other gifts I probably missed that day, and how many I might miss *every* day. It would have been easy for me to go back to sleep that night and not write down the phrase "Creating Wealth from Within" and probably not remember it in the morning. It would have been easy to not get up at 5 o'clock that morning, as I did, and go into my office and write these words.

I've spent hours contemplating the new subtitle, and am feeling more and more passionate about aligning my life to be in harmony with this expression. I think you will see that there are a lot of things you'll read that will show that I'd actually been on that track anyway. I have created the intention to one day have the opportunity to share with JT what an important gift he gave me, and if I don't connect with him soon, I will find a way to write him and thank him.

As I write this, it is January 20, 2012, and I have already finished most of this book. I am just going over everything one more time and adding some thoughts in places that are appropriate. I write from a stream of consciousness (as you've probably already figured out), and try not to edit myself too much so that I can experience the "exhilarating imperfection" that Carol talked about earlier in that seminar we were listening to in the car. It would have been easy to just continue reading and not take the effort to write. But just sharing this with you has helped me come to a deeper understanding about what happened, and I hope you have found some value in it as well.

Attaining Goals

I've set some pretty audacious financial goals for myself this year, and if I don't take steady and consistent action, there's no way I will ever approach any of the milestones I've set. I've written down goals for each of the areas in my Wheel of Life, and I've shared with others what I think they need to know in relation to these aims. As for my financial goals, I know that if I am to accomplish them, I will absolutely need to create that wealth from within, because there's no way I want to feel like I'm struggling to achieve something I don't really need.

My financial ambitions stem from the fact that I'd like to be able to give more and help more. I want to use the money to finance building a team who can get Sidi's teachings to a larger audience. Every day I ask God to direct me toward the fulfillment of my goals, if they're in alignment with His will. I accept that part of this ambitious goal stems from my own ego, but it's not as important as His favor.

"But the greatest reward is the good pleasure of Allah. This is the sublime felicity." — QUR'AN 9:72

So many things in our lives can be accomplished by taking small actions today, and taking these small actions can significantly reduce the intensity of so many challenges. If we can detect something early on, we can remedy the situation a lot easier than at a later date.

I remember one time I wasn't paying attention and flew to Raleigh, North Carolina, instead of Richmond, Virginia, and had to take another plane to compensate for the oversight. I don't know how the flight attendant didn't catch it when I boarded the plane, but I ended up on the wrong one. If I'd taken the small action step of paying a bit more attention before I got on the plane, it would have been a simple adjustment to correct; but the longer I waited, the bigger the action I had to take to correct the situation. The same holds true for our health, our jobs, our family relationships, and our love lives. By making some small change today, we can avoid larger problems later.

Take small, valuable actions now
to prevent larger problems tomorrow.

Real Wealth, Real Integrity

I believe that we have to do everything in our power to stay totally honest in every single moment of our lives. Sometimes this can be extremely challenging, because it might mean we have to admit to mistakes, or other things that aren't easy to admit to. Even though this might not always be the easiest thing to do, in the long run it will make us feel more at peace. When we don't have to worry about what we said to people—for example, that they'll discover that we might have misrepresented something, we can then feel safe in our relationships. The more people know you as someone who is honest and who has integrity, the more they'll open their hearts to you, and the more they'll share with you. As a result, you'll have better relationships, both socially and professionally. It is my belief that wealth is created when we offer enormous value to people without thinking about what we'll get back.

Real wealth is in the joy we feel when we open our hearts in the act of giving and sharing. Think about all the people you love most. Doesn't your real happiness and well-being come from what you can *give* them? Aren't some of your most joyful moments those times when you felt their hearts open to you because of your generosity? It's easy for God to give you what you need if you open your heart and abide by the Divine laws, and want for others what you want for yourselves. Sidi has said to me many times that if I had $10 million, would I be able to go to the market and buy children like the ones I have? Of course not! So what is real wealth? It certainly isn't some pieces of paper with numbers on them.

It says in the Bible:

> *Love is patient, love is kind. It does not envy, it does not boast, it is not proud. It is not rude, it is not self-seeking, it is not easily angered, and it keeps no record of wrongs. Love does not delight in evil but rejoices with the truth. It always protects, always trusts, always hopes, and always perseveres. Love never fails. But where*

there are prophecies, they will cease; where there are tongues, they will be stilled; where there is knowledge, it will pass away. For we know in part and we prophesy in part, but when perfection comes, the imperfect disappears. When I was a child, I talked like a child, I thought like a child, I reasoned like a child. When I became a man, I put childish ways behind me. Now we see but a poor reflection as in a mirror; then we shall see face to face. Now I know in part; then I shall know fully, even as I am fully known. And now these three remain: faith, hope and love. But the greatest of these is love.

1 CORINTHIANS 13:4-13

The message is the same everywhere, in all the religions, and in all the great traditions. The same truths are written in all our hearts if we know how to access them and then apply them to our lives. We should not think of wealth as something we have to go out and *get*. We learn about wealth and how to manifest it by learning how to *give*.

I remember during one period of my life I was living in Paris working as a magician in clubs, and I got into a fight with my girlfriend at the time. In one of her angry moments, she asked, "Why should I believe anything you say when you make your living deceiving people?"

I must admit that I was a bit taken aback by her comment, and it has stuck with me all these years—more than 40 years, in fact. Today I make a serious and concentrated effort to be as truthful as I can in every moment, yet I still perform magic as a hobby. I'm also in the process of making some videos using magic effects to illustrate certain concepts of this book, which will make up the modules of the membership site; and I am definitely doing and saying misleading things to execute some of the magic effects. I tell myself that this is for entertainment purposes, so I allow myself to continue. When I look at the end result and the pleasure that people find in magic, it makes the deception acceptable, especially since everyone *expects* a magician to be deceptive.

But, of course, in real life, when I'm not performing magic, I avoid saying misleading things—not only to others, but to myself as well. I try to be brutally honest with myself at all times so that I can hold myself accountable. I believe that one of the reasons why I'm so successful in inviting people into business partnerships is that others trust me. They know me to be someone who does what I say I'm going to do. I believe that the financial wealth I've reaped has been the result of what I've given to others without thinking of getting something in return. I have to believe deep in my heart that when I ask people to partner with me in my business, it's because I totally trust in my heart that this is good for them. I feel I could easily retire with the residual income that my wife and I have now, but I want other people to be able to arrive at the same place, so I carry on. Almost everyone who has joined with me has done so because they want to have financial freedom and focus on living their life purpose.

I send e-mails to the owner of the company I'm involved with when I hear how someone has benefited from our products, and one day he said that it's these stories that keep him from retiring to his ranch. He doesn't need more money; his wealth lies in sharing his message of wellness. Do you think he'll be remembered more for how much money he's made, or for how many people he's helped by distributing products that help them with pain and inflammation?

My wife and I are so grateful for the opportunity to create wealth in order to live our life purpose! Financial freedom allows me to assist my teacher in spreading his message, building schools, and helping thousands of people discover their true nature. All the treasures of the world exist within us. We just need to forget our material selves and allow our hearts to experience Divine love.

The company I'm involved in is basically a health-and-wellness company, but the company mission statement is: "To help people experience wellness and create wealth to live their life purpose." I think you know me well enough by now to see how I resonate with this statement and how it is in alignment with my beliefs. The literature says that in order to be healthy, we need to follow the following ten principles:

Breathe deeply, drink water, sleep peacefully, eat nutritiously, enjoy activity, give and receive love, be forgiving, practice gratitude, develop acceptance, and develop a relationship with God.

Think about this for a minute. Isn't this also a message about how to create wealth from within? When you know how to give and receive love, aren't you experiencing wealth? Doesn't this open the door to receiving all the money you will ever need?

Recently I accompanied Sidi to a seminar, and I was staying in a beautiful house near the workshop location. Trees surrounded the home, and it felt good to be connected with nature. We are given so much by Mother Earth; and so few people, myself included, know how to send blessings back. We take so many things from the earth to sustain our bodies, to nourish us, to heal us, and often just to amuse us. Once we open a doorway to receive, this opening is not intended for energy to just pass in one direction. Imagine if you're in an airtight compartment and you punch a hole in it so that you can breathe. This opening will also be a way for more air to leave.

Once an exchange of energy is created, the energy does not necessarily flow in just one direction. This is especially true with love. If I open my heart to send you love, there is a doorway for you to send it back into my heart.

All of our connections are like this. When we open our hearts to accept Divine energy, we then have a doorway straight to the heart of the Divine through which we can send love and gratitude. As I sit here and write these words, wanting to connect with many people, I am energetically opening a pathway of communication that will allow things to flow *to* me as well as *through* me. When I conduct seminars and stand in front of people, I become open to them. The more each of us opens up to each other, the bigger the passageway and the less chance of experiencing the pain of blocked love. So it's important that we learn to love one another, and that we increase our awareness around what happens when we exchange this love. Every time we meet someone, we are opening a doorway of possibility for exchanging energy with that person, and often I see people creating these pathways without conscious realization of what is happening.

When you go into a situation looking for work and you don't feel good about being in a certain place, you're not honoring yourself or anyone else. Suppose you accept a job because you need money, but you wish you were doing something else. Every day when you go into that place of business, you're a conduit for all the pathways you've created; and the other people come in contact with your life history, just as you come into contact with theirs. If you're not happy, you will bring this unhappiness with you, and this negative energy will slowly start to permeate the environment. So I might not know you well, yet I will get plugged into your unhappiness, start to feel bad, and have no conscious idea why.

Now if I'm strong, living with a sense of purpose, and vibrating at a high level of wellness, I might not be affected too much. But if I'm having a weaker moment, I might be more susceptible to your moods. An analogy is that when your immune system is weak, you catch a lot of flus and colds; but when it's strong, you resist these types of illnesses. That's why it's so vital to live your life with conscious intent and a positive attitude.

Equal Opportunities

Each one of us has enormous potential, and the possibility through grace to experience Divine unity. It's not because certain people are richer or stronger, or faster or smarter, that they have a head start over you. Good card players become good when they learn how to play weak hands. When everything comes easy, people don't always learn how to deal with adversity. For all we know, the person born with a physical challenge might successfully integrate this seeming deficiency and get enlightened, while someone who's blessed with apparent physical prowess might develop nothing more than the ego.

I believe that we're are all born with certain gifts, and it's up to all of us to work on ourselves and discover what those gifts are. Sharks are born swimming, birds are born knowing how to fly, bees are born knowing how to make honey . . . and none of them allow the material world to confuse them as far as where their abilities lie. Yet many of us humans seem somewhat baffled by who we really are and why we're here. Of course, more and more we see children recognize their gifts and act on them right away. The media is full of stories about child prodigies who express their talents in phenomenal ways. As the world goes through different stages, and as people are turning more and more inward, they are discovering their own unique gifts to a greater extent.

When I was in school, my writing style was always graded very poorly because it didn't conform to certain people's beliefs as to what made a good writer. There are surely a good number of people who could and would criticize my writing, but I'm now in the process of finishing my fourth book, and there are many people who really seem to love my work. I enjoy expressing myself through the written word and the sharing of stories, and do not concern myself with people's negative opinions. And, of course, I would never have become aware of my ability to help others through writing if I hadn't one day sat down and followed my heart. I would never have discovered my ability to start and run a nonprofit if I hadn't followed my passion for something, and a desire to share it with the world.

I strongly encourage you to make a list of things *you'd* really like to do, and start doing them. Don't quit just because others give you negative feedback. Listen to your heart and trust in your abilities. You will eventually figure out if you're on the right path or not.

We create in our lives what we expect, and this is what we manifest. It is our vision that creates our reality. We need to learn to be wherever we are and to own the fact that our thoughts and our mind-set got us to that point. We can't blame others for our circumstances and expect those circumstances to change. It took me years to learn that after the breakup of my marriage. It wasn't until I could accept that I'd been responsible for what I'd created and stop blaming *her,* that I could move on. It wasn't about what I wasn't *receiving* that made me unhappy; it was about what I wasn't *giving.* My heart wasn't loving as it was created to love—that is, unconditionally. I wasn't creating wealth from within, so there were a lot of limitations in my life.

There's a wonderful Sufi saying by Abu Sa'id. When he was asked, "What is a Sufi?" He replied, "Whatever you have in your hand, you give away, whatever you have in your head, you put aside, and you do not flee from whatever befalls you." It is also said that a Sufi is a person whose every act is aimed at pleasing God, with the result that every act of God pleases him or her. In this last sentence, you can experience the truth of how energy flows back and forth.

We have a choice when we don't seem to be getting what we want in our lives. We can either develop more faith that what we want is on its way, or we can lessen our desire to match our faith. The way of the warrior doesn't always lead to romance and an easy life.

As I said before, when we accept the Divine presence more fully in our life, that's often when we enter into the real dark areas; but without the Divine, it's an even tougher journey. People seem to think that once you have wealth of any sort, life becomes a piece of cake. It doesn't matter if it's financial, spiritual, emotional, or physical wealth. Granted, all of these things are wonderful, but because we're always in a process of change, growth, and transformation, it's all relative. The more we *become,* the more we're able to do more, and the more we're challenged. After all, it was because of Gandhi's remarkable spiritual power that he was chosen to lead the struggle for independence. His challenges were magnified examples of many of ours. We learn to manage *personal* responsibility, whereas he assumed responsibility for a nation.

I'm not suggesting that we compare ourselves to Gandhi, but rather, that we experience a sense of our unlimited potential. We need to rid ourselves of worry about what other people think. We have to forget about the past and even stop stressing about the future.

**We have to assume the mantle of our greatness
and wear it every moment, every day,
living each moment as if it were our last.**

Not every battle is easy. One time I was talking to a friend with a scientific background as well as a strong spiritual sense, and he shared with me that when people romanticize spirituality, they tend to lose the sense of the spiritual warrior who has to do battle with the demons trying to hold us back.

Every time we encounter conflict or resistance, it's an opportunity to experience where we are and who we are, and I don't think I've ever met any kind of a master who wasn't a warrior as well. Gandhi was a total pacifist but a spiritual warrior, and he went to war with an army of pacifists, and won. It's a huge contradiction to think that we can make peace through war. The only way to have peace is to be peaceful. And this is true whether we're talking about individuals or nations. For me, in order to feel at peace when I'm involved with any type of conflict, I must let go of every tendency to fight. I have to decide to give up being *right,* and just try to feel *good.*

Maintain a powerful belief system and a positive attitude.

I truly believe that every single person has the possibility to live his or her greatness. That doesn't mean that we will all win a major golf tournament or an Academy Award, but it does mean that we're all potential winners. If we all developed our powers to the maximum, I don't think that that many people would even *want* to use their powers to win big contests.

We're all so unique, so special, and each of us has a gift to offer. I haven't written much about my past, about what kind of kid or young adult I was, and how mixed up and confused I was. Maybe that will be another book someday, but I'm sure I would have been the last kid in my class to be thought of as someone who would one day write a book about personal growth and transformation. Sex, drugs, and rock 'n roll, maybe, but nothing along the lines of *this* book.

One year as I watched Tiger Woods outperform everyone on the golf course by 12 strokes, he still got upset with himself when he didn't hit one shot exactly as he thought he should have. Even the best want to be better. The will to grow and be more is part of who we are. The people who *do* become more are those who learn to focus their energy, and I feel that the disparity between those who have and those who have not, has to do with their drive and intensity. Tiger Woods spent thousands of hours intensely focused on who he wanted to become, on who he knew himself to be. I'm sure that when he put on the famous green Masters jacket, he had visualized the entire sequence already. He'd already seen, felt, and experienced what it felt like to walk off the green at the end of the tournament as the winner.

Similarly, the reality that I experience today was already decided a long time ago. This was a vision that became reality. I remember standing in my bedroom when I was a kid, imagining Vin Scully, the Dodgers announcer, giving the "play-by-play" on a World Series winning grand slam home run by yours truly, and then I heard him describe in detail my striking out the side in the last inning to preserve the victory. But something in me knew this was a fantasy, because I knew I didn't believe as strongly as Tiger that I would be a world champion in my sport. I didn't have the same intensity or desire that he had, because if I had, I'm convinced I would have accomplished a lot more in that sport.

When I was involved in photography, I had a high opinion of myself in the early years and took a lot of great photos. But as I got older, I saw myself as a *good* photographer, not *great,* and I know now that this was because I lost some of the intense passion I had for taking pictures.

I had great ability, but when the passion dies, there's not enough energy to go through the challenges. I'm passionate now about sharing information with respect to personal growth and spirituality, and I know in my heart that nothing can stop me from being truly great at this. This may not sound humble, but it *is* my truth.

I've made an internal decision to follow my passion, which at this time in my life is to help people help themselves. I'm committed to helping people experience the Divine. I want everyone to feel what I feel. I'm committed to sharing home-based businesses with people so they know that they can work for themselves, and that they can make a *life* rather than just a living. I want people to truly see that they can live their dreams and help others do the same. There's no need to lead a life of quiet desperation, because there are many people waiting for someone to teach them how to be their own bosses and follow their passion. I'm committed to sharing information about the business I'm in because I believe that so many people will benefit from it.

One evening years ago, I was talking with my friend Kathleen, and she was saying that she would continue to do almost everything she's doing in her life even if she had millions of dollars, and that's what I feel. I want to do these things because I have an intense, burning desire to make a difference, and because I really love what I'm doing.

Nothing can stop the force of love.

There's no way that my energy will not be expressed. All these things will happen because I will never give up, and I will hold my vision. When I worked in photography, I was really working by myself. I had jobs that took one or two days, and some that would go for a week or two. On the longer jobs, there was a feeling of teamwork; in fact, people would often refer to the group as a team. After spending a week or two with a particular team, there was often a form of bonding that would occur, and over the years I established quite a few friendships. I was exposed to people who worried about this or that, but most of those in the industry didn't have a chance to affect my life with their fears because I never really saw them much. Consequently, even though I knew a lot of people, I never got too involved personally.

As I travel around the country, I constantly meet new people, and because of the work I do, the connections are intense and personal; and I share a lot of feelings with a number of people in the community. There have been many periods of my life when I've been almost paralyzed with fear, but I've kept it to myself. I'm careful about who I share my concerns with because I don't want other people to worry.

At the time I felt this way, I wasn't aware that other people worried, also. I would have moments of deep distrust with respect to my abilities, and wonder if I'd be able to support my family. I've never been very organized in terms of financial records, and even though I was always good at making money, I was also good at spending it, so I always seemed to be in debt. Sometimes I would feel as if there was no way out, so I'd lie awake at night feeling depressed and lonely, with no one I felt I could talk to. There would sometimes be periods where I would go a few weeks without a booking and wonder if my career was finished. Working for yourself takes away one's support system. In a way, it's the price you pay for the freedom of not having a boss.

During those months, I really felt like I worried alone because I felt very disconnected from everyone. There was no one to talk to since basically everyone hid his or her fears. So when I lay awake at night, worrying, I didn't realize that it wasn't just *my* fear I felt, but that my thoughts were congealed with lots of other people's thoughts.

Since I've grown in awareness, I realize that if I feel fear or worry start to creep into my life, it's not necessarily mine, but someone else's coming my way and scanning my thought processes, so to speak, to see if there are any sister thoughts that the fear and worry can latch onto. Now that my faith feels more secure, and now that I feel plugged in to Divine energy, I don't get so attached to that worry anymore.

A few years ago I got way behind on my taxes, and knowing that I was $60,000 to $70,000 short would have created nightmares if I hadn't utilized some of the processes I've mentioned here. I knew that if I just worked as hard as I could, eventually I'd find a solution, and that worrying about it and forcing the issue simply wouldn't be productive. I wanted to focus on the positive so that I would attract good things into my life; and in a very short time, things worked out better than I could have imagined. Before I knew it, the debt was gone.

When you come face-to-face with a big problem of your own, you can either let fear and worry overtake you and make you totally miserable, or you can allow the fear to motivate you to make positive changes so you can avoid the situation in the future.

I know that the universe always takes care of me. And I know that feeling fear and worry do not serve me. Now, I focus on solutions, not problems. I do not let the threat of fear galvanize me into action. Back then, I saw my debt as an opportunity to go out and increase my value in the marketplace. There are millions of dollars floating around out there, so I put myself in situations where some of those millions passed through my hands into the hands of the tax people.

I share this with you because I want you to know that I'm just like you. I worry, and I have fears, but do not let them stop me—or even slow me down. I work through the fears and worry because they don't serve me. And if *I* can do it, you can, too.

If I were to focus on the fear and the worry rather than bless it and move on, I would only attract more of it into my life. I don't want to just deny it either. I truly acknowledge it, for I trust that there's a great gift in it for me. When I tap into the universal consciousness, I am tapping into a power much bigger than I am. I can connect with all the empowered consciousness that has overcome every challenge that has ever existed. I know that faith and love is much better than some technique or strategy, because if I don't think that something is possible, there's no strategy that will allow me to accomplish it. Fear and worry is blocked love, and blocked love translates to pain.

Pain is not the truth, love is. Pain is what we go through on our way to love and truth.

One enormous challenge for me back then was patience. My impatience has been an asset in some cases, because it has helped me get things done. By wanting something done immediately, I usually took the action steps necessary to obtain it. But being impatient can also be a detriment if it prevents someone from doing things in their own time and space. I believe that patience is a tool to get what we want when properly used. I just want to leave you with this thought, because patience is such a valuable asset to cultivate. I will discuss this in more depth in the next chapter.

Real Wealth Creation

When it comes to creating wealth, which most people are interested in, I think with all the changes in the world we have to look at things differently. I subscribe to a lot of financial newsletters, as well as Mike Dillard's evolution group, and because of this I can educate myself and stay up-to-date as far as what other people are doing.

I don't necessarily use all the strategies I read about, but I still like to know what others are doing. Personally, I've chosen to continue participating in the co-op advertising campaign with the company

I work with because I love the wellness industry, and it's currently the most lucrative thing I know of with respect to using any extra capital I have. It has proven to be a tremendous wealth-building experience for me, and I've never done nearly as well with any kind of investment such as stocks, options, IRAs or Keogh accounts. Just recently I read the following headline in *The Palm Beach Letter*. It said: "Don't invest your money if you want to grow rich."

I thought that was a strange headline for an investment-type newsletter. What was interesting is that they talked about how long it took to create wealth through investing. It mentioned that if you had $50,000 to invest, even if you got 10 percent a year for 10 years, that would mean you would have $129,687 by 2021. Extend that to 30 years and you'd have $872,470 in 2041, which would give you, at 10 percent, an income of $87,200. After taxes, you would take home about $65,000 a year, hardly enough for most people to say they're wealthy. And if you're anywhere near my age, waiting 30 years is not really an option. Instead, here are some thoughts from the newsletter, which I hope you'll find helpful:

> Building wealth involves much more than just investing in stocks and bonds. Most rich people get that way by consistently doing the following five things:
>
> 1. They understand and manage their debt. They don't let debt manage them.
>
> 2. They spend their money wisely, getting maximum value for every dollar.
>
> 3. They continually work to increase both their active and their passive incomes.
>
> 4. They are aggressive savers, far outpacing their peers.
>
> 5. They are disciplined investors. When they find a good strategy, they stick with it.

The newsletter goes on to suggest spending only one hour a week checking investments, and the rest of the time working to increase income, which is basically what I do. I spend that hour reading more than doing anything else, because as I mentioned, I'm a big believer in self-education. Fortunately, due to the nature of my business, I don't need to spend many hours adding to my net worth, another positive reason why I love residual income. So I can spend my time doing things I'm truly passionate about, such as building my nonprofit and raising money for the disadvantaged.

In his book *Who Took My Money?*, Robert Kiyosaki mentions that the best thing you can do is find a business that produces a cash flow at a rate that gets all your cost capital back within five years. This means that if you put in $100,000, then you should own an asset that should have a cash-flow profit of $20,000 a year.

My experience has shown me that since our company's introduction of a new juice that helps people manage pain and inflammation, the capital used to acquire customers through co-op advertising is being recuperated very quickly. When I acquire customers, I usually find that 30 percent of my costs are recovered within 90 days, and the rest in anywhere from 20 to 24 months, depending on a number of factors. Thereafter, we are seeing many people earning 2 to 5 percent a month, which translates into over 20 percent or more a year, depending on the structure of their business, the number of customers acquired, and their commitment to sharing the business with others.

Also, I mentioned earlier that often if we want to change the way things are in our lives, doing the opposite of what we're doing can lead to the desired changes. What if in these times of gloom-and-doom predictions for the economy, we did the opposite of what the masses did? That's how some people get rich.

And what about the amazing potential and creativity of the human being we hear about from all the great teachers and mentors? And do you not believe that God will send us inspiration to help turn things around? Maybe we're going through tough economic times so that we can learn that to truly prosper, we have to return to what was taught in our holy books. Look how many corrupt regimes are being overthrown these days. Corrupt dictators who stole billions from their people are being exposed, just as many people in our own country now have to face the music.

Last night my wife watched the film *Miracle on 34th Street* with our granddaughter and heard a great line, which she shared with me:

"Faith is believing in things when common sense tells you not to." Well, I have a lot of faith, and I act on that faith. I will continue to do the things I believe in and not focus on fear and worry. I often think about how much I get from God, how much He has blessed me in this life, how generous He has been (and not just to me but to so many), and what an immense difference there is in what we give back. When I think about all the wisdom He imparts to us, all the immense love and caring, all the great prophets and teachers and messengers He sends our way, I see no way I could ever give back but a tiny drop in the ocean of His splendor.

When we start to master our desires, when we learn to surrender to Divine will and Divine principles, when we learn patience and the value of restraint, we are on the road to self-mastery. And if we sense that our appetites control us, that we feel insecure about ourselves and possible outcomes, and if our lives are dominated by fear and worry, we should see that it's because we lack faith and are led by our egos. We need to eliminate those qualities that separate us from feeling connected to the Divine. If we follow Divine laws, we'll have a much greater chance of experiencing life fulfillment.

Sidi says in one of his teachings:

> So throw out the fear of poverty out of your heart and do not expect to fulfill your needs with people. Beware of being overly concerned with your provision; rather, be confident of your Lord's promise. Your Lord is the one handling your affairs.

> God says, "And there is not a creature on earth save that the responsibility for its provision is on Allah." And you are among the creatures on the earth. Therefore, busy yourself with what you have been asked to do and this will grant your provision because God, your Guardian Protector, will never forget you and he has already informed you that your provision is on Him. And He has asked you to pursue it through worship of Him.

When I was growing up, I was really rebellious, not connected with God or with many people, for that matter; and there were times when I felt like crying because I felt rejected so often. Now I celebrate this, because those situations turned me into who I am today, and I feel so good and so grateful to have been able to experience life as I do. I know there are many things outside my control; but due to my faith, I am able to trust that if I live in alignment with the teachings of the holy books, I won't have anything to worry about, and all will continue to go well.

How Helping Someone Helped Me

Recently one of Sidi's students sent an e-mail asking Sidi to pray for her because she was going through some challenges. I have a lot of affection for her and her husband, and I know that this lady spends her life serving others as a spiritual healer. So, I wrote her and told her that if she liked, she could call me and maybe I could help her because I'd gone through something very similar. Even though she had many things to be grateful for, she felt stuck and didn't feel she was moving forward spiritually. I mentioned a certain prayer I'd memorized when I, too, felt lost, and told her how that prayer had helped me. She mentioned another prayer that she'd been thinking of learning, something called the "Orison of Tender Mercy," a prayer with which I was familiar and loved a lot.

I asked her to let me know in a few days if she was feeling any better, and she wrote back saying that things were still the same, so I got out my copy of the poem and read it again; and then sent her some quotes from it and suggested that she memorize just these few short lines and spend time allowing the phrases to really sink into her heart. I also decided to re-memorize those passages myself.

What happened to me was truly magical, as the prayer helped me open my heart even more to appreciate my connection with God and my faith in His protection. So, I'd like to share these words with you now. I love how trying to help someone I care about ended up really helping me. Here are a few lines of this prayer:

> *Oh Allah. Your unseen tender kindness is infinitely more subtle than what can be seen and you are the one who is tender to all beings. . . .*
>
> *Cause us to witness the secret of this protective tender mercy perpetually and eternally. . . .*
>
> *Yet open to us the doors of your hidden infinite tender mercy that shields, and fortifies us, from every misfortune. . .*

Cause us to enter by your graciousness into those citadels. . . .

Oh our Allah. You are tender with your worshippers, especially the family of your lovers and (those) dear to you. . . .

So by the family of lovers and beloveds, single us out for the most subtle tender kindness. . . .

More from Mentors

If we want to build anything, whether it's a business, a relationship, or anything, we must believe in what we're building. When we're passionate and intense; and totally love what we're doing, our beliefs are correspondingly strong. With strong beliefs, unshakable faith, a positive attitude, patience, and a totally loving heart all focused in the moment, we're able to *create,* because we're an extension of pure creative energy. As we all learn how to transform ourselves, we can collectively join together to transform the world.

I originally met Rick Tonita through a really close friend at the time, Garrett McGrath, a fellow networker who is also very successful. We both learned a lot from Rick, who has also been influenced by Robert Fritz, whose books I studied extensively. As I mentioned earlier in this book, Robert is one of the best teachers I know, and he understands how to help people create more of what they want in their life. Rick and Michael Ellison, (whom I mentioned earlier, is also the owner of the company I work with) are both *big* believers in research. Rick once said that 98 percent of people responded positively when asked if they'd like to be personally invited into a business and be mentored to success. I always like it when I see commonalities in successful people, because I can model those same attributes in my own business life. I always do a lot of research to learn as much as I can about the best people to follow, and diligent research allows me to see whether those who follow them are also successful. As I mentioned, my friend Garrett did very well using Rick's teachings.

Rick taught me so much about how to present a business to top-level people in an elegant way, without shutting down their receptivity before I was done. Much of what he teaches is on my website.

EXERCISE

Make a list of three to five of your own qualities that you'd like to focus on and develop. When you've identified each quality, write down the benefits you derive from it.

For example: **Patience:** *As I develop more patience with my partner by trusting that I am doing every action in the highest way, I feel comfortable that I will have a positive outcome. As I open my heart more and give more love and more caring, and pay more attention to my partner by being fully present, I have faith that eventually our relationship will grow in every way and I don't need him to change for everything to be better.*

_____

_____

_____

_____

_____

_____

_____

_____

_____

_____

_____

_____

_____

_____

_____

_____

_____

_____

Chapter 18

❧

Patience

"The human being is at a loss except for those who faithfully believe and perform good deeds and counsel one another in the truth and counsel one another to steadfast patience." — **QUR'AN 103:1–3**

I don't know if you've read *Siddhartha*, by Herman Hesse, but there's a moment when Siddhartha is coming back into the world and applies for a job, and when asked what he can do, he says, "I can think, I can wait and I can fast." And then he uses these qualities to create abundance.

Sidi says that if you're patient, wise, and gentle, many things will come to you. There's a difference, though, between being patient and just waiting for something to happen. Too often I see people who don't do much, yet who expect a lot.

I already mentioned the African proverb "When you pray, move your feet." This is a reminder that purpose-driven individuals take action in harmony with their purpose, and they fill that action with love and excellence. When they do so, the process itself is filled with rewards, and the outcome will be what it should be.

So patience, here, is not forcing an issue, but letting it unfold in the way it naturally should. Being wise about the actions you choose, being gentle so that what you do harms no one or no thing and is in alignment with Divine laws, and patiently waiting till everything reaches its conclusion . . . will bring you to a place where you're feeling at peace with everything.

See what happens when unnatural methods are used to make animals grow fatter faster, or crops are forced to look bigger and better. We end up with millions of people getting sick from all the chemicals, and with all sorts of natural disasters creating huge losses of life and billions of dollars of damage.

We should allow nature to unfold in the way God intended. We live in a world where the need for instant gratification doesn't allow for the natural unfolding of things. People plunge instantly into intimate relations without allowing for the unfolding of their love, and this type of promiscuity has led to many diseases. Sports teams are rushing athletes so much that injuries occur, some of them career-ending. I think you get the point.

I had to practice a lot of patience in the development of my businesses. So many people quit in the early months because they're not making enough money, but when this happens, it's usually because they started with unrealistic expectations. Think about how much money is spent sending people through formal education processes in order to get their MBA's or Ph.D.'s, and how many years it takes. Then look at how many years it takes to build up a practice to a six-figure income. Yet people start a home-based business and quit soon after if they're not making thousands of dollars a month. If everyone could just understand that if they work hard for a number of years and be patient, persistent, and consistent, they could end up with life-changing income.

Change is uncertain, sometimes quite frightening, and always unpredictable. It does not come when *we* want it, but when *God* wants it. Michael Port says in one of his books that the only people who like change are babies in messy diapers. I think that there are many people who would love change because they're not in a situation that makes them happy. But they tend to stay in the same place because they fear the unknown.

We can attract change by changing ourselves. We really can change our lives in an instant through a simple shift within ourselves in the direction where we're headed.

If you don't like where you are and don't feel good about where you're going, what is stopping you from changing direction? If you're driving down the road wanting to go north and realize you're going south, in an instant you can change your direction. If you can do it physically, you can also do it emotionally, spiritually, and financially. Just look inside, be truthful with yourself, and then make the decision to change.

Many people today have coaches who help them with important decisions. I chose to work with a spiritual guide, because for me, everything I want in life originates in my spirit; and I don't want to be associated with anyone or anything that doesn't harmonize with Divine law. But if you can't find a spiritual teacher, then start with a coach, as they're pretty easy to find these days; and most of them are doing this work because they love to help others.

If you want to change, then do something to make change happen.

After I went through my divorce, I waited more than ten years before remarrying, and the reward of that patience has been an immensely satisfying relationship that was definitely worth the wait. When people are in long-term relationships, usually one of the partners, or both, will have to be patient as the other goes through certain cycles of development. The same is true for those of us who have children. We need patience to wait for the maturation of their qualities. Patience implies trust: trust in the unseen, in accepting something that is not yet apparent. So sometimes we have to trust the process we're in and wait for the results. Sidi often speaks about how humans should have the same qualities of dogs. They are trustworthy, faithful, disciplined, sincere, patient, and love us unconditionally.

A Story about Moses

I want to share something with you that has had a great impact on my life. It's a story about patience, and it is in the words of my teacher Sidi. This is a transcript taken of a lecture he was giving in Texas, and he was speaking in Arabic with a simultaneous translation in

English. The transcription is verbatim, to stay as close as possible to the flavor of Sidi's language. *Al-Khidr* is a legendary Islamic figure and spiritual guide, endowed with direct inner knowing, and *Allah* is the One God of monotheistic religion.

As with all of Sidi's teachings, it is highly recommended to read multiple times. I have personally found great benefit in writing out these teachings as well. I hope you enjoy it.

Moses one day was claiming that no one had more knowledge than him.

He thought that he had a lot of knowledge

But his knowledge stopped with the outer law, but he had not really arrived at the ultimate reality, and the presence of God totally.

So Allah heard him saying that, and He said, "Go to that teacher."

And when he went to that gnostic teacher, the teacher al-Khidr, told him,

"I don't think you will be patient enough to handle my teaching"

And Moses said, "No, I promise to be patient."

This is because God said that he gave direct knowledge, gnosis, to al-Khidr, which Moses needed to know

And if anyone had looked at al-Khidr, that great prophet that taught Moses,

you would find him a simple man, like walking there as if he was insignificant.

He's hidden, but he was a gnostic, a great gnostic

If he said, "O, my Lord," his Lord answered him immediately.

It is the wisdom of Allah to hide his gnostics so that he can teach us, to teach us how to humble ourselves

For look at that great gnostic; he was walking among people as if he was insignificant, humble, not recognized

So Allah wanted us to learn through this, that we must be humble

So Moses promised to be patient, and while they were travelling they wanted to cross a river so they came upon a small boat

And they went in that boat to cross the river

So al-Khidr, all of a sudden, he makes a hole in the ship, he breaks it; he breaks a little bit of it

And Moses thought that was so evil

He said, "How come you are doing this to the people who own the ship? That is not right. It is not permissible."

And he was talking the truth, from his perspective, because you don't own this ship, how come you break it like that?

And Moses was very strong at heart,

And very strong in speaking, because he was a prophet and he had to speak the truth in his heart

So al-Khidr, the gnostic, told him, "I told you, you would not be able to be patient with me, with my teaching. If you keep asking questions, you will not be able to accompany me. You have to be patient."

So Moses said, "I promise; I'll be patient next time."

Because he was a noble prophet, he really wanted to learn more

So they continued in their journey

Then they arrived at the city and they were hungry and the people there refused to offer them food.

They said, "Can we buy some food from you?"

They said, "You're strangers and we don't deal with strangers. Whether you pay or not, we can't offer you food. We don't welcome people we don't know here. Please leave."

But they were hungry; and no one helped them.

However, al-Khidr continued his journey in the city until he arrived to a particular house that was old.

And there were two teenagers living there, about 12-13 years old, with their mother.

She was a widow, living there with her two sons. And she offered them food and allowed them to sleep in the barn. And there was a man there who was drinking a lot and very mean to the children.

The house was very old, and there was a wall that was falling down and in the morning when he woke up Moses saw Al-Khidr out in the hot sun working on fixing the wall and starting to renovate it and strengthen it, because it was about to fall.

And Moses said, "I don't understand what you're doing. The people in this village refused to offer us help. But you come and for free you are building a wall in that village? I don't understand why you're doing this. We can ask for a salary for fixing the wall."

So al-Khidr answered Moses, "I told you, you would not be patient with me."

He said, "It seems you're an impatient one. So you should leave me."

He said, "O please, excuse me this time again. And I promise to be more patient. But I don't understand it and it's very difficult for me to endure this, to bear it."

However, they continued on their journey.

It was a divine journey; it was a godly journey, a walking, walking towards Allah.

The student, the seeker, must be patient with the walking, must learn from the teacher, no matter how the lesson is difficult, because he doesn't have that knowledge of the teacher's, so he must trust him and be patient and continue his walking

Because the teacher can tell you to do something and your ego refuses it.

"Why should I obey this? Why should I do this?"

For example, your spiritual teacher, your guide can tell you, "You need a retreat; you have to go for 10 days, or for 40 days you shouldn't eat any meat."

Like tough requests he will make of you, and don't do this and don't do that

And you say, "Why is he asking me this?"

You shouldn't object because you don't have the same knowledge.

He's trying to heal you and to help you arrive at the Divine presence.

So Moses continued to walk with his spiritual guide, until they came across a youth that looked handsome, but he was really a monster inside.

And the youth raised a knife to the throat of al-Khidr, and demanded all his money.

So what happened was, al-Khidr killed him.

And Moses said, "No, that's it. I can't endure this anymore. Why did you kill an innocent spirit?"

Because Moses always followed the law, and he wanted to understand why al-Khidr killed someone.

So the spiritual guide said, "This is the point where we have to separate, because you can't tolerate this teaching." He said, "But I will explain to you things before you leave. I will make you understand why I did what I did. I will answer your questions."

So he said, "In the first case, I made this hole in the ship, because the owners were really kind faithful believers, loving people, good people, and they were very poor. And they always raised the flag of unity and justice and love and compassion for all.

They were beloveds to Allah and Allah wanted to protect them. That's why I cared for them.

What I did was care, because I know that there is this ruler, tyrant, oppressor who takes everything from people. And he was about to take the ship, every ship in good shape, he takes it to work for him. He enslaves people to work for him.

So he would have never left them alone with that ship, until I made the ship look old and ruined.

Any new ship, he will take it and enslave the people to work for his benefit, but that would deprive the poor people from their source of provision, because they use this boat to make a living and feed themselves.

This is the way of the gnostics. They care for everyone, the poor and the hungry and the homeless, the suffering.

That's why I wanted to make this hole, so it will appear as old and the tyrant will pass by it and leave it for the poor people, so they can continue to have provision."

So that's what happened, the tyrant came and he said, "O, this ship is no use," and he left it to the poor people.

"And then we will go back and we will fix it. It's easy to fix and they will keep their source of provision.'

So the gnostics always work to build, not to destroy, and to protect, not to deprive.

Because they are the beloveds of Allah, the are the messengers of Allah,

They never deviate from His way. They never mean destruction, they mean service, to help people in any way they can.

So if the inspiration came to them to do that,

Then that was a teaching for Moses, to understand more that he needs to help people in any way he can, to spread peace, justice, freedom, compassion and mercy and love for everyone, for all people regardless of if are you Arab, non-Arab, black, white, whatever ethnicity and nationality you have, you're all the same and the gnostic treats you the same.

So the ship was just an metaphor to see the Divine mercy.

He can make something that might look harmful, but it is really beneficial, because that saved the people and their source of provision.

So al-Khidr told Musa [Moses], "We have to defend the poor and the helpless. We have to make sure that justice and protection is granted for all who need it and cannot stand for themselves.

This is the true message of God.

You are not created to just eat and drink and have pleasure and play.

You're created to serve yourself and others, to serve God, and fulfill your duty on earth. This is a lesson, that teaches you how to walk, how the messengers walk.

They are inspired by God to serve the people and to protect them in the wisest way."

Then al-Khidr went on to explain the second case.

He said, "I have built this wall or renovated it, repaired it, without any salary, because of a wisdom."

He said, "Moses, you're foolish. We cannot ask for a salary from this house, because it belongs to a single mother with orphans. We serve them; we don't take anything from them.

You saw how the other citizens of this city were; they are misers. They will not take care of those orphans and widow. And they have no hearts, no mercy in their hearts. They deviated from their humane way.

And these two children are orphans, and their father was righteous and a pious man who carried the message of unity, mercy, peace, justice, and love for all. And that's why Allah sent me to serve his family.

And the father hid some money and treasures for his children underneath that wall.

So we had to build it, because if someone else finds it, they will take it.

Those are evil people; they will take it; they will not care for the orphans or for the widow. They will take their wealth that their father left.

So we needed to protect that wealth for the orphans so when they grow up they can have it, and the mother can have it."

So that is the way of the gnostics, to protect people from those who are willing to destroy their houses and unrightfully take their wealth and resources.

The people of God serve those people and protect them.

So al-Khidr protected those orphans so that they can grow strong and be able to serve themselves and protect themselves.

So Musa said, "Ok, I understand now some of what you did.

What about the third case, where you killed that young man?"

He said, "That young man was an evil one.

He was causing a lot of destruction and he was like a tyrant.

He was terrorizing the people; he was violating their rights and oppressing them,

And it came to us with a divine command to stop his transgression and aggression and oppression for people.

So the one who wants to destroy humanity, should we just leave him doing it?

If someone's coming to burn your house, and take all of your resources, you just stand there helpless, and no one defends you?

Or does someone have to stop that, stop the oppressors and the tyrants?

We should not be selfish and live only for ourselves.

We should also serve the helpless and the poor

Otherwise the tyrant will come someday to our house too."

So al-Khidr informed Musa, "I did not do that out of my selfish ego.

I did it for a Divine command, inspired by a Divine command to protect the helpless and the poor from the tyrants and the aggressor."

Because Allah commanded us to save the resources, to protect them, to purify them, to protect everyone and not to allow people to pollute them, or take them for themselves selfishly, and destroy humanity.

Allah wants us to preserve all the good on earth and all of its resources, to share it.

I hope you've gotten as much out of this teaching as possible, and suggest you go over it a number of times, because the more time you spend with it, the more you will get *out* of it. There have been so many times in my life that my immediate reaction to something has been similar to what happened in this story, and it's only after time has passed that I've seen the wisdom of why certain things happened as they did. Often things drop out of our lives in order to leave a space for something new to take its place. And without patience, it's impossible to reach the point of being able to see the value.

Good Luck, Bad Luck

Another favorite story of mine involves a rancher who has a couple of horses that do all the work on the ranch. He uses them to plow the fields, to gather his sheep, to go to town to do the shopping, and so on. One day the two horses bust out of the corral and disappear, and his neighbor John comes by and says, "So sorry, Pete, that's such bad luck," and Pete responds "Good luck, bad luck, who knows."

Then Pete goes out in search of his horses and finds them with a small herd of wild horses, which he gathers and brings back; and John comes by and says, "Wow, Pete, that's such good luck," and Pete responds, "Good luck, bad luck, who knows."

The next day Pete and his son are working on breaking the wild horses so they can ride them, and the son falls off the horse and breaks his leg, and John comes by and says, "Pete, that's such bad luck," and of course Pete replies, "Good luck, bad luck, who knows."

Then the next day the army comes by to gather all able-bodied young men to take them to war, and the son gets passed over because of his broken leg and…well, you can see how it goes.

As Yogi Berra says, "It ain't over till it's over."

We don't always know when something is happening if it's good or bad. But when you're patient and wait for something to follow its course without forcing things, then more often than not a positive outcome will result if the effort is in harmony with Divine laws.

The three holy books: the Bible, The Torah, and the Qur'an, all have essentially the same teachings. They all believe that there is only one God, they all agree that we all come from Adam and Eve, they're all against killing and hurting others, and so on. So when we live in alignment with these principles, things will start to go a lot better in our lives.

Remember when I spoke about Ava Brenner (the therapist), and she said one day that I would build an altar to commemorate all that was happening as I went through my divorce? Well, now that I have a different perspective, I understand what she meant. All the pain of what I went through pushed me into looking so much deeper at myself than if it had never happened at all. It made me really reach out and connect with God and find the source of Divine energy deep within my being, which I feel is the "inner magician" we all have. Our inner magician can make pain disappear, turn pain into pleasure, and totally transform us into someone different. Once we truly learn that we can control how we react to what happens to us, we can influence our reaction to numerous situations.

I don't think there was much I could have done to alter where my ex-wife, Nathalie, was going, but I sure had a lot of choices as to where *I* could go with what happened. Looking back, I realize that one thing I did not practice was patience. I was not in a space where I could sit back and wait patiently while she went through the processes she was experiencing.

When I look back at everything and take stock of where I am today, I really find it difficult to imagine a better life than I have. Because of everything that happened, I met Sidi, who has been a major influence for me. Would I have met him anyway? I guess there's no way of knowing. But his teachings have led me to completely revamp the way I think, feel, and act. Nathalie and I are still really close, and even though we're both in other relationships, I don't sense any friction or conflict between us at all.

I am now at a place where I really am a lot less concerned with outcomes than enjoying a process; and as a result, I feel a lot more patient. I rarely find myself in a situation where I feel I want to force an outcome, so I'm content with just letting things unfold naturally.

I suggest taking stock of your current situation now, and seeing if there are places where *your* impatience is creating conflict for you. A lot of our challenges come from getting out of the present moment and worrying about the future, but if you allow yourself to really enjoy the process and not try to force things outside the natural laws, I think you'll feel better.

Impatience is a sign of disconnection with our faith in God, and patience is a sign of relying on that trust.

EXERCISE

Write down a few instances where you've had a negative reaction to something that actually turned out to be more positive than you thought, and then write down a few instances when you thought something was actually better than it turned out. This might refer to someone you met and liked initially and then realized this person wasn't so nice, or someone you didn't like at first but then who turned out to be wonderful. Or maybe you lost a job only to get a better one. Look for the hidden meanings you might have missed.

_____

_____

_____

_____

_____

_____

_____

_____

_____

_____

_____

Develop the Divine Qualities of Patience and Trust.
Join me in our 8-week program for in-depth support.
www.MakeYourLifeMagical.com/explore

_____

_____

_____

_____

_____

_____

_____

_____

_____

_____

_____

_____

_____

_____

_____

_____

_____

_____

_____

_____

_____

_____

_____

_____

_____

_____

_____

Chapter 19

Forgivenesss and Leaving the Past

"Do not judge, and you will not be judged. Do not condemn, and you will not be condemned. Forgive, and you will be forgiven."
— LUKE 6:37

"On no account brood over your wrongdoing. Rolling in the muck is not the best way of getting clean." — ALDOUS HUXLEY

One of the most transformational things in my life occurred when I got to a point where I not only felt authentic forgiveness toward Nathalie for leaving me, but finally could leave all the bad emotions in the past and feel nothing but good feelings about her. The same is true for a company I worked with. I was making a high-five-figure monthly income, but then they actually stopped my checks because they said I'd violated some part of a distributor agreement. They also terminated a number of other distributors. That company has since gone out of business and was taken over by another firm, and I have gone on to do really well. Some of the other people who were terminated are also doing really well in other companies, while those who weren't terminated have watched their residual income drop down to a fraction of what it was before.

"Forgiveness is not an occasional act; it is a permanent attitude."
— MARTIN LUTHER KING, JR.

Because this company stopped paying me, I was forced to build another business and develop new skills, which have served me well. This is another example that mirrors the story of Moses, because when it happened, I couldn't understand anything. First, I didn't think I'd done anything unethical, and I could never understand why they would want to terminate the people who had the talents and abilities to build the company. But looking back on it all, I am eternally grateful that they pushed me to pursue a different path.

Often we find our future on the road we took to avoid our destiny. It's difficult to see the workings of what's really happening at the time, just like looking at a skilled magician perform an effect. We look at something and don't really understand how it's possible, but if the magician were to break it down step by step, then we'd be looking at something completely different and seeing things we wouldn't see if we weren't exposed to the truth.

One of the major tenets of Sidi's teachings is repentance, or forgiveness.

Here's another excerpt from one of his talks:

> *Know that everything depends upon repentance. Repentance is your first step, and it is a continuous step. It is like changing the oil in your car. Can you actually drive a car without oil or when it has a problem? No, you have to fix it in order to drive it. You are like this vehicle, and you are full of things that need to be fixed and rectified and washed and cleaned in order to drive and to arrive at the Divine presence.*

> *The path to God is full of obstacles and danger, and you must continue to purify yourself by walking this path until you become fully conscious of the Divine presence. You must purify the body and the soul through repentance from their illnesses, because our bodies and hearts and souls accumulate dirt that causes illness. We must purify ourselves and truly follow the Divine way by following His commands and following His prohibitions. Do not fear anyone except God. Revere God and walk to Him through the essential gate, which is the gate of repentance.*

So what he is saying here is that before we can forgive others, we must ask for forgiveness ourselves for all we have done that is not right. Sometimes we hurt others without even realizing we've done so; so when we ask for forgiveness, we must ask for it not only for what we've done wrong intentionally, but also for all the unintentional things.

Here is more from one of Sidi's talks:

And all the prophets said, "All the doors we knocked on were closed.

There's only one door that stayed open,

And that was the door of piety and surrender, filled with lights,

And that's the door of the repentance."

And God said about it,

"O, my worshipful slave, if you did not make mistakes,

I would create another creation that would make mistakes and that would repent to me,

And I would give them repentance and forgive their mistakes."

O worshippers of God, if any of you comes to God with sins that filled the entire earth,

And if a person comes to repent, an honest, true repentance,

And comes to the mercy of Allah with a pure, sincere intention and a clear heart and all pure senses,

He will open to him or to her the door of repentance and the door of mercy,

And He will come to him or to her with the lights of His Divine lights, equal to what would fill this earth.

And He will give him the repentance that will purify him.

One should not be stopped by something that he did or she did, to come forward towards Allah.

Because Allah said, "O, My worshippers, who have transgressed against themselves,

Do not give up on the mercy of Allah,

Because Allah forgives all sins."

And all those who come forward through the door of repentance and regret what happened,

And who promise that they will not return to what they have done before will be forgiven

Because the person who repents and returns to do what he was doing before,

It's as if he was being dishonest with his Lord.

And for this reason, when you declare your repentance to your Lord,

Do not deceive yourself that you can repent and go back to do what you were doing,

Do not think, "As long as this door is open we can make mistakes and come back and repent."

No, this is not how it works.

When you take this promise, it's a solid oath,

And if you break it, it's as if you broke your promise with Allah.

So don't go back to what you have done before.

All the prophets, and the prophet Muhammad, (pbuh) said, he was asking for forgiveness every day seventy times.

So are you ready for a true repentance?

If this is the case, Allah said,

"Only those who repent and ask for forgiveness,

Those I will replace their mistakes with good deeds

Because I am the most forgiving, the merciful."

This is a small tradition to explain to you how great this door of repentance is.

This is the door of the poor who are returning to Allah.

And "the poor" here are the ones who are in need of the Divine Mercy and the Divine Love

And the state of those in complete surrender to Him

And who put themselves in this place of humility.

And they come promising Allah that they are giving everything to Allah,

So He can purify them with this water of mercy

This is the meaning of the repentance."

So how does this relate to our own lives and what difference this can make in building a business? For these kinds of teachings to have any use in the real world, they need to be applied on a consistent basis. Here are some thoughts to live by:

COLOSSIANS 3:13:
Bear with each other and forgive whatever grievances you may have against one another. Forgive as the Lord forgave you.

BUDDHISM:
Hatred does not cease by hatred, but only by love; this is the eternal rule.

MATTHEW 6:14-16:
For if you forgive men when they sin against you, your heavenly Father will also forgive you. But if you do not forgive men their sins, your Father will not forgive your sins.

MARK 11:25:
And when you stand praying, if you hold anything against anyone, forgive him, so that your Father in heaven may forgive you your sins.

FROM WIKIPEDIA:
In Judaism, if a person causes harm, but then sincerely and honestly apologizes to the wronged individual and tries to rectify the wrong, the wronged individual is religiously required to grant forgiveness.

"It is forbidden to be obdurate and not allow yourself to be appeased. On the contrary, one should be easily pacified and find it difficult to become angry. When asked by an offender for forgiveness, one should forgive with a sincere mind and a willing spirit . . . forgiveness is natural to the seed of Israel." (MISHNAH TORAH, TESHUVAH 2:10)

Swami Vivekananda wrote:

"The Lord has declared to the Hindu in His incarnation as Krishna. I am in every religion as the thread through a string of pearls. Wherever thou sees extraordinary holiness and extraordinary power raising and purifying humanity, know thou that I am there."

In the Sermon on the Mount, Jesus repeatedly spoke of forgiveness:

"Blessed are the merciful, for they will be shown mercy."
— MATTHEW 5:7

"Therefore, if you are offering your gift at the altar and there remember that your brother has something against you, leave your gift there in front of the altar. First go and be reconciled to your brother; then come and offer your gift." — MATTHEW 5:23-24

The Qur'an makes it clear that, whenever possible, it is better to forgive another than to attack another. The Qur'an describes the believers as those who, "avoid gross sins and vice, and when angered they forgive." — QUR'AN 42:37

The Qur'an also says that "although the just requital for an injustice is an equivalent retribution, those who pardon and maintain righteousness are rewarded by GOD. He does not love the unjust."
— QUR'AN 42:40

Sidi teaches: To receive forgiveness from God there are three requirements:

 1. Recognizing the offense itself and its admission before God.

 2. Making a commitment not to repeat the offense.

 3. Asking for forgiveness from God.

If the offense was committed against another human being, or against society, a fourth condition is added:

4. Recognizing the offense before those against whom offense was committed and before God.

Committing oneself not to repeat the offense.

Doing whatever needs to be done to rectify the offense (within reason) and asking pardon of the offended party.

Asking God for forgiveness.

There are no particular words to say for asking forgiveness. However, Muslims are taught many phrases and words to keep repeating daily asking God's forgiveness. For example:

Astaghfiru-Allah, "I ask forgiveness from Allah"

Subhanaka-Allah humma wa bi hamdika wa ash-hadu al la Ilaha illa Anta astaghfiruka wa atubu ilayk, "Glory be to You, Allah, and with You Praise (thanks) and I bear witness that there is no deity but You, I ask Your forgiveness and I return to You (in obedience)".

There are also a lot of examples in Buddhism, Hinduism, Jainism, and most other religions. It seems universally accepted that forgiveness and repentance help cleanse us spiritually.

Applying Forgiveness in My Business

Let me share a personal example. In my business, my company allows people to acquire customers through a co-op advertising media program. This sets my company apart from any other business model I know. In every other business, people have to build their own customer base through friends and family or marketing efforts on their own. The co-op advertising program allows us to acquire a significant number of customers through whom we can establish predictable, sustainable, and long-term residual income. I have also created a customer-service center that my partners can use to make sure their customers are handled in a professional and courteous manner. In addition, my company mails catalogs and journals on a continual basis to every customer, so the follow-up is quite extraordinary.

I've come to learn that unless people have pretty significant discretionary income and can acquire a significant number of customers, there is not enough momentum created to earn something really substantial, unless they choose to actually contact and invite a considerable number of people to the experience, just as you see done in a lot of other MLM companies. If someone is willing to do this, the program can be fantastic. If someone acquires a small amount of contacts, say 25, and gets a significant number of people to do the same, then they can do very well. That is actually how I started.

Since, statistically, the average person will recruit between two and three people, the ability to acquire 25 customers is really phenomenal. If someone were to come in and spend a few thousand dollars, I would personally benefit, even if they didn't end up doing well. This has happened in a number of companies where I did well, but only a small percentage of my downline did as well as they'd hoped.

Of course, most people don't understand that it's called netWORK marketing, and they forget the *work* part. In order for it to work for them, it would be important for them to invite other partners, which most people aren't very good at doing. Whereas when people have more capital, they don't need to share the business with others to have a viable business.

When I first came to this realization, I thought that it would be much more difficult to ethically grow my business because *I* would probably be successful, but a lot of other people would fail; and if I cut out all the people who could afford a small amount, I would not grow as much as I had in other companies. But I made a conscious decision. I decided to stop inviting people into the business if I wasn't sure they'd be successful.

I then asked God to forgive me for inviting people into the business in the past who would eventually lose money, and I made a commitment to stop doing that. I did acknowledge that it would mean a loss of income for me as well.

I then arranged to buy out those who hadn't done well as a way of asking for their forgiveness. And I did stop sharing the business with people unless I found those who either had more discretionary income so they could earn enough to allow them to get a return on their capital; and create some predictable, sustainable, long-term income.

By sharing the wellness business with people who had significant capital, it became more like sharing an opportunity, which was similar to buying a franchise, but without employees, brick and mortar locations, and so on.

In the past few months, I've found many more people than I expected to join me as partners, and I truly believe that this is a result of asking for sincere forgiveness, changing the way I conducted business, and committing to continuing in this manner in the future. Also, returning the money to those who were dissatisfied opened doors to success I could never have imagined.

Now I'm finding it a lot easier to find people with enough discretionary income who are looking for something similar to what I'm doing. And my business has grown a whole lot faster than it ever has before. Not only that, but I'm surrounded by really happy people who love being a part of this experience.

Forgiveness in Relationships

This principle also holds true for our relationships. If we do something that hurts others, and we ask them for forgiveness and promise to never do it again, my experience is that this really heals the relationship and allows it to blossom into something very beautiful. We are all humans, and humans make mistakes. So it's vital that we learn about forgiveness, and practice it on a daily basis. There are also different levels of forgiveness/repentance. There is the repentance for the body, the heart, the mind, and the spirit.

Here are more of Sidi's words:

> You move forward, after you purify your body and repent with your body,
>
> And purify your heart.
>
> And you purify your body and your heart with tears of regret,

Promising your Lord that you will not return to what you have done,

And you promise an absolute promise, that you will not return back to what you have done before.

And to purify this body so that it comes back to the point where Allah said,

"I am creating a human."

This body, Allah created the human being with His divine light,

And put in it a divine light of love, peace, and mercy and unity.

For this body to be beautifully pure, it must only contain purity in it,

So don't put anything in it that will bring impurities to it.

Then you'll be pure in your body, and pure from all that Allah does not want you to be, to have in your body.

From that point, Allah said that He loves them, and they love Him,

That Allah has loved you before you loved Him,

When He created you and filled you with divine fragrance,

That Allah is very keen and very caring for you.

Allah wants you to be with Him;

That's why He gave you this light within you

And perfected your creation.

Don't you see how He created you and perfected you in the perfect picture that He wanted for you?

We have to be very careful with the body,

Because it's a vehicle that Allah created

And ordered you to use this vehicle and taught you how to use it,

And how to be in it, and how to walk in this life

And how to use this vehicle to serve you,

Use the hands, use the eyes, use the legs and to use the hearts.

And this is the true meaning of repentance of the body.

And Allah said in the Torah, He said, "First, worship Me, and do not associate others with Me.

Do not kill.

Do not steal.

Do not commit adultery.

Do not lie.

Do not betray, be honest, be truthful."

These are holy words,

And those words are confirmed in the Qur'an also.

There He said, "Worship Me and establish salat.

And avoid all sins.

And do not steal.

And fulfill My promise,

And I will fulfill your promise."

And also in the Gospel; it's also there.

It's only one message.

You have to be responsible for how you use your senses. The person who backbites, lies, speaks badly about others, refrains from speaking good about others, spies on people and/or ruins people's reputations by speaking badly about them, is not following Allāh's order. Know that Allāh says that whenever a human utters a word, it is recorded by angels. There are two angels: one to the right and one to the left, and they record everything you say [SEE QUR'ĀN 50:17].

There is also the sense of hearing. Hearing could be used to listen to gossip, but this is a deviation of Allāh's way. Also, seeing can be used in the wrong way, in deviation to what Allah commands, by looking at what people have and envying them. The envious one looks at what people have and thinks, "Look at what they have. They have so much," and he envies them. This envy hurts people."

So what he is saying here is that we must be careful what we put in our bodies. Today we fill our sacred vessels with tons of chemicals, as well as drugs and other intoxicants. This destroys the purity of our bodies. The same goes for our hearts, minds, and spirits. We can choose to only fill our minds with positive thoughts and feelings, and when we do so, we'll find that our lives will transform to an amazing extent.

"All we are is the result of what we have thought. The mind is everything. What we think, we become." — BUDDHA

Many years ago when I met Sidi, I made a promise to God to stop using any kind of intoxicant, and this was a big change for me. Yet here it is, 20 years later, and I don't even think about it anymore. As a result, I enjoy pretty fantastic health. I also have had a complete turnaround with my life as a whole. How much can be attributed to my healthy way of life is a question I can't really answer, but in my heart I feel it contributed greatly to why things changed so much for me. I asked for forgiveness, and then kept my promise not to do drugs again, and I feel great about myself as a result.

As for our hearts and our spirits, the same holds true. Once we make a promise to be kind to each other, and once we ask forgiveness from those we've hurt, something special happens in our hearts. And when we ask God's forgiveness for things we've done that violate spiritual laws, and promise not to return to any of those behaviors again, our lives improve radically. The more we act in accordance with Divine laws, the more our lives advance and improve, and the more abundance we create for ourselves and for others.

This is a teaching of the prophet Muhammad:

> *There is a self within the body*
> *and within the self there is a heart,*
> *and within the heart there is a spirit,*
> *and within that spirit there is a secret,*
> *and within the secret there is a concealed secret,*
> *and within the concealed secret there is the most concealed secret,*
> *and within that there is Me.*

When we revere the body, the heart, and the spirit, we open up a door to the different levels of all the secrets hidden within us; and as the veils are lifted, we begin to access our true selves and our true power.

The other thing that is so important is to really leave the past behind. I think so many people are caught up in the past that they cease to look ahead. If you walk with your head turned around looking behind you, then you will never be able to see where you're going.

Another teaching from Sidi:

> *Anything the hand does for evil will be brought to account. If the hand does anything in deviation of Allāh's command, it will be brought to account. Whoever wants to walk toward Allāh must repent a sincere, honest repentance, and he must never commit those past actions again. He must purify his senses. As mentioned in the Qur'ān, Nūḥ (Noah) said to his people:*
>
> *Ask forgiveness from your Lord; for He is Oft-Forgiving;*
>
> *He will send rain to you in abundance;*
>
> *Give you increase in wealth and sons;*
>
> *and bestow on you gardens and bestow on you rivers*
>
> *(of flowing water).* **(QUR'ĀN 71:10-12)**

This means that you have to purify your senses and not return to committing past wrong actions. God will not accept repentance from someone who harms others, someone who steals, or someone who deceives people and takes their money without right. God will not accept repentance just given on the tongue. He must take action; he must return the money he took from the people he wronged.

If you backbite someone and you want your tongue to repent, it is not enough to say, "Forgive me, God." You must go to the person and say, "I mentioned you in a way that I should not have. Please forgive me." Whenever a person does something that harms another, he must go to that person and ask for forgiveness. Then he must go to God and ask for forgiveness and he should ask for Allāh to help him sincerely repent."

Quietly forgiving and moving on is a gift to yourself.

"When one door of happiness closes, another opens, but often we look so long at the closed door that we do not see the one that has been opened for us." — HELEN KELLER

Here are some more quotes I looked up on the web about forgiveness and leaving the past.

"Letting go doesn't mean giving up...it means moving on. It is one of the hardest things a person can do. Starting at birth, we grasp on to anything we can get our hands on, and hold on as if we will cease to exist when we let go. We feel that letting go is giving up, quitting, and that as we all know is cowardly. But as we grow older we are forced to change our way of thinking. We are forced to realize that letting go means accepting things that cannot be. It means maturing and moving on, no matter how hard you have to fight yourself to do so." — UNKNOWN

"To be able to move on, one has to learn to forgive not only the person (or people) who have done one wrong but also oneself."
— EUGENIA TRIPPUTI

"This only is denied to God: the power to undo the past."
— AGATHON (448 B.C. – 400 B.C.), from *Aristotle, Nicomachean Ethics*

"The farther behind I leave the past, the closer I am to forging my own character." — ISABELLE EBERHARDT

"We can draw lessons from the past, but we cannot live in it."
—LYNDON B. JOHNSON

"Do not dwell in the past, do not dream of the future, concentrate the mind on the present moment." —BUDDAH

"If we open a quarrel between past and present, we shall find that we have lost the future." — SIR WINSTON CHURCHILL

"I like the dreams of the future better than the history of the past."
— THOMAS JEFFERSON

"We have one life; it soon will be past; what we do for God is all that will last" — MUHAMMAD ALI

"No man is rich enough to buy back his past." — OSCAR WILDE

These quotes are from a really diverse cross-section of mostly well-known and successful people, so spend some time thinking about them and applying them to your life.

My Wife, Dr. Elizabeth Rose

My wife, Elizabeth, who teaches about repentance and forgiveness, shares a few thoughts with you here as well:

> *Forgiveness and repentance is one of my favorite topics to teach in my classes as well as share with my clients, because it is so powerful, healing, and freeing.*
>
> *Sometimes people have a negative reaction to these concepts. For people whose spiritual training came with a lot of guilt, the idea of repentance can feel heavy and loaded with a lot of shame and guilt.*
>
> *One thing that helped me with this was to understand that the Arabic word "tawba," usually translated as "repentance," literally means "return." So when we "repent," and seek forgiveness, we are actually returning to Divine Love and returning back to the original pure, holy, loving essence of our own nature. And, as many have pointed out, even the English word "repent" literally means "re-think." So when we are invited to repentance, we are really being invited to re-think our mistakes and return to our original state of wholeness and unity with our Creator and our fellow creatures.*
>
> *Islam offers some very beautiful and hopeful teachings about forgiveness. The Prophet Muhammad (saws) said, "The repentant one is as one without sin; for repentance erases what happened before it." What a beautiful thought. Take a moment and imagine what it would be like if your slate was wiped clean, all your mistakes completely erased, and all the negative repercussions evaporated!*

The Qu'ran offers an even more hopeful and merciful concept: "... the one who repents (tawba) and believes and performs righteous deeds: for such, Allah will change their evil deeds to good. And Allah is Ever-Forgiving, Singularly Compassionate." (Q25:70) Now the negative repercussions are not just eliminated but transformed into positive consequences!

Imagine what your life would be like if all of your mistakes were actually transformed into good deeds? In other words, once you repent and return to love, instead of the results of your mistakes harming you and other people, they would actually bless you and others! This is what I mean by how freeing repentance can be.

There are important conditions given here in this teaching from the Qur'an; we need to not just repent and return to love and follow the steps that Tony outlined above, but we also need to believe and trust in Allah's mercy for us, and then step out in faith and take positive, beneficial action as well.

People sometimes have an uncomfortable response to the idea of forgiveness as well. They may be afraid that forgiving means that they accept or approve of someone else's harmful behavior or that it means that they have to continue sharing their life with someone who repeatedly harms them.

But forgiveness doesn't mean accepting someone's harmful behavior or continuing to put ourselves in harm's way. It means we set ourselves free from the pain and anger and grief that we've been carrying around, sometimes even decades after the other person has died, which really only hurts ourselves. As a wise person once said, "Holding resentment is like drinking poison and waiting for the other person to die." That resentment, pain, and anger keeps us in a prison of the past, disempowers us, and deep down comes from a belief that the other person's power to harm us is greater than Allah's power to heal and uplift us and bring something good even out of the most challenging life situations.

If we forgive someone's past harmful behavior, it doesn't mean we approve or accept that behavior as okay. It just means we have decided not to let ourselves suffer and be eaten up with anger, resentment, and bitterness anymore. We can forgive someone's current harmful behavior and still decide not to subject ourselves to it anymore. For example, someone may decide to leave an abusive marriage or an abusive employer, but also choose not to hold on to bitterness and resentment over the situation.

When we forgive, we free ourselves from the stranglehold we've allowed other people and painful situations to have on our psyche. We affirm that God's love and healing are more powerful than anything that any human being has done to us. We make our hearts available to experience that Divine Love and healing and be transformed by it. We also allow others who may be seeking forgiveness to experience the transformative, healing power of Divine Love and mercy, to have their slates wiped clean as well as their own mistakes transformed into good deeds. So imagine now, what if the mistakes that others who hurt you made, were also transformed into good deeds, so that even those things that seemed like your deepest wounds ultimately brought about only blessings?

Repentance and forgiveness are such powerful forces for transformation that applying them sincerely does indeed make our lives magical!

— **DR. ELIZABETH ROSE**

One of the traditions that Sidi helps us to understand more comes from the story of Abraham when God asked him to sacrifice his son; and when he was willing, and with his son's permission, at the last minute God changed the knife to water and Abraham sacrificed a sheep in place of his son. The meaning of this sacrifice has profound lessons within the story.

Abraham was willing to give up something he loved completely because his faith in God was so strong. The word *sacrifice* comes from the Latin word "sacrificium" (sacrifice), also related to "sacrificus" (make or offer sacrifice), which comes from "sacer" (sacred/holy) and "facio" (do/make), so we can see that a sacrifice means "to make holy/sacred."

This is commonly understood as offering something as a gift to a deity. It also implies giving something of value to receive something of greater value. For example, in chess, you have strategies where a player might sacrifice a queen in order to take an advantage and win a game.

In the Bible it says in John 3:16: "For God so loved the world that he gave (sacrificed) his one and only Son, that whoever believes in him shall not perish but have eternal life."

As you can see it is not just the Qur'an that teaches forgiveness (think of this also as sacrificing or giving up holding a grudge); it is in almost every spiritual tradition. Here are some more quotes from the Bible about forgiveness:

"And whenever you stand praying, forgive, if you have anything against anyone, so that your Father also who is in heaven may forgive you your trespasses." — MARK 11:25

"Pay attention to yourselves! If your brother sins, rebuke him, and if he repents, forgive him, and if he sins against you seven times in the day, and turns to you seven times, saying, 'I repent,' you must forgive him." — LUKE 17:3-4

"Then Peter came up and said to him, 'Lord, how often will my brother sin against me, and I forgive him? As many as seven times?' Jesus said to him, 'I do not say to you seven times, but seventy times seven.'" — MATTHEW 18:21-22

"Be merciful, even as your Father is merciful. Judge not, and you will not be judged; condemn not, and you will not be condemned; forgive, and you will be forgiven." — LUKE 6:36-37

"But I say to you, love your enemies and pray for those who persecute you." — MATTHEW 5:44

"Be kind to one another, tenderhearted, forgiving one another, as God in Christ forgave you." — EPHESIANS 4:32

And in Judaism

Ideally a person who has caused harm needs to sincerely apologize, then the wronged person is religiously bound to forgive. However, even without an apology, forgiveness is considered a pious act (*Deot 6:9*). *Teshuva* (literally "returning") is a way of atoning, which requires cessation of a harmful act, regret over the act, confession, and repentance. Yom Kippur is the day of atonement when Jews particularly strive to perform *teshuva*. Two relevant Jewish quotes on forgiveness:

"It is forbidden to be obdurate and not allow yourself to be appeased. On the contrary, one should be easily pacified and find it difficult to become angry. When asked by an offender for forgiveness, one should forgive with a sincere mind and a willing spirit."
— MISHNEH TORAH, TESHUVAH 2:10

"Who takes vengeance or bears a grudge acts like one who, having cut one hand while handling a knife, avenges himself by stabbing the other hand." — JERUSALEM TALMUD, NEDARIM 9.4

Because God Has Forgiven Us, We Must Forgive Others

And here is a beautiful prayer from one of the great Christian mystics:

Prayer of Saint Francis Assisi

> *Lord, make me an instrument of thy peace!*
> *That where there is hatred, I may bring love.*
> *That where there is wrong,*
> *. . . I may bring the spirit of forgiveness.*
> *That where there is discord, I may bring harmony.*
> *That where there is error, I may bring truth.*
> *That where there is doubt, I may bring faith.*
> *That where there is despair, I may bring hope.*
> *That where there are shadows, I may bring light.*
> *That where there is sadness, I may bring joy.*
> *Lord, grant that I may seek rather to comfort,*
> *. . . than to be comforted.*
> *To understand, than to be understood.*
> *To love, than to be loved.*

For it is by self-forgetting that one finds.
It is by forgiving that one is forgiven.
It is by dying that one awakens to Eternal Life.

I know that I thought many times before my marriage broke up that I had surrendered to God and was willing to give whatever I thought He wanted of me, but when it came time to give up my relationship with my wife, I realized that I was not nearly as willing as I thought, not nearly as surrendered as I thought. There were many times when my faith was seriously challenged during the years of working things out. One of the biggest changes I've felt in the past years is that with the deepening of my faith and my connection with God, I am a lot less attached to things than I was before. As happy and grateful as I am for having a lot of good things in my life, my main passion is working to please God and to feel the warmth of His love and acceptance.

When I was single-parenting my kids, many people would say, "You are sacrificing so much for them," and I would correct them immediately by saying, "They are nothing but a total plus in my life, and there is nothing that I feel I give up for them. In fact, they give me everything."

As I've mentioned, it was my love for them that allowed me to hang on and find my way back to connecting with God. What I've released is all feelings of resentment I ever held about my ex-wife for leaving; and I feel that my heart has forgiven, not just *her*, but myself as well. In its place is a deep love and gratitude for the great years we had, and the four beautiful children she bore.

There are now two little granddaughters, Layla, 6, and Anais, almost 2, who bring joy to so many hearts. Changing maybe one tiny and seemingly insignificant thing in my past might have brought about a completely different life, and I cannot imagine not knowing all these wonderful beings, especially Sidi and my present wife. So I leave the past to the past and look to what I want the present and future to be. I also rejoice in the fact that I have so many things to be thankful for and so much more I yearn to do.

Rainbows follow storms, and sometimes the storms of our lives produce the most positive results for our personal growth.

If you really want to experience change, put these ideas into practice and you will see how well things start to go for you.

EXERCISE

Make a list of people you feel you'd like to apologize to, and make a point of asking for their forgiveness. Take some time to sit quietly and ask for God's forgiveness, too, and promise not to return to negative patterns of behavior that you may have engaged in.

Do the same for your body, heart, and spirit. Basically it's like immersing every part of your being in a warm spiritual bath. You will feel a lot different, I promise.

_____

_____

_____

_____

_____

_____

_____

_____

_____

_____

_____

_____

_____

_____

_____

_____

Would you like help in letting go of past pain, anger and grief?
Join me in our 8-week program for in-depth support.
www.MakeYourLifeMagical.com/explore

Chapter 20

Being Present:
Being Present:
Being the Son or Daughter
of Your Moment

"Either appear as you are or be as you appear." — RUMI

I cannot emphasize enough how important being present and being the son or daughter of my moment (that is, overcoming procrastination) has been in helping me attain the success I've experienced so far. Procrastination can slow progress faster than almost anything I know, and one of the best and most productive habits I've developed over the years is to do something as immediately as possible when the thought comes to my head. And if I can't do it at right at that moment, I will either write it down or make an audio note on my iPhone. I keep a constant to-do list going, and it's always open on my desktop and available on my laptop, iPad, and iPhone, so I always have it with me.

Very often I will think about calling someone, or I'll have a thought for this book or something else I'm working on, and I am relentless about being sure that I carry through on those ideas. I have a file on my desk with pages from magazines, postcards of offers I want to look into, brochures with things that I want to research; and on my desktop browser, I keep info on different websites I want to explore.

Just like everyone, I get a ton of e-mails, and even though I have a folder with these messages that I want to peruse when I have time, I keep the link to that e-mail file open 24/7 so I have a double reminder.

Recently I started receiving e-mails from Jeff Walker, who is one of the great teachers on product launches. Even though I have all of Brendon Burchard's courses, including one of them called Total Product Blueprint, Jeff's name always comes up from the top internet marketers I follow, and I intend to buy one of his programs.

Additionally, I follow Michael Port, Eban Pagen, Frank Kern, Mike Koenig, Ann Sieg, Mark Hoverson, Pam Hendrickson, Joe Polish, Tellman Knudson and Jimmy Harding; and I invest in their programs because I love learning from the best. I look for the commonalities and the differences, take a lot of notes, and have learned so much from them collectively. The price points of some of their programs run into the thousands, and I have to admit that because I don't always manage my time in the best way, I don't often get to look at all the material I buy. The main reason is that internet marketing has never been a very big source of income for me, so it has not been that great a focus. However, when I decided to create this book and program, I developed a renewed interest in learning about product launches, so I'm paying more attention to how this is done.

Launching a Product

Maybe you're someone who also wants to share a gift you have with the world, and one day you might want to launch your own product, so I hope understanding my process will help you. Or maybe you want to market some of the available information products, such as this one.

Most people have an affiliate program allowing them to earn income from promoting their products. This is a great way to build an additional income stream.

I had a number of links from Jeff Walker's e-mails about his new product launch, and every day I would see them but simply didn't take the time to watch them. But he has always emphasized the value of list building, so I was very conscious of the importance of doing this, step by step.

Then one weekend I was scheduled to fly to Florida with Sidi for a seminar, and for the first time in more than 15 years, something came up that prevented us from flying that weekend, but we still wanted to put on the seminar. So at the last moment I decided to try to put everything together over the internet. Because I'd been building a list of people who could help me with this for over a year, I started contacting some of them to see how this could be done. The only reason I had this list was due to my habit of being the son of my moment; and every time I came across something related to web presentations, I would add it to my file. I was doing what Jeff Walker and others taught.

One thing that every great internet marketer seems to have in common is that they all stress the value of list building. I had a feeling that one day I would need this info, and I was just acting on that feeling.

I had only a few days to learn everything I could about how this could work, and because of the list, I had everything under way within 24 hours, and in the end it worked out perfectly. Sidi sat in my office, and his image was projected on a large screen to over 100 people in Florida, all of whom got great teachings over the weekend and really loved the experience.

In fact, it all went so well that I started thinking about expanding on that idea. We had just projected from my office to a large conference room, but now I wanted to figure out if I could do that at a reasonable cost so that 1,000 people could watch Sidi on a video, rather than just a traditional webinar where you hear the voice and see text on a screen but don't see the person. I also wanted to have a second video of someone translating, if possible, and that person would be in a different location. And lo and behold, I get an e-mail from Jeff Walker that he was about to do a five-hour live web broadcast explaining his new launch, and he was also going to have guests from a different location on the broadcast with him.

So I tuned in to the broadcast, which was really awesome, and sent the link to my webmaster, who reverse-engineered things and saw how Jeff was doing it. So I found the technology, bought it, and have installed it on my computer. Later, I will start to test it and figure out how it works, and then set up a broadcast where we will have a seminar with hopefully 1,000 or more people attending.

Now when I first started paying attention to Jeff, I had no idea that this would be one of the doors he would open, but because each time he sent me something I built a file, and then actually acted upon the information when I needed to, I ended up in a position to do something that could greatly influence the future of my nonprofit.

I think I mentioned that we've built a school in the Holy Land for orphans and children from poor families, so I plan to use this special broadcast to raise money for the school. I also plan to use some of the launch techniques I'm learning from Jeff and Brendon to augment the number of attendees at Sidi's seminars, so I'm really excited. I know that if I hadn't taken notes, kept a to-do list, and then been the son of my moment, none of this would have come to pass.

The Value of Small Daily Actions

An added point of interest is that I also got an e-mail from a company I used to work with that I keep a file on, and I've stayed up-to-date on their progress. They once mentioned that they'd be doing a worldwide webinar for the launch of their new product, and that they would have video streaming; so I called a friend of mine, Don Karn, who is now their vice president, and he ended up telling me that the name of the company they used was exactly the one Jeff had.

So again, keeping track of things and people and being organized, and following up on things as they happen, really works for me; and if I miss something, I trust I'll find the answer in another way.

What I want to impress upon you is that I actually took action when I came across these two e-mails about streaming video. I wrote both items in my to-do list, called Don, and was sure to log in to Jeff's broadcast, and then I followed up by sending the link to my webmaster. I also sent it to the people who organized the Florida webcast and asked them to tell me how it was done, so I had three different lines in the water, so to speak. This is also an example of how when you really want something, it's important to follow up on it. When you get in the habit of performing these small daily actions, you'll see how they can lead to positive results.

And even though I kept Don Karn's name on my to-do list, I know him well enough and respect his professionalism so much that I knew he would return my call without any reminders from me. This is not the case for many people, so I sometimes have to follow up a number of times. But when I want something, I am relentless in pursuing it until I attain the outcome I desire.

The other quality I mentioned, being present, is equally important. I am, like a lot of people I know, a huge multitasker, but I've also spent considerable time and effort learning how to be completely present when I need to be. When I was working as a photographer, I was able to focus all my attention on my viewfinder and would simply ignore all the activity around me. Fashion shoots are full of highly creative people in the throes of a lot of activity, so I had to be cognizant of everyone's wants and needs, yet at the same time stay focused on the image I wanted to create. And I also needed to be completely present with the model during the moments when I was shooting, because these men and women were placing themselves in very vulnerable positions at times, which I was sensitive to.

I've used this skill so much when sharing my business with others; and have gotten very adept at paying close attention to their needs, fears, desires, and vulnerability; as well as being 100 percent present for them. The same goes when I'm speaking or leading a seminar. I've learned to be truly present in each and every moment and sustain that intensity for an entire day.

Recently I was watching a tennis match and was amazed by how present Rafael Nadal is every single second the ball is in play. That's one of the reasons he's one of the most accomplished athletes in the world.

When we're really present with those around us, they appreciate us so much more. I believe that when we show up in others' professional and personal world, we have to maintain integrity, be consistent, follow through, and continually be the honorable individuals they've experienced us to be in the past so that they can feel safe in their relationship with us.

The Secret

I'd like to share something I wrote for my blog after the book *The Secret* came out, and it feels as true to me today as it did back then. These are some ideas I've developed from the various teachings I've learned, which I feel could be very helpful in making the concepts presented in this book bring positive results into your life. Sidi has written extensively on these things, but in a different form.

Here is my interpretation and assimilation of how it all works, and how our thoughts develop along these lines:

You are an extension of Divine thought; all nonphysical language is a kind of vibration; and we radiate that which we vibrate, so in this sense you are the creator of your own reality. As much as possible, you can choose to allow your true Divine nature to always flow through you; and when you do that you are consciously allowing your full connection with God to express itself, and this is a joyful feeling.

This well-being is what God intended for us, because He created us with Divine love. The better you feel, the more you are allowing Divine love to flow through you; and the worse you feel, the less you are allowing your connection with the Divine to flow through your heart. When you feel bad, you are resisting this connection. When you experience feelings of insecurity and anger and hate, they are born from a disconnection with who you truly are; and when you remember who you are through prayer and remembrance (repetition of the Divine Name), you then can intentionally reach for thoughts that will hold you in a vibrational harmony. Then your world will fall into alignment, and a sense of well-being and Divine Love will show itself to you in all areas of your experience.

Your emotions will always show you whether you are allowing your true connection with God to express itself. No one who is truly connected to God and in the flow of Divine Love could ever do anything to hurt you. They can only do this from a place where they are disconnected, and if you don't allow it, they cannot cause you to be disconnected.

What happens is that often we allow our fears or negative thoughts to dominate, and so our vibration is from a place of fear rather than the joy and light that we feel when we are focused on our dreams. And here is a very important point: God is love, and when we live from a place of love, then we are living as an extension of our Creator, living the way we were created to live. And thus we can feel peace. But when we focus on our fears, we are not trusting this love, and so we are disconnected from feeling good.

What I have found is that when I am feeling really good and have strong, positive emotion flowing through me, when I focus on what I want, I can actually feel a genuine excitement as I move toward the fulfillment of what my heart is seeking.

Remember when you fell in love how excited you were about everything and how powerfully you experienced emotions? If you meet someone and there is not that spark of powerful emotions, then the relationship usually doesn't go very far. And if you focus on negative thoughts such as "I am not good enough for this person," or "This person could never like me," then the relationship doesn't work either. You attract the dominant thought, and the dominant thought is the one with the strongest emotion tied to it.

There are also many references in The Secret *about the law of attraction. One of the important aspects to understand about this law is that if the thing you are seeking is right for you, this thing is also seeking you. This is what makes it a match. If you are looking for change and growth and transformation in your life, there are people who want to teach and share and mentor people like you. Great sports teams are seeking the athletes that are also seeking them. If you are married, your wife was looking for you while you were looking for her. So if you are challenged now and thinking of doing something else, there is definitely an opportunity looking for you.*

I am always looking for people to mentor, just as there are many people who desire to be mentored. The fact that you're reading this means that we have attracted each other into our lives, and this is because I'm seeking people like you, and you are seeking something that I have to offer. And as Sidi would say, "If you didn't feel in your heart that God was calling you, you would not be here now."

EXERCISE

Make a list of those you'd like to be totally present with the next time you meet. Write down your plans for connecting with these individuals within the next month or so.

Then write down several activities that you're going to do while being fully present, and visualize how you'll feel when you're doing so.

_____

_____

_____

_____

_____

_____

_____

_____

_____

_____

_____

_____

_____

_____

_____

_____

_____

_____

_____

Learn to strengthen your direct connection to the Divine Love
in our 8-week program with in-depth support.
www.MakeYourLifeMagical.com/explore

Chapter 21

.ૐ.

Factors of Success

"Nothing can stop the man with the right mental attitude from achieving his goal; nothing on earth can help the man with the wrong mental attitude."— **THOMAS JEFFERSON**

My success in life—whether it be in relationships, business, sports, spirituality, family, recreation—or any other area of my life, has always been determined by certain factors that always seem to show up. Desire and motivation always play a big part, but without resolve they don't bring about consistently strong results. Other factors are love, commitment, belief, giving, self-confidence, and hope.

Let's start with love and commitment. Until we're committed internally to something, we have very little chance of eventually seeing a positive outcome. My experience has been that commitment only really comes about when we truly love something and are truly passionate about it. Love awakens something special in our hearts and gives life to things. Love is the basis for everything that has value to me. Here are some excerpts of a talk given by Sidi, this one focused on love:

> *First we will start with love, because no one across the earth can live without love. There is no one in existence, no creature—even birds or other animals—who can live without love. There is not even a plant on the earth that can live without love. Even the worlds of solid matter need love.*

Do you not see the water gush forth out of the rocks? It is the mountain that you live by and drink. It sometimes comes out of the mountains. This water has everything the human needs. All mountains contain minerals, and underneath them are metals that the human body needs. These resources can be used for the happiness of the human being, or to destroy the human being.

Do you not see that underneath the surface of the earth there are all of the metals and materials the human being may need? There is: oil, fire, all metals, gold and silver, charcoal. And even this matter cannot live without love.

What is love? Love is water. Do you not see that tremendous fires cannot be calmed down except by water? Why? Because water is full of love. When water is sent down to fire, what happens? It turns the fire off. So water prevents suffering. If fire spreads, what happens? For example, we see the volcanoes gushing forth burning lava. What prevents this from happening is the water across the earth. If it happens, it is water that turns it off. This means that water is an indication of love. It is a sign of love. If water is used in the right way, it is a sign of love and it will revive life. Even in the mountains, everything becomes calm and safe from water.

From where does water come? It is sent down from the sky. It comes down by the Lord of Love, the Lord who created love within our hearts. The name of that lover is Allāh, which in your language is "God." Is that not true? In all languages there is a name that refers to that Being Who is the Creator, the One and Only.

Let us now search in love. We explained the different signs of love across the earth. If people used water in a holy way, then the whole earth and its people would be happy, but if people use water to destroy and harm, then it will make the human sick and miserable. We must use the water of love that God sent down to earth in a good way.

God fills the oceans and seas with this water of love. Look at the oceans and seas. What do they contain? The vapor from these oceans rises into the skies. By the command of the Almighty, the Wise, the water accumulates and forms clouds. The clouds are led by winds to the parts of the earth that are barren and without plants. When water is sent down as rain to these lands, it brings forth things that carry the fragrance of absolute beauty that the human being needs. It is a sign that shows the love of God for the human being. It talks to the human being and says, "Look at me. Do not pollute me. Keep me beautiful so that you can become beautiful, too."

When you walk by fruits and flowers, they call you to witness their beauty. They say, "Come to me. I will teach you about love. I will teach you to be beautiful." Everything in creation talks to you. God also says in the Qur'an: "Everything in creation knows its prayer and glorification of Allāh." **[SEE QUR'AN 24:41]**

Do you not hear the trees talking as they sway back and forth? They chant with the Divine tongue. Do you not also hear the birds singing and chanting the praise of God?

God wants you to be a beloved, not a destroyer or a corruptor. He wants you to be beautiful, full of mercy for everything. He wants you to be merciful to the birds, to the trees, to everything. Do you not hear the currents of water running in the river praising God and thanking Him? He waters all the fruits and vegetables and trees for you. Isn't that the essence of love? God serves you. God made everything for you. He offered you the water of love. People need love. They need the pure and clean water of love.

This heart must be full of love and peace and security. The house of your heart must become the mercy. Those are three things: love, peace, and mercy. Fill your heart full of these qualities.

Whoever does an atom's weight of good will receive its reward and whoever makes an atom's weight of evil will suffer the consequences. **[QUR'AN 99:7-99:8]**

For the one who does not have love, it is better if he throws himself into the Hellfire because he actually wants the Hellfire. He must pursue love so that he can find the Garden. If he does not pursue love, he will continue to be in the Hellfire. He has free choice. Does he want to be in the Garden or in the Hellfire? Only through love can you live in the Garden. You cannot find sufficiency without love.

Do you know the seven qualities of a dog?

The first one is love. The dog carries love because he loves his friend with the pure love of eternity. He teaches you about love.

Surrender

Sincerity

Truthfulness

Faithfulness

Friendship

Patience

Do you see these seven qualities in one human? Show me that human! If I see him, I will kiss his feet, because that would mean he is one of the saints, one of the loyal friends and allies of Allāh.

Personally, I also love the qualities we see in children.

Curiosity

Wonder

Trusting

Open hearted

Live in the moment

Non-materialistic

Non-judgmental

Of course there are more, but I think you get the point.

Develop these qualities within yourself, and one of the things you will find is that you will start to attract others with these qualities into your life and partnerships. Be the type of person you would most like to associate with, and continually ask more of yourself than you do of others.

Are you still childlike? Are you truthful, faithful, sincere, patient, and so on? Do you give to everyone what you would like them to give to you?

I never expect anyone to give me something I would not be able to give them if I could. I never expect someone to work harder at something than I would unless I am paying them to do so. I don't work harder on building an addition to my house than the people I hire to do it, but I like to pay them before the sweat dries on their brows, as the saying goes. And I like to pay them fairly.

Someone might say, "Well, it's easy for you because you can afford it," but it wasn't always that way, as there were times in my life when I didn't have much money. But I believe that one of the reasons I have some today is because even when I didn't have it, I always tried to be generous.

I also mention belief, because this is one ingredient that is always very present in the successful areas of my life: belief in myself, and belief in not only what I am doing, but why I am doing it. I need to believe in the fact that if I'm spending hours every day involved in something, it is a worthwhile way to spend my time and energy.

A yogi friend of mine once said that we should measure our lives by how many breaths we take, as when we stop breathing, we stop living. He believes that relaxing and taking slow breaths actually prolongs our lives, and that he values his ability to be able to breathe clean air and work on his body so that he can take deep breaths that fully oxygenate his entire being. He also feels that when we do things pleasing to us, we breathe better and deeper, and this keeps us healthy.

So if you're going to take a certain number of breaths every day, it makes sense to make them count as best you can. If you're stressed and just taking short, quick breaths, you're going to use up your life force a lot faster. When we really love what we're doing and have a belief deep in our being that it's worthwhile, we're making every second count.

Belief in what you're doing gives you the power you need to overcome the many challenges you encounter in your life. I see a lot of people who start out doing things—whether related to business, relationships, a sport, or something else—and I can usually discern their level of belief in what they're doing and whether they'll have a successful outcome. For example, if you start out in a relationship *wondering* whether this person is the one you'll spend the rest of your life with, it's a very different feeling than when you're so attracted to someone that you *can't wait* to spend the rest of your life with him or her.

Likewise, when I initiate a new business endeavor, if I start with negative thoughts or doubts and am unsure about my decision, I find that things don't usually have the best outcome. Also, when I truly love something or someone and believe 100 percent in it or them, I'm much more focused on being in the moment and enjoying the experience, which almost always produces positive results. It's important to enjoy the journey; and when you're worried about the outcome, then it's not really easy to enjoy the moment.

Giving

I am such a huge believer in giving, as the door to opening everything in our lives. As Sidi says, "The love you give is the love you get." The act of giving opens our heart so much and feels so good. If you're like me, you get a lot more joy out of giving than getting. I wrote a lot about this in the chapter on abundance, so I won't repeat it all again, but if you're ever in situations where you're not happy, and not really satisfied with the way things are going, I would suggest looking at how much heart you're actually putting into that situation and where you're holding back. The level of your giving will be tied to your belief in, love for, and commitment to, what you're doing; as well as your passion for helping others. If you're not getting enough, it could well be that you're not giving enough.

Back when I was living in Paris, I was taking sitar lessons, and I brought my sitar teacher, Pramod Kumar, to play a particular type of music called a *raga* at a gathering of people who had come to listen to some teachings of Swami Satchidananda. It was a really cold day, and Pramod was having a difficult time tuning his instrument. I was getting really nervous because I felt everyone *else* getting impatient. They were all waiting to hear the talk, and each time Pramod would start to play, his sitar went out of tune and he would start over. He refused to play an instrument out of tune, and the people in the room were getting really agitated.

Indian music is a free-style type of music, but ragas have something called a tonic, and a lot of it depends on how all the notes relate to that tonic. Each raga has a time of day, a particular emotion, a season, and of course, the tonic; and out of respect to his art, Pramod had to be sure everything was correct. Of course, Swami understood all this and was extremely patient. Finally, Pramod got everything to his liking and played a superb instrumental piece that really moved everyone.

After the recital, the first words out of Swami's mouth, after thanking Pramod, were to make a lesson out of the tuning experience. He shared how the entire instrument is tuned to the main string, and if that string is out of tune, all the strings will be out of tune. This is similar to tuning a guitar to the top string, but if that string is out of tune, the entire guitar will be out of key. Anyway, Swami went on to say that if you yourself are out of tune, there's no way you can really help others get in tune, so we had to work on ourselves like Pramod worked on his first string, and we have to take care to get ourselves in tune if we want to help others.

A lot of the material I have shared in this book has been the things that have helped me feel "in tune," and I hope that you have resonated with what I've presented here.

When you have developed the traits I've mentioned, what happens is that it builds your self-confidence, and once your self-confidence gets strong, there's very little that can defeat you. Self-esteem and self-confidence go hand-in-hand, and they are qualities that come about after achieving a certain amount of success through practicing and developing many inner qualities.

For example, I am utterly convinced that home-based businesses are a worthy endeavor because I have so much confidence in my ability to make such enterprises work due to my previous success. People often tell me that multilevel marketing is a scam and a pyramid scheme and can't possibly work, but the fact is that I've seen it work, so it's going to be really hard for someone to shake my confidence in my belief in this industry. Why? Because I love it, I believe in it, I am passionate about it, I've given 20 years of my life to it, I've gotten so much back in return, and I am committed to sharing it with others because I see that it is really the solution to the challenges that so many people are facing in these challenging times. It might not be for everyone, but it is definitely for me.

As the writing of this book comes to a close, it is February 2012. and it feels like I could easily write for another month, but I know that it's time for me to start working on the modules; and I'm really excited to start creating the membership program. I've never done something like this before, and I'm finding the entire process quite exhilarating.

Adversity Can Lead to Greatness

I was watching the two football league championships on TV today as I was working, and both games ended due to errors. The Baltimore Ravens missed a fairly short field goal going for a tie, and the kick-off returner for the San Francisco Forty-Niners fumbled the ball in overtime, giving the New York Giants possession within field-goal range. It made me think about how difficult the next few months will be for the two players involved, as they might feel that they let their teams down. Individual losses don't carry as much weight as being responsible for a *team* loss, and I hope they both have a strong spiritual belief to be able to overcome what happened with grace and acceptance. My prayers are with both of them.

I know that adversity can really bring out the greatness that lies within everyone, so I hope that all of you who are reading these words remember all the difficult times I've gone through and know that all it takes is a small step in another direction, a small shift in how someone thinks, or a small opening in the heart, to shift things in a positive way.

I want you to ask yourself if you're hesitant about moving toward what you want because of something in your belief system, because you fear change, or because you're not sure of a particular outcome. When you can alter your belief system, then your decisions will change; and when your decisions change, your actions change, and when your actions change, your results change.

As I've mentioned earlier, the way I've overcome fears when they surface is to first establish whether what I want is in alignment with my purpose. When I find that it is, I then set goals with specific steps, and dates by which I will accomplish those steps. I then make a list of people whom I might ask for accountability if it involves them.

I have developed a lot of habits that I believe serve me really well for staying on track with things, and I count on these habits to keep everything moving forward. Something I'm proud of is my ability to keep my commitments, and the reason I can keep them is because I've developed the ability to undercommit and overperform.

There's a huge difference between making a decision and making a commitment. People who simply make New Year's resolutions usually don't keep them, while those who make *commitments* will find that they carry through on their intentions. When I look at some of the dialogue I use when setting goals, I make an effort to use the most positive words possible. Instead of struggling *against* something, I work on *allowing* what I would like to see manifest. Instead of struggling *against* debt, I *allow* wealth. Instead of fighting *against* being judgmental, I *allow* more love. Instead of fighting *against* being overweight, I *allow* more wellness.

Don't think for a moment that the limiting beliefs you have experienced in your life—because of what other people have told you or that you have allowed yourself to believe—have anything to do with who you really are as a person. At any moment you can change your life by changing your beliefs, and the only one who has the ability to control that is *you*. You can't blame others if you choose not to change; you need the courage to realize that you have the ability to make whatever changes you truly desire; and decide in your heart that you will no longer live at a fraction of your potential.

Make your commitment to change more than just a decision. Make it from deep within your heart—with passion, emotion, and a refusal to accept any other outcome than the one that feels in harmony with your soul. And then stay consistent and persistent, and don't let anyone limit your belief in yourself. Learn to manage your expectations so that you don't get discouraged if things don't change overnight. Rather, be proud that you've embarked on a whole new journey. And be sure to enjoy the voyage as you head for your new destination.

Decide to replace any negative self-talk that has held you back with empowering and powerful thoughts that lead you to freedom. Use your inner magician to make all negativity disappear. And when you face dark moments of self-doubt, turn to God . . . because with God, everything is possible.

This is a poem that I learned from my daughter Jessica, who learned it from Ray Hunt, a man who taught her to work with horses in a superbly gentle manner.

When you get what you want in your struggle for self

And the world makes you king for a day

Just go to the mirror and look at yourself

And see what THAT face has to say

For it isn't your father or mother or spouse

Whose judgment upon you must pass

The person whose verdict counts most in your life

Is the one looking back from the glass

Some people might think you're a straight-shooting chum

And call you a great gal or guy

But the face in the glass says you're only a bum

If you can't look him straight in the eye

That's the one you must please

Never mind all the rest

That's the one with you clear to the end

And you know you have passed your most dangerous, difficult test

If the face in the glass is your friend

You may fool the whole world down the pathway of years

And get pats on your back as you pass

But your final reward will be heartaches and tears

If you've cheated the face in the glass.

Hope and Magic

And what does the development of all the qualities mentioned in these pages lead to? *Hope!* And, as I've talked about earlier, hope is a crucial ingredient for creating successful outcomes. As vision becomes reality, it's important to not only feel hope in our hearts, but we must develop the ability to instill and promote hope in the hearts of others.

Because I have a deep belief in God, I am extremely hopeful that there will be a positive outcome to everything, and I've been told numerous times by numerous people that I've helped them experience more hope as well. I know in my heart that because I've developed this ability, this is a major reason for my success. People love to experience hope in their hearts, and they love to believe that things can be different.

This is also what I love about magic, and why it has also been such a big part of my life. With magic we can tell a story; we can explain real life in a way that appears magical. We can make things disappear, and when we do, people marvel, and then some of *their* despair can disappear.

Magic is a way to enchant people; and when they're experiencing difficult times, this enchantment can help them reexperience joy, if only for a moment. They can forget their sadness for a minute and believe in miracles.

So if *I* can help people, even for a moment, experience a feeling of magic, then I can work on expanding that moment to a minute, and then an hour, and then a day, and beyond; and the result might be that I can help them make others' lives feel more magical, too.

I hope that if anything in this book has touched your heart, you will check out the modules online, where a lot of what I mention here is illustrated with magic. Each effect is meant to be a metaphor to help you understand the principles and values that form the basis of personal growth and self-development.

As with everything I do, I always appreciate feedback and thoughts so that I can continue to grow and serve others more, so do feel free to contact me.

It is through living a life of service that I feel I have made my life magical and have awakened my inner magician, and I fervently pray that I have helped you do the same.

My deepest prayer is that you will take your chance and be the "Son or Daughter of your moment" as Sidi would say, and join us on the journey through the interactive media modules that I have created to enhance this book.

The complete program will help you to integrate and implement everything in order to achieve change and transformation as it takes you step by step through applying the concepts. I look forward to meeting you and supporting you as you begin to Make Your Life MORE Magical.

Live to love,

Love to serve, and

Make Your Life Magical.

Many thanks and many blessings!

— Tony Kent

tony@tonykent.com
www.tonykent.com
www.makeyourlifemagical.com

Join me in our 8-week program for in-depth support.
www.MakeYourLifeMagical.com/explore

TESTIMONIALS AND ENDORSEMENTS

"Tony has a huge desire to help people from all walks of life improve the quality of their lives; and has used his time, talent and resources to make that difference. He is not only a wealth builder but a wealth giver to the greater benefit of mankind."

May your life be full of God's blessing as you reach out your generous hand to help others."
— **MICHAEL ELLISON,**
   CEO; AUTHOR OF *10 KEYS TO WELLNESS AND WEALTH*

"I have experienced Tony re-creating himself personally, professionally, and spiritually during the time I have known him. He is always transforming to a higher level of understanding, growth and peace. In his new book Make Your Life Magical, Tony provides GPS directions for others who want to realize the magnificence of themselves and life. Tony, wishing you all the best of success and happy trails as you promote your work globally."
— **RICK TONITA, GLOBAL PARTNERS, INC.**

"Wherever you go, whatever is happening around you, there is a magic door that, when you open it, will take you to a world so beautiful and overflowing with love that it will astound and delight you. That magic door is the door of your heart. Go through it!"
— **DR. ELIZABETH ROSE**

This is a quote from my guide, Sidi, dictated to his wife, Halima, in December 2011:

"I look for what is in my beloved holy son Salih [he is using the Sufi name he gave me], and I see he has a big heart and he works very hard and helps the poor people and he serves many people thru the work that he does. He has worked with me nearly 17 years and I see he is a very good one, having the deep sincere and honesty. He is like the bees, he does not stop. He knows where he is going and walks in the right way, and in what he writes in this book I see his goodness in it,

295

and he gives in it many useful things for anyone who is interested in this topic he writes about. I ask God to help him to continue to give more always. I call anyone and everyone if he like to know what is in this book, it will feed you in the right way. Thank you, Salih, about what you write. I ask Allah to bless you always and keep you in the complete health to continue working.

"The guide of peace, love, mercy, justice, and freedom for all the people without separation."
— SIDI SHEIK MOHAMMAD AL JAMAL AR RIFAI

"Thank you kindly for your wonderful book Art of Abundance.

I found it very impressive and inspiring and would like to thank you sincerely for the inspiration I received from your writing. I agree with you wholly when you say: "For me, wealth is having an abundant connection with God and being full of Divine Energy."

I am working on writing my purpose statement, with the guidelines from your book. Thank you sincerely again.

The point you have made about gratitude is also so poignant and reminds us how we tend to take things for granted in our lives. I also like the beautiful picture of the tree laden with fruit on the cover of your book.

With deepest thanks and many blessings."— MARGARET JOSEPH

"The moment you meet Tony Kent, you know he's the real deal. Honest, inspirational, sincere, and encouraging; anyone can feel a bond with Tony from their first encounter. Tony believes in motivation through genuine concern, connection, and commitment. I recommend Tony Kent to anyone looking to change their life in positive ways."
— DAREN FALTER,
    AUTHOR OF *HOW TO SELECT A NETWORK MARKETING COMPANY*

"Tony has mastered one of the most important aspects of life, caring about people, and he knows how to help people discover this force."
— CHRISTIAN DRAPEAU

"After achieving great success, Tony Kent has dedicated his life to offering a wealth of information and opportunities to enable others to realize their own dreams."
— A. ADLEMAN: WWW.BOOKWRITINGEDITING.COM

"Tony gave a workshop in Argentina a couple of years ago. The clarity and depth of his speech, and the heartfelt connection with all of us, made it a wonderful experience.

I personally felt it nourished my heart and it helped me see and change some patterns of behavior that helped me to lead a happier life. I'm very grateful for it. He is a great leader and communicator."
— ADELA AGUIRE

"When I think about Tony, I think . . . peaceful, spiritual, teacher, generous with his time . . . someone I would like to know better and hang out with so that I could learn from him." — CAROL ERAMO

"Tony is an all-around "can do" person. He is so upbeat and positive…a great leader and motivator. If I wanted to know how to make my life magical, he would be the first person I would ask. . . . I look at how he lives his life and touches the lives of others for my inspiration." — GAIL JOYAN, BUSINESS CONSULTANT

"Tony is an incredible mentor. Anyone wanting to learn how to network and build residual income for themselves would do great to study and work with Tony. He is passionate, fiery, loyal, and like getting a force of Nature on your side. I've learned an incredible amount from him." — JEFF BRONNER, VETERAN NETWORKER AND HOME-BUSINESS CHAMP

"Having been in business with Tony Kent during the past 10 years, I have found him to always do what he says he will do. Tony doesn't over-promise and he delivers every time. Working with him has been a blessing, and I look forward to continuing our business relationship for many years to come." — MITCH LOVER, SCOTTSDALE, ARIZONA

"With Tony Kent the sky is truly the limit, or perhaps only the beginning. Tony has been a friend and a teacher. He is always there at the other end of a telephone or internet line, come rain or shine, during moments of the worst inner chaos and turbulence. He forever connects when most needed. His excellence is in a loyalty and a loving concern that are unquestionable. Tony, and to know him is to love him, sees only the highest truth in my innermost being, and in reflecting this beauty back to me helps make it my daily life. And he is not afraid to translate this vision into practical reality, giving much-needed advice to help make the best choices possible. How easy it is then to carry the same truth to others around me in my life and my clinical practice. Thank you, dear friend. Forever in gratitude."
—NAOMI MILLER, PH.D., LCSW, DEPT. OF PSYCHIATRY, MT. SINAI MEDICAL CENTER, NEW YORK CITY

IMPORTANT REMINDER

This book was conceived and written as part of a complete program and I invite you to visit www.MakeYourLifeMagical.com to learn more. Although I feel that the book will also stand alone, the exercises, ideas and teachings—especially those from my spiritual teacher—will have greater value and deeper significance if you go through the interactive multimedia modules. The complete program will help you to integrate and implement everything to achieve change and transformation, as it takes you step by step through applying the concepts.

RESOURCES

Please visit www.MakeYourLifeMagical.com for a list of the different resources I have used to create and market Make Your Life Magical, and for the contact information of the people who have helped me.

ABOUT THE AUTHOR

Please visit www.tonykent.com and www.MakeYourLifeMagical. com to learn more about me.

NOTES

CPSIA information can be obtained
at www.ICGtesting.com
Printed in the USA
FFHW010959170319
51084404-56501FF